PROFESSIONAL HR

A new breed of HR Professional is needed who can offer the sort of effective people management that can change the way organizations work. They will first have to resolve the legacy left by an absence of professionalism in people management amongst both operational managers and the HR departments that serve them. Much of the problems that currently undermine capitalism and governance today can be traced back directly to insufficient attention being paid to the professional management of human capital.

This text offers an objective scale to gauge levels of professionalism that can be applied to management in any sector. Paul Kearns has also developed a clear 10-step guide for anyone looking to develop their HR professionalism in a practical way. With these tools, readers will be encouraged to move away from the old world ineffectiveness of people management by looking towards a New Norm and the huge potential it offers for value and wealth.

Suitable for managers and students studying HR, *Professional HR* provides the answer for what could be the next iteration of the capitalist system, with professional, evidence-based people management at its heart.

Paul Kearns is a career HR practitioner and founder of the PWL consultancy. He has specialized in HR measurement, metrics and evaluation for over 20 years and delivers Masterclasses and keynote conference presentations around the world. He teaches HR Strategy at MBA level and is a leading authority on evidence-based HR and human capital reporting. He is now the British Standards Institute's Principal Expert on international HR standards and chairs the UK's National Committee.

PROFESSIONAL HR

Evidence-based people management and development

Paul Kearns

 Routledge
Taylor & Francis Group

LONDON AND NEW YORK

First published 2013
by Routledge
2 Park Square, Milton Park, Abingdon, Oxon OX14 4RN

Simultaneously published in the USA and Canada
by Routledge
711 Third Avenue, New York, NY 10017

Routledge is an imprint of the Taylor & Francis Group, an informa business

© 2013 Paul Kearns

British Library Cataloguing in Publication Data
A catalogue record for this book is available from the British Library

Library of Congress Cataloging in Publication Data

Kearns, Paul.
Professional HR: evidence-based people management and development/Paul Kearns.
  p. cm.
Includes bibliographical references and index.
1. Personnel management. I. Paul Kearns.
HF5549.K33 2013
658.3–dc23

2012039045

ISBN: 978-0-415-63231-7 (hbk)
ISBN: 978-0-415-63232-4 (pbk)
ISBN: 978-0-203-37112-1 (ebk)

Typeset in Bembo
by OKS Prepress Services, Chennai, India

Printed and bound in Great Britain by MPG Printgroup

CONTENTS

LIST OF ILLUSTRATIONS

Figures

Tables

ABOUT THE AUTHOR

Paul Kearns is a career HR Professional and founder of the PWL consultancy. He has specialized in HR measurement, metrics and evaluation for over 20 years and delivers Masterclasses and keynote conference presentations around the world. He teaches HR Strategy at MBA level and is a leading authority on evidence-based HR and human capital reporting. He is now the British Standards Institute's Principal Expert on international HR standards and chairs the UK's National Committee.

For more information visit www.paulkearns.co.uk.

For online Professional development visit www.paulkearnshr.co.uk.

For Evidence-Based HR visit www.evidencebasedhr.com.

For the Institute of HR Maturity visit www.hrmaturity.com.

Other titles by Paul Kearns:

HR Strategy: Creating Business Strategy with Human Capital (2010) 2nd Edition, Oxford: Routledge.

The Value Motive: The ONLY Alternative to the Profit Motive (2007) Chichester: Wiley.

Evaluating the ROI from Learning (2005) London: CIPD.

FOREWORD

Some years ago a senior executive in charge of talent management for a large US financial institution called me to request my help as she set about, at the request of her CEO, to design a program for the bank's 'high potential' people. 'Why did she need a program?' I asked. Was there evidence that the bank was losing more talented people than in the past, or more than its competitors, in other words, was there any evidence of a problem? 'Jeffrey', she replied, 'the CEO has asked me to design a program for our high potential people.' Without baseline information, or measurement of the problem and a diagnosis of its causes, how could she and the bank know what to do or how much progress it was making, I noted. Her reply was the same – she was charged with putting in a program for the company's high potentials because, after all, most of the bank's competitors either already had such initiatives in place or were designing them, and that's what she was going to do. I told her to go get a HR consulting firm to design a high potential program, that's what they do and I was sure they would be untroubled by the absence of data showing the problem or its causes as long as they could get paid for putting a program in place.

That's the state of play in human resources today mindless imitation of what others are doing, little to no systematic evaluation of the effectiveness of management practices and programs, infrequent data-driven diagnoses of the problems HR is expected to address, in short, little of the professionalism now almost taken for granted in medicine, to take just one example. Nor is it the case that everything is so wonderful that no one needs to worry. Evidence from surveys conducted by Towers Watson, Gallup, Hewitt, and the Conference Board, among many others, show pathetically low levels of employee engagement, widespread distrust of management, dissatisfaction with leadership, and strong intentions to look for new jobs, thereby increasing turnover and draining talent, as soon as the economy and the job market improve. Fear and workplace bullying seem endemic.

The result? Company underperformance and, indeed, shocking levels of corporate malfeasance as employees are too distrustful and fearful to speak up and prevent mistakes.

These circumstances make Paul Kearns angry and determined to do something to improve organizational management, and who can blame him? It is not just that the problems are pervasive, although they are. It's that research on the effects of people management on company performance consistently shows its importance and these findings are scarcely new. And the conditions Kearns bemoans, autocratic leaders who want to be told they're right rather than having issues surfaced, human resource practitioners who seem more concerned with keeping their jobs and growing their budgets than in being effective, are long-standing.

Kearns wants management in general, and human resource management in particular, to professionalize. Part of the professionalization project is to pay attention to the evidence while making decisions – to, simply put, think more like a scientist or, dare he use the word, an 'academic'. Professionalization entails critical thinking and analysis – becoming an expert diagnostician of the causes and possible remedies for organizational dysfunctions. Professionalization entails knowing the research literature and keeping up, something expected of most doctors, for example. And professionalization requires the professionals to speak truth to power, not just go along with fads and fashions or what the boss wants to do, because professionals have an obligation to those they serve – in this case, employees and investors – to advocate for the best policies regardless of what is in vogue at the moment or what the boss's personal predilections are.

Even as *Professional HR* lays out suggestions for moving practice and practitioners down this path, the obstacles seem daunting. Pick up a popular management book and what you mostly get are stories. Statistical analysis or even data are amazingly rare, let alone the sort of sophisticated analytical work necessary to separate correlation from causation and rule out alternative explanations for the observed results. Some prominent management writers tell me that they write books without feeling *any* compunction at all to consult any research evidence other than their own experience or whatever casual research they may undertake for their particular project. When I ask them why, they tell me that this is how the popular management book market is so why should they break the mold.

Meanwhile, management education at any level, bachelor's, master's, or executive, is not much different. Unlike the clinical, hands-on experience expected of doctors, management programs operate under what I have to call the 'airline model', with one instructor at some given cost at the front of the room, the more people you put in the room (the more seats), the higher the profit margins. Evaluations mostly measure inputs or 'happiness', not if students actually learn anything and implement that learning. Decades ago there was discussion of management being a profession and the phrase 'management science' was more prominent. Indeed, Frederick Taylor was a proponent of scientific management in the early 1900s. Although one might fault Taylor's simplistic conception of human psychology and his emphasis on time and motion studies and separating planning from doing, Taylor did collect, and pay attention to, the evidence and, more importantly, ran experiments, something that one sees today in internet marketing but seldom in other management domains. If management is to become more scientific, it logically follows that managers, including human resource managers, must think more like scientists and, as importantly, have the skills that can make them at least somewhat competent adopting a scientific mindset.

An accounting colleague at Stanford, David Larcker, frequently tells me that most companies do not know how they make money. Yes, they understand that profits are revenues minus expenses, but their cost accounting systems, activity-based accounting prescriptions notwithstanding, are rudimentary and incomplete. And few companies have the data, or use it, to understand the profitability of different customers or different strategies. When I asked Dave what companies did with the enormous amount of data sitting in and produced by their ERP systems sold by Oracle and SAP, he replied, 'they use it mostly for budgeting and control, not for strategic, competitive advantage'. This may be changing with all the talk of 'big data', but change is coming slowly and possibly not at all to human resources.

The financial shenanigans and corporate meltdowns do not merely destroy economic value and cause investors to suffer. As even a casual reading of the business or general press shows, for the most part, those who suffer from bad decision-making are not the decision-makers but the rank-and-file employees who lose their jobs and even their pensions and, in the US, access to health care when companies fail or lay off people by the carload. The consequences of bad decision-making are both severe and widespread. This makes the professionalization project Kearns outlines imperative. Too many have suffered for too long because of the neglect of evidence-based management.

Jeffrey Pfeffer, Thomas D. Dee II Professor of Organizational Behavior, Graduate School of Business, Stanford University, September, 2012.

"Kearns wants management in general, and human resource management in particular, to professionalize … those who suffer from bad decision making are not the decision makers but the rank-and-file employees …. This makes the professionalization project Kearns outlines imperative."

Professor Jeffrey Pfeffer, Stanford University, USA

"This is an important book that provides a positive road map for the future of the HR profession. Its importance lies in its willingness to address the big questions: why has Human Resources been at the crossroads for over a decade? What does it mean to operate as an HR professional? How can HR apply evidence-based practice to be more systematic in its priorities and evaluate the business impact of its activities?

The book, a combination of analysis, argument and anecdote, checklists and case studies, ranges far and wide in exploring the debate about the role of Human Resources, the nature of professionalism and the utilisation of evidence-based practice.

Professional HR is also a refreshingly authentic book that provides a candid insight into the connections between academic research, consultancy activity and HR practice. Paul Kearns takes on with insight and courage: snake-oil consultancies selling solutions of dubious value; the academics that gave their blessing to any number of flawed research wheezes; those HR practitioners who valued prize winning more than the implementation of processes that 'worked'; and the various professional bodies that stood on the side-lines rather than take a lead in raising and reinforcing standards.

For some, this book – with its willingness to 'name and shame' several of the players who contributed to HR's current reputation – will be an awkward reminder of a past that missed opportunities to establish Human Resources as a critical component of organisational success. For the emerging HR practitioner who wants to make a positive impact through a combination of a professional ethos and evidence-based practice, *Professional HR* will be indispensable reading."

Andrew Munro (MA, C Psychol), Director of AM Azure Consulting

"Kearns' book is a timely reminder that neither precise, legally enforceable regulations nor reliance on human moral points of failure can address the paucity of moral courage and deliberate systemic myopia of our political and corporate leaders or of academic experts. What he is seeking is a widening of the purpose of management to include value to society, humanity and stewardship and to resist the corrosive effects of relying on narrow performance measures like profit. Kearns is advocating that his brand of professionalism be central to organisational life. He asks the right questions, itself doubtless a process of testing hypotheses and paying attention to the quality and relevance of data, blending critique of methodology with topical examples and practical checklists. Kearns' *Professional HR*, to be sure, is worthy of a wide managerial readership."

Dr Wilson Wong, Academic Fellow, CIPD

"*Professional HR* is every bit as ground breaking as his previous book *HR Strategy: Creating Business Strategy with Human Capital*. Kearns' new work points out clearly that the lack of professionalism and standards are destroying the public's faith in business, and in many cases, businesses themselves. He makes it clear that evidence-based professional HR management is the way to stem the tide. This book is a blueprint for training a new generation of true HR professionals."

Patricia Turnham, Kaplan University, USA

"Amidst the fallout of a deep economic depression, the malaise organisations find themselves operating within affords a very real opportunity for HR professionals. HR has the chance to become what it has failed to do since its strategic aspirations were first voiced in the 1990s; the chance to become a value proposition for organisations. This value proposition is about demonstrating that the very best people management is a route to healthy, vibrant and sustainable organisations that produce real value for all stakeholders. Paul Kearns' book shows how and why HR professionals should take this opportunity and reposition both themselves and their own organisations to succeed in the 21st century."

Stuart Woollard, Kings College London, UK

"In this book Paul Kearns provides a compelling vision for the future of the HR professional and the HR profession. This vision challenges the HR professional to approach their role in a far more reflective and evidence based way. Kearns provides a convincing prescription for how a more professional and mature HR practitioner can deliver on the potential and value of human capital which remains untapped in many organisations."

Prof. David Collings, Professor of HRM, Dublin City University,
Editor, Human Resource Management Journal

1

THE VALUE OF THE PROFESSIONAL

Beware the HR 'professional'

If you are looking for professional HR advice be very careful. Managing people is a really serious business and your search will not be made any easier by the fact that anybody can work in HR. That is because the professional institutions have no powers to restrict entry and their qualifications are not always required. There are many reasons why HR is in this predicament but it will only be able to put matters right when it has clear evidence to distinguish between the professional and the unprofessional; between best practice and malpractice. Once those distinctions can be made we will have the basis for a General HR Council (GHRC), with similar powers to a General Medical Council. Gathering the right evidence is not that straight forward though and measurement in HR is notoriously problematic. This is why the most well-established professional bodies (CIPD, SHRM, ASTD), with a combined world membership of over half a million practitioners, have so far failed to become evidence-based. Changing times now make change imperative: people management might never become an exact science but there is a real need for a much higher level of HR Professionalism. The ultimate challenge for us all is to convince ourselves that we are achieving the best returns possible from our human capital. Professional HR will play a major part as soon as it starts dealing with the real problems, which start right at the top.

When Stephen Green, former CEO and Chairman of HSBC, was asked whether the bank had any regrets about its disastrous purchase of Household International, which resulted in record losses in subprime lending, he replied[1] 'It's an acquisition we wish we hadn't done with the benefit of hindsight, and there are lessons to be learned'.

So what has HSBC learned from its experience and what wisdom does hindsight bring? When Green referred to 'we' did he just mean he and his executive colleagues or did he mean everyone at HSBC? What about the managers who did the Household deal and their investment banking colleagues who advised them? Then there are all the other thousands of people involved in the global financial system, including those at the lowest levels who were close enough to the actual coalface to realize, well before their masters, that this was always likely to be a bad deal? They are the ones who saw the poor quality mortgage applications going into the system. While we ponder that we should not forget the journalists at the press conference; what did they learn? That assumes, of course, that the journalists want to learn so that they can spot any bad deals in the future, before they happen. Foresight is much more valuable than hindsight. Would HSBC's mergers and acquisitions team have been better served by interviewing the mortgage administrators at Household rather than the accountants? Have any lessons been learned at all, by anyone? Apparently not.

In 2012 Green was under pressure again, although he was now a UK Trade Minister after retiring from HSBC. He was under the spotlight this time because there was some explaining to do concerning HSBC's diligence in its anti-money laundering procedures.[2] The *Wall Street Journal* reported that 'Lawmakers said money laundered through HSBC-linked accounts benefited Mexican drug lords and terrorist networks, and skirted US sanctions on Iran.' It appears that lax management controls are endemic at HSBC; one part of its system probably infected another. The problem with systemic infections is they spread very quickly and HSBC is part of a much larger system; the entire, global financial system.

Before anyone gets the impression we are picking on HSBC let us stress that we chose them because of their good reputation. No organization is perfect and HSBC has come in for its own share of criticism but it weathered the financial crash of 2008 better than most. Its previous Chairman at the time of the Household acquisition, Sir John Bond, is highly respected and Green was at least willing to admit to some mistakes. Green is actually our example of a 'good' CEO and such animals are rarely sighted. He is an ordained Anglican priest and manages to reconcile his own deeply-held convictions with his personal ambitions and responsibilities as a commercial banker. He even writes books on the moral aspects of capitalism with titles like 'Good Value: Reflections on Money, Morality and an Uncertain World'. So if large organizations like HSBC, with principled CEOs and respected chairs, can become so mired in illegal and highly questionable deals and practices, what should we expect from the rest who are likely to have less integrity? Maybe we are onto something here?

We are not implying that Green or Bond have necessarily done anything wrong. What we are suggesting is that to manage large organizations, in a global marketplace, is getting decidedly tricky in the twenty-first century. The scale of the damage that can be caused is now potentially so great we can no longer afford to get it wrong. The answer, in principle, is relatively simple; we need much more professional management to minimize the risks. CEOs and Chairmen cannot know every detail of every transaction so they need every bit of help they can get. They need to feel absolutely confident that their people are only doing what they are supposed to be doing and are doing that to the best of their ability. They need to combine commercially-sound decision making with a moral form of corporate governance. In the hard-nosed world of banking that is an extremely difficult balancing act to pull off, which is why so many banks are no longer fit-for-purpose. The same balancing act also applies to every other global corporation because banking is only one part of the complete global system. Maybe getting that balance right requires a much higher form of Professional management; especially people management?

The global system needs Professional people management because any system can only be as watertight as the human beings who run it. Financial regulators know that their main purpose is the stability of the financial system and have learned, both in theory and with hindsight, that asset bubbles should be avoided at all costs. Yet history has an unfortunate habit of continually repeating itself because we fail to apply these lessons in practice. We should not need reminding that some unscrupulous human beings will follow their own short-term selfish interests, to the detriment of society as a whole, unless there are sufficient constraints in place to curb their worst inclinations.

These lessons are not rocket science. Any reasonably intelligent, objective observer will witness human beings behaving in irrational ways, on a daily basis, if they keep their eyes open. Despite this, successive generations of managers in mortgage companies, banks, financial regulation bodies and governments have failed to influence or stop such behaviour. Historians, or at least those with a sense of humour, tell us that the most significant events in history can all be perceived as either a conspiracy or a 'cock-up' (badly managed). So is the global financial system one big conspiracy or just an almighty cock-up? If it is a conspiracy then perhaps many financial dealings today, that are deemed to be legally acceptable, will one day be declared illegal? Conversely, if it is just the result of bad system design, then someone should have known better and, if HSBC had educated its senior managers to higher Professional standards, maybe none of this would have happened. So what level of professionalism have you reached so far?

So how Professional are you?

To answer this question you obviously need a definition of Professionalism but note the capital 'P', which signifies the very highest form of Professionalism; governed by a General Council that monitors standards and has the authority to strike off those who are guilty of malpractice. If you cannot pass this test then maybe you can still reach a lower standard of professionalism with a small 'p'? At that level it is more a case of personal conduct and minimum standards of expected basic behaviour. We could refer to the lowest level as the Entry point to the world of the professional. The following list offers a sample list of the types of behaviours we would all like to see and expect from any professional:

- Listening to your customer's needs.
- Respecting others and their views.
- Fulfilling your commitments.
- Turning up to meetings on time.

- Being properly prepared.
- Being courteous and having good manners.
- Maintaining confidentiality.
- Being prepared to listen to constructive criticism.
- Keeping any criticisms you might have of others objective.
- Being honest and having integrity.
- Informing those who need to know.
- Ensuring you have communicated clearly.
- Being impartial and making others aware of possible conflicts of interest.
- Maintaining self-control in any meetings, debates or disagreements.

There is a simple, over-arching principle here: 'treat others as you would like to be treated yourself'. Not everyone will manage to satisfy this most basic requirement because human beings are fallible and will have occasional lapses. Nevertheless, you can try applying this standard to someone you know, right away. Think of someone who you regard as very professional but who also exhibits 'small p' failings? For example, your doctor may be a brilliant physician but perhaps they are unpunctual, forget common courtesies or their bedside manner is not what it could be? So what do you expect from your doctor, a good bedside manner or effective treatment? Ideally, we want medical excellence combined with all of these professional niceties but if we had to make a trade-off then presumably we would value a cure above common courtesy?

This begs the question of whether professionalism can be dissected and deconstructed in this way. For a doctor, is 'listening' just courtesy or a necessity? How can they apply their medical knowledge and expertise without having first undertaken a thorough diagnosis; including the patient's own description of their symptoms? To start answering these difficult questions we had better set out our Professional stall more clearly. Our aim is to define, shape and develop a total, people management version of Professionalism, with a capital P. This will also be the highest value version because value creation is our ultimate purpose.

A Professional statement of purpose and value

Being Professional means being sufficiently disciplined to achieve your declared purpose. Our declared purpose is as follows: 'The purpose of a Professional is to ensure they offer the highest probability of the highest value solution to their customer's needs.'

The 'customer' is anyone receiving your Professional help, whether they have to pay for that help or not. Customers can also include patients, students, clients or any service user.

We then define 'value' as: 'The cost of a product or service that is fit-for-purpose.'

'Fit-for-purpose'[3] is a standard definition in quality that will work with any conventional, quality management system. Under ISO 9000:2000 lead auditors are taught that quality is defined as 'the degree to which a set of inherent characteristics fulfils requirements'. In other words 'will it do what it is supposed to do?' The value requirement asks 'will it do it at the lowest possible cost?' Sticking to these strict definitions is an important discipline that works well in manufacturing. The customer is always the ultimate arbiter of 'value' and can vote with their wallet, or their feet, if they believe they can get better value elsewhere. Taxpayers, who might decide they are not prepared to pay for poor value government services, will vote accordingly.

These same definitions and terminology can be applied to any sector, product or service. They can be used as a yardstick, for example, to judge the value of financial advice. When the adviser recommends a pension product, all that matters to the customer is what returns they receive. In the final analysis, the customer's judgement of professional advice will come down to what they expected to get for their money and what they actually received. Of course, there are many other factors outside of the financial adviser's control, and we can understand that some of these might not be foreseeable, but we still tend to judge people by results.

Let us take this idea further by looking at the case of a doctor's patient wanting a second opinion. If the second doctor's diagnosis turns out to be identical to the first then whichever doctor charges the least for the treatment is offering the best value for money. This should be just common sense because rational human beings are unlikely to pay more than they have to. We should just add here that this definition of value does not impose any condition, on either doctor, to charge the lowest price for their services. A Professional doctor can charge what they like in a free market and, assuming the market works well, those regarded as being the most Professional should attract a premium.

But how do we judge professionalism if there is no market or price mechanism in operation? Take the example of someone looking for free legal advice from a citizen's advice bureau. The professional adviser will do whatever they can to ensure that the quality of their advice is the best it can be, in relation to the cost of the service. If a taxation-funded, or charity-based, advice centre costs more to run than an equivalent, private law practice then the state version is of less value, and vice versa. This is a general principle of value that will apply in any context and can be expressed in simple equation form, as shown in Figure 1.1. If you achieve more output, more revenue or better quality per dollar spent then that is extra value. If you receive the same output, revenue or quality at a lower cost that is also better value. Now let us consider the potential for extra value from more Professional people management.

Applying the test of value

If you ask a football or baseball team manager what creates 'value' they would probably include everything from picking the right players, training them well, motivating them to perform and instilling team spirit. Yet all of this is neatly summed up in one, ultimate, objective – scoring goals, or home runs. If Manchester United never scored goals the club would eventually cease to exist. For

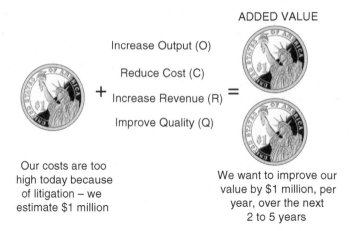

ADDED VALUE

Increase Output (O)

Reduce Cost (C)

Increase Revenue (R)

Improve Quality (Q)

Our costs are too high today because of litigation – we estimate $1 million

We want to improve our value by $1 million, per year, over the next 2 to 5 years

FIGURE 1.1 Added value is always in dollar's linked to OCRQ

a Manchester United fan it might mean that life itself is no longer worth living because they value their team so much. As Bill Shankly, a famous Liverpool FC manager once joked: 'Some people think football is a matter of life and death. I assure you, it's much more serious than that.'

Shankly was known for his witty quips but there was usually some fundamental management truth in his jest. If he did not take his own management job as seriously as life itself, how could he expect his players to give their all? If he placed a limit on the club's ambition, how would the fans react? This is the mindset of a true Professional, there are no limits, their Professionalism is more important than life itself. So how does a company that produces cans of beans apply this philosophy?

Imagine this food processing company is facing litigation over sub-standard products (e.g. customers have discovered contaminants in their beans) and wants advice on how to reduce this cost; currently estimated to be $1 million per year. Any adviser asked to help with this single issue, legal or otherwise, can only add more dollar value in four ways.

They can advise how to:

- Increase the number of tins of beans (O) that are of an acceptable quality (Q).
- Reduce the cost (C) of producing the beans (including litigation costs).
- Increase the price or revenue (R) received from existing sales of beans.
- Improve the finished quality of the beans themselves (Q) that should reduce cost (C) and improve margins (R).

There is no complexity in this eminently simple model because it is just a statement of a very obvious fact of life. However, it serves a very practical purpose: it provides an objective point of reference for comparison of value. The formula is a simple technique for assessing the dollar value of anything, tangible or not. Yet, paradoxically, it is particularly useful where intangibles are involved, such as people management problems. Managers who do not assess the value of their people accurately succumb to a form of management cancer that can destroy the value of people. When such a cancer takes hold in very large organizations, like banks, the extent of the damage can be immense. For now though let us return to the case of the legal counsel to the bean company. They can only apply their expertise to reducing the immediate cost of litigation, option (b). This will do nothing to resolve the underlying problem of food contamination in the production process but we will only deal with one problem at a time, in this instance.

The value equation is intended to highlight one of the main barriers to improving professionalism in people management, a failure to see people issues in hard, dollar value terms. To illustrate this point we need to apply the same equation to a different example. Imagine the same dollar figures shown in Figure 1.1 now refer to a private hospital that has a problem with litigation from patients who are unhappy with their treatment or care. It is costing the hospital $1 million per year and it wants to reduce that cost over the next two to five years. The adviser they engage this time is an HR Professional but, unlike the legal adviser, she does not take a narrow, specialist's view of the problem. Maybe the hospital management need to improve the quality of care (Q) first? That might involve an immediate increase in costs and push up prices, which could result in fewer patients and lower revenue. Table 1.1 shows the math for such a scenario, including some assumptions.

In this specific example reducing the litigation costs to zero does not produce a higher value organization, in terms of net profits. It just shows how tightly connected these four variables (OCRQ) are. The HR Professional uses this discipline of what we might call 'value logic' to eliminate any solution that does not make any economic sense. The full implications of this logic model might still not be apparent yet but should become so as we develop more applications of these same principles. Put very bluntly, for every dollar spent we want Professional doctors to give us the highest probability of surviving; Professional lawyers to ensure the highest probability our case will get a fair hearing; and HR professionals to guarantee the highest probability that we will achieve the greatest value from our people.

One general objection to this approach is that organizational life is just too darned complex to be reduced to such an apparently simplistic formula. Objectors point out that it is impossible to *prove* that any improvement in value (e.g. the overall

TABLE 1.1 The simple math of added value

Before any improvement action	
Hospital revenue from patients	$100,000,000
Net profit	$10,000,000
After action taken	
Cost of 10% improvement in quality of care	$ −1,000,000
Drop in patients/revenue due to 1% price rise	$ −1,000,000
Drop in litigation cost to zero	$ +1,000,000
Net profit	$9,000,000

value of the hospital in net profit) is directly attributable to the intervention (Professional HR advice). Such objections mistakenly view the value equation as simplistic when in fact it is the opposite: it is entirely holistic and incorporates all aspects of organizational complexity. This should all become clear but for now let us just take a simple stance. The HR Professional does not set out to **prove** anything; their standards and practices are based on probabilities. Luck does not come into it.

Professionalism and probability

Golfing legend, Gary Player, when asked what part luck had played in his success, remarked 'The more I practice the luckier I get'. Some believe the origin of this quote should actually be attributed to Hollywood mogul, Sam Goldwyn, who said 'The harder I work the luckier I get'. The Professional manager's version is 'the more disciplined I am the luckier I get'. It does not matter whether Gary Player actually did more practice than any other golfers, or Sam Goldwyn worked more hours than other film producers, what matters is that they put their success down to factors other than luck. They were acknowledging that probability plays an important part in success: sustained success does not happen by chance.

A doctor cannot rely on luck or chance if they want to cure someone. All they can do is to offer a much higher probability of curing a patient than a quack. That higher probability can only be built on evidence of what *seems to work*. The HR Professional is duty-bound to follow exactly the same principle of being evidence-based but will admit, from the outset, that they will not be providing any proof to anyone. The Professional has to manage expectations, they are not infallible, and their credibility will be gauged by the extent to which they match those expectations. The other essential rider here is that the Professional will explain to their customer why this is a valid stance, otherwise it will be seen as a cop-out.

Of course, an HR Professional would prefer to work from proof but will be pragmatic enough to accept that a burden of perfect proof would very quickly stymie their decision-making. Ask any accountant, marketer, production manager, engineer or even researcher whether they base their decisions on proof and there would be some very rapid back-pedalling. If managers could never act without absolute proof then they would rarely act. When the time comes to make a decision it should be based on a balance of probabilities, after weighing up the best evidence available. For example, will that machine break down soon or should we take a chance it will last until the next, scheduled maintenance check? Does that mortgage book already consist of fully-vetted mortgagees or should we do our own detailed checks first?

In a perfect world we might all look for perfect answers and the HR professional is no different. Indeed, they might have the most optimistic, even idealistic view of the type of society we might achieve one day. There should be no incompatibility between an HR Professional's idealism and their pragmatism though. The Global Polio Eradication Initiative[4] has a vision of a world without polio and some sceptics might regard such visionary idealists as naïve, even irresponsible, to hold out such hope. Yet even impossible goals can produce enormous value by reducing the incidence of disease, and relieving human suffering, even if total eradication is unattainable. The HR professional will work towards the best possible world whilst keeping their feet firmly on the ground.

Now, if you understand basic probability, and are well acquainted with the bell curve in Figure 1.2, please resist any temptation to skip this next section. First, we need to quickly re-visit the theory. A very rough interpretation of probability theory tells us that if you toss a coin an infinite number of times the chances are it will turn up heads as often as tails. If it turned up heads 999,999 times you would be right to be suspicious about the coin. We might call this intuitive grasp of the subject of probability 'common sense', but the HR Professional cannot rely on intuition or common sense alone; they need a much deeper understanding of the practical implications of applying probability theory to the management of people.

One aspect of probability theory that might appear counter-intuitive is its prediction that, regardless of how many times you toss the coin, it will never alter its chances of being a head or a tail on the next toss. On the 1 millionth toss there is still only a 50:50 chance of it being a tail or a head because coin tossing is a totally random action with only two possible outcomes. That is all well and good when there are only two possible outcomes but what about more complex situations, with many more possible outcomes and many more variables? This is the world the HR Professional faces and they can only cope with it if they adapt probability theory, and the bell curve, to the infinite complexity of the human race.

The bell curve can only address one variable on the x-axis, one human attribute, at any one time. This particular graph shows the range of competence for people, from the least competent at '1' to the most competent at '10'. On the y-axis will be the number of people measured. Imagine we were able to produce such a curve for a very large population, say the driving ability of all car drivers in the world, what does the theory predict? It will predict that the majority of drivers will fall in the

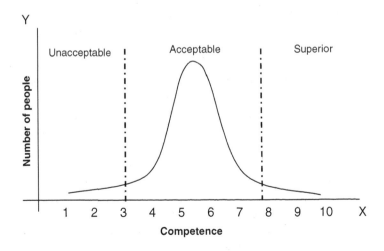

FIGURE 1.2 The basic proposition of management professionalism

middle range (4 to 7 on this chart), being reasonably competent relative to the whole group, and much smaller numbers of drivers will be at the two extremities of the scale. Using this as our **baseline**, a crucial concept both in EBM (evidence-based management) and for the HR Professional, we can now start to ask a generic set of very focused, searching and potentially serious questions about how to set standards of human (driving) competence.

Three basic performance questions:

(1) Have we chosen the best criteria for the x-axis? (Safe driving?)
(2) What test has to be passed to achieve the minimum acceptable level of 4? (The driving test?)
(3) What should we do with those who fall below this minimum level? (Fail or improve?)

The bell curve is only as informative as its choice of measures for the x-axis. Poor measures will produce a misleading curve. Drivers who regard the measures as invalid or irrelevant will not be encouraged to change their bad driving habits. In the worst cases people will just ignore the evidence and flout the laws or rules imposed on them. So the first real lesson for the Professional HR manager is to ensure that the people being managed buy into the data being used.

Professionally managing the complexity of probability

Performance management can become a mechanistic chore if we are not careful. Ignoring the uniqueness of human beings does not bring out the best in them. Although Figure 1.2 reduces human complexity to a simple 1 to 10 scale it expects improvement to come from holding a meaningful conversation with each individual about their own particular driving skills. If we want to refine the process further we could produce several curves for different driving attributes (speed, handling, hazard awareness etc.) but we need to be mindful that people come as a complete 'package'; we cannot just choose the attributes we like and ignore the ones we do not.

Because performance management is problematic, organizations can be tempted to ignore the complexity of human performance altogether and set a very limited number of predetermined grades or performance statements (e.g. 'meets, does not meet and exceeds expectations'). This type of simplistic thinking is also drawn towards the use of simplistic psychometric tools such as the Myers-Briggs Type Indicator which has become so popular in HR circles. The MBTI divides the world's population into only sixteen possible permutations, in much the same way as an astrology chart only allows for twelve signs of the zodiac. Anyone who believes in astrology, and reads their horoscope every day, will tend to identify with the predictions that match their experiences on that particular day and happily ignore any inaccuracies. The main attraction of these instruments, simplistic categorization, is their main failing. They encourage managers to look for similarities rather than the unique differences that might be the source of new ideas and innovations.

The most professional performance managers are well aware of all of these weaknesses but use other insights to make the most of what the bell curve has to offer. These include the fact that the curve is always:

- *Relative.* It might appear counterintuitive but even in the 'best' organizations, where they employ the most talented and highly paid people, there will still be a normal distribution of the total workforce. Goldman Sachs pays its people better than most companies but still gets rid of the bottom three to five per cent each year because they are not good enough *relative to their own, internal peer group.* The same person who scores a three with Goldman Sachs may well score an eight or nine with another bank, where performance expectations are lower.
- *Dynamic.* A score of ten out of ten today may well be worth only three out of ten tomorrow. The performance of fax machine salespeople must have suddenly looked very poor when the internet and email arrived on the scene. The underlying philosophy that has to underpin the bell curve is the need for continuous, never-ending improvement simply because the world around us is changing all the time. No one can afford to stand still; not even those scoring a ten.
- *Non-judgemental.* This does not mean that the fax machine salespeople suddenly had worse sales skills. It means those skills were no longer creating value. This is why the HR Professional will be very careful not to use the curve in a judgemental way. Often there are many other factors outside of the individual's control that come into play.
- *Dependent on buy-in and ownership.* If people think they are going to be judged by measures that they cannot control or influence they will not buy into their own score. Operational managers who have to manage this curve need to take ownership of it and they will not be able to use it effectively if it is not credible.
- *Naturally split into three categories.* You will have noticed in Figure 1.2 that there are two 'goalposts' at 3 and 8, representing the boundaries between unacceptable, acceptable and superior. There is no fixed rule or immutable law that says these have to be at these particular points. However, there are natural divisions and levers for improvement at these points. The unacceptables have to change, the superiors always want to and the biggest group in the middle, the acceptables, see no reason to move out of their comfort zone of acceptability. A complete HR strategy will incorporate different tactics for each group. We need to be particularly creative, even inspirational, to encourage the 'acceptables' to move forward.

Now let us practice using these insights by applying them to a firm of lawyers.

Applying the HR Professional's insights into the bell curve

We have to start with a measure of performance for lawyers on the x-axis (basic performance question (1) above). This could be something as obvious as professional examination results as long as we acknowledge that legal knowledge is not automatically an indicator of practical competence. A lawyer who scores very highly on technical knowledge might have very poor social or communication skills that mean they fail to attract or retain clients. So we would need at least three curves, working together, to create a more complete picture of each individual. Perhaps we should combine measures of technical competence, client relationship skills and individual fee income? The score for relationship skills could be based on observation, client retention data and even direct client feedback. In Table 1.2 we have produced the scores for one lawyer in hypothetical law firm 'Smith, Jones & Wilson'.

If they employ 100 lawyers this data can be used to produce a bell curve but we need to ask basic performance question (2) – where should the minimum standard be set? The partners who run the firm can either do this arbitrarily or consciously aim to raise their own level of management professionalism, more scientifically, by following the statistician's convention of calculating standard deviations, or intervals. We have done so in Figure 1.3 with the percentage of people who would fall within each standard deviation (x-axis 1) superimposed over our simple 1 to 10 range (x-axis 2). We can now choose where to place the unacceptable and superior 'goalposts'.

The partners might set these goalposts according to their own judgement, values and experience. However, they would also have to take into account any external standards of competence demanded by the professional registration authority for lawyers. The standard deviations on x-axis 1 show the approximate percentage of lawyers that will fall within each interval. So if the partners at Smith, Jones & Wilson choose to introduce a more professional performance management system for the first time, they might set the bar of unacceptability at 3 out of 10 (as suggested in Figure 1.2). If so, they would know that they might have to remove approximately two per cent of their total lawyer population (two lawyers). Now, having refreshed our memories on basic statistics, let us leave the legal profession and apply the same principles to management in general.

TABLE 1.2 Collecting data to produce a bell curve

Name: Beryl Steep

Attribute	Raw score (1 to 10)	Basis of measurement
Technical competence or knowledge	9	Based on their exam score relative to the other 99
Interpersonal skills	4	Based on observation and subjective assessment
Client retention	3	Actual client retention relative to that achieved by colleagues
Billed hours	4	Actual $'s billed
TOTAL SCORE	20	

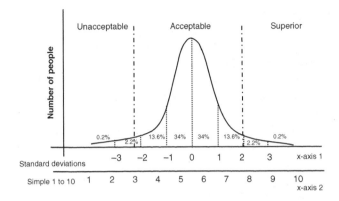

FIGURE 1.3 Connecting statistical theory to a simple, practical, scoring scale

Professionalism and transparency in managing people data

For any recent MBA student this might be a good point to refer to one of the most well known uses of the bell curve in recent management history. This was GE's forced ranking policy introduced by its former CEO, Jack Welch. Welch used a simple split of the bottom 10 per cent, the middle 70 per cent and the top 20 per cent. Welch wanted the bottom 10 per cent to be replaced every year. As Welch is an engineer he would be very well acquainted with sophisticated statistics but his bottom 10 per cent would equate to point 4 on x-axis 2 in Figure 1.3. If Welch's HR adviser was a true Professional they would have wanted to know the philosophical and scientific basis for Welch's scheme. Why did he choose this particular, asymmetrical split as a management tool when he drew his 'vitality curve'? Was that not immediately contradictory? Or was it just easier to talk about 'round' figures of 10/70/20. Was there any particular reason for identifying the top 20 per cent rather than just the top 10 per cent? Also, would Welch's ego have welcomed someone implying that he had a rather cavalier attitude to people management?

The professional HR adviser would have other serious questions about the practical problems of introducing Welch's 'vitality curve' including the most obvious one; having to replace 10 per cent of managers every year. They would also caution that potential damage could be done, in hard dollar terms, through disruption and by increasing the organizational fear factor. No doubt, at the time, Welch thought his performance ranking system was in the best interests of shareholders and GE's stellar share performance appeared to support his hypothesis. However, GE's subsequent share performance under Welch's successor has not been so attractive. This leaves another question hanging in the air about how 'vital' and sustainable the theory and practice of forced ranking is? Perhaps this whole area of producing and handling people data is much more problematic than Welch's simplistic twist on probability theory would have us believe?

Treating people as statistics is not to be recommended if you want them to give of their best. Not everyone's ego is as unassailable as Welch's; people have feelings and their perception of how they are being scored by the organization really matters to them. The HR Professional will always consider the 'PR' aspects of performance management as much as the ER implications. Individual performance data is very sensitive and has to be handled carefully but hard-nosed managers might dismiss the need for sensitivity as 'pussy-footing'. Of course, effective managers will never skirt around individual performance problems but Professional managers realize that value is often an organization-wide, rather than a purely personal, issue. They understand the interdependencies that connect performance to value and accept that everyone is dependent on everyone else pulling their weight. The organization therefore has to believe in transparency if it is to design the best performance management system. In a Professionally managed organization transparency is not an option, it is a principle. So is your organization transparent enough?

Should every employee know how they are doing, in performance terms, and should they also be able to see how every single one of their colleagues is doing as well? Transparency has to apply to everyone and that includes every senior executive; who should also know the consequences of failing to be transparent. How can hiding information from colleagues or 'covering up' be regarded as Professional behaviour? Yet there is still an unwritten rule in the CFO's 'manual' that salting money away for a rainy day, hiding it in lots of different pots, is an essential part of their job. They see it as the right thing to do: an indicator of effectiveness rather than an admission of organizational weakness.

Only a Professional CEO, confident in their own management abilities and humble enough to admit their mistakes, will foster a culture of transparency. The opposite of such a transparent culture is one of obfuscation and mistrust. This is not an environment in which to give birth to a high performance, Professional, people management culture. Nonetheless, we are going to assume away this huge problem of transparency for now so that we can ask more straightforward questions about the use of people data. If HR Professionals start producing people data that exposes accounting conventions for what they are then maybe the power balance in boardrooms will start to shift?

Damn lies and statistics is a game we can all play. So should we regard the accountants' version of the organization's performance as the accurate version or should we remain highly sceptical? On the other hand, should engagement surveys by HR departments, not known for their numeracy or their business focus, be trusted at all? HR Professionals are naturally sceptical of simplistic correlations between the way employees feel and the way they perform. The only answer is to start producing really convincing evidence about how the organization is managing the performance of its people. This is not just a different emphasis though, it is a fundamentally different management paradigm, based on a totally different philosophy. While damn lies are devoid of human content, Professional people management is replete with it.

There can be no better example of how far apart these paradigms are in practice than to refer once again to the sub-prime mortgage fiasco that contributed to the financial collapse of 2008. The short version of that complex story is that experienced human expertise and insight, in appraising the quality of mortgage books, was replaced with a detached and mechanistic use of statistical formulae to bundle the mortgages into cold, financial, derivative products. The human version views mortgages in both financial and human terms; mortgage applicants are real people who sometimes struggle to make ends meet. The purely financial view is a purely cynical calculation that aggregates default risk and aims to maximize returns in the short term, before exiting. We now know what happens when human accountability and responsibility are taken out of the equation in this way. The mortgage salesperson, the mortgagee and the banker, who ends up buying toxic debt, are all part of one single system and that system is only as good as its weakest person. Only Professional human governance can resolve these inherent conflicts of interest and prevent further catastrophes on this scale.

Human governance and the organizational fear factor

One human factor that is never made explicit in financial accounts is how organizations are perverting the natural behaviour of their employees. HR Professionals are acutely aware that survival is the strongest of all human instincts and never underestimate the part that a fear of extinction plays in human behaviour. There is no point in passing judgement on innate instincts; they cannot be changed but they can be managed. If survival is of paramount importance an employee will be prepared to disengage their brain and ignore any other, natural, inclination to do good. We need look no further for evidence of this phenomenon than the 450-page report[5] of the UK's Financial Services Authority (FSA) into the collapse and subsequent nationalization of the Royal Bank of Scotland in 2008. The report is damning in its criticism of ex-CEO Fred Goodwin's management style and devoted a whole section to the importance of management, governance and culture noting that:

> the FSA had identified a risk created by the perceived dominance of RBS's CEO. While it was recognized that the CEOs of large firms tended to be assertive … in the case of RBS, the 'challenging management culture led by the CEO raised particular risks that had to be addressed'.

Those issues were never addressed. Underlying issues are rarely addressed while profit figures are good and giving an impression that the organization is being well managed. Whatever talents Fred Goodwin might possess, his management style is not one of them. It was the culture he created, above everything else, that condemned RBS, its shareholders and the UK taxpayers to their eventual fate. This is the most convincing argument for placing HR Professionals on the board, with the specific remit of developing the right culture in the organization. Such a person has to be appointed directly by and reporting to the main Board, so that the relationship between the HR Professional and the CEO does not become one of meek, unchallenging obedience. The added advantage of this proposal is greater reassurance of cultural continuity; especially when evidence tells us that the average tenure of a CEO is only between four to five years.[6]

If we leave powerful CEOs to their own devices, without strong governance, we will suffer the consequences. That is why we have Boards of Directors in the first place but if they have not been Professionally trained for the role of human governance then the risks remain. Professional HR management is sustainable management. HR Professionals will have to fight their corner, along with every other director, and vigorously resist any narrow, short-termist tendencies, but there is now a clear case to be made. The HR Professional will have to be able to demonstrate though, with evidence, that Professional people management offers a much better alternative.

This leads to the next obvious, logical and ground-breaking recommendation: all managers in the system have to be equally Professional in people management, otherwise the whole system is too weak. The insecurity of one manager (bullying an employee to pass dodgy mortgages or fiddle overcrowded hospital waiting lists) will completely undermine the foundations of transparency and trust. In order to assure the requisite level of management professionalism we need to ensure they are receiving the right education, based on the best principles of EBM.

Re-defining Professional management performance

If we take a hypothetical company that makes a range of own-brand juices for several large supermarket chains, the Nectar Fruit Juice Company, we can start to see the initial signs of how different this new management education might have to be. Nectar is constantly under pressure from its largest customers, the dominant players in the supermarket sector, to keep lowering its prices. The Production Director at Nectar has three managers (Bill, Dave and Sue) who run the different fruit juice mixing and packaging lines. He tells them they need to reduce their costs by ten per cent within six months. The business objective is plain; lowering costs will enable the company to make the margins it needs to stay profitable. So how might each manager react to this imperative?

Bill

Bill is thinking of leaving the company over the next six months so achieves his own ten per cent cost saving by cancelling the orders for fruit pulp from regular suppliers and changing to slightly inferior products from an alternative source, offering lower prices. He also changes the machinery maintenance schedule slightly to bring down monthly maintenance costs; taking a gamble that this will not result in any more downtime while he is still there. He also calculates that it will take at least six months before the marginally, inferior quality of the product sent to their largest supermarket customer starts to show up in negative customer feedback and deteriorating sales. Not only does he achieve the full ten per cent savings target he gets a good reference from his boss when he leaves.

Dave

Dave is a very experienced manager who has no plans to leave the company, even though he knows how difficult it will be to take this level of cost out of the operation. Nevertheless, he knows he has to hit the target so works on reducing inventory and wastage. However, as this is a company that has been cost conscious for some time, he acknowledges there will be no significant savings immediately and believes he will just about reach his target through tighter controls. He only manages to save seven per cent and just accepts the unfavourable impression this creates between him and his 'more successful' colleague, Bill, who the Production Director says he was sorry to lose.

Sue

Sue is a working mother who has to structure much of her life around this particular job in this particular location, for a mix of personal reasons. She calculates that, at best, she might be able to shave a further five per cent off her costs. She knows only too well that this will impose even greater strains on her team, who she has recently been developing to have greater involvement in the day-to-day management of their production lines. Sue always knew things were never likely to get any easier. She now realizes the time has come to sit down with the Production Director and re-visit the factory layout, because she knows that the company has hit a wall on cost reduction efforts. She knows the only other alternative is to go against her own principles and cut corners but that would risk them losing the contract altogether. Discussions with the Production Director get nowhere, partly because the Production Director has always resented having to accommodate Sue's personal circumstances. Sue only reduces costs by five per cent and her commitment is now being questioned.

So which of these managers should receive the highest performance rating and who is the most professional manager? This is a fictitious and admittedly pointed example but it is based on real life, on genuine testimony, and is designed to highlight the fundamental principles for designing performance management systems:

- Hitting your target in the short term is a very narrow definition of performance if you know it will cause longer-term problems. Bill is not Professional because he is putting his own interests before the company's and is only looking at the cost aspects of value, in isolation.
- Even the more responsible, more professional, approach of Dave will not, on its own, resolve future problems.

- The rounded view of Sue could be regarded as the most professional in the sense that she is concerned with the company's long term survival. Her approach offers the greatest chance of sustainability, even though it might not have achieved an instantaneous result.
- Regardless of Sue's own, innate professionalism the company's future will depend on everyone working to the same set of principles and professional standards, not their own agendas.
- If the Production Director has a different agenda to the most professional manager, Sue, then she will be squeezed out.
- Only the highest level of management Professionalism, at the highest levels of management, is going to give the Nectar Fruit Juice Company the best chance of surviving in the long term.

The higher plane of Professionalism

Having earlier established some minimum standards of professional behaviour, and now acknowledging that Professionalism requires a more sophisticated view on performance management, we can start to sculpt the Professional role to which HR can aspire. So is there a standard framework we can use? Perhaps we might learn something from professions that are much older than HR? Are there any generic points of commonality with the medical and legal professions? If so, are they also generic to all other professions such as teachers, architects, airline pilots, social workers and even professional footballers? Or is there something peculiar to certain professions that sets them apart?

Arguably, the medical profession is held in the highest esteem, with practitioners who are generally trusted by their patients. So what are those 'magic' ingredients that make medicine the most respected profession of all? What standards have to be added to medicine's Entry Level list? In the list below we move up a notch of professionalism to Level 1, where the standards of professionalism become more challenging.

The Level 1 Professional standards in medicine:

- Dedication, lengthy training periods, hard work and years of experience leading to valuable and prized qualifications.
- A higher duty or calling, a vocation, with a strong ethical code, including the doctor's Hippocratic Oath.
- Diagnosis, advice and treatment is based on a large body of evidence-based knowledge.
- Limits of basic competence are acknowledged by the existence of specialist consultants for higher referral.
- Highly developed skills including medical procedures, tests and surgical techniques.
- Working to the highest quality standards of patient care and wellbeing within a clean and sterile working environment.

- The patients' or clients' needs are of paramount importance and placed ahead of any personal interests.
- Maintaining the reputation of the whole Profession is crucial so non-evidence-based methods and unproven therapies have to be outlawed.
- Registration as a practitioner with a General Council is mandatory.

This probably covers most, if not all, of the main distinguishing features. Although it might be worth emphasising that the one, over-arching feature not explicitly mentioned in this list is the simple fact that doctors deal in matters of life and death. That could be the single most important element: our lives are in their hands.

In January 2012 the cruise ship Costa Concordia ran into rocks just off the Italian island of Giglio. The captain was fully qualified and had competently sailed the same ship in these waters before. So the accident was not a question of technical incompetence. Also, the ship appeared to be in working order and the weather played no part. So whether this can be called an accident or not is still open to debate. Whatever the cause, the effect was that some passengers died. Inevitably, questions were asked about the captain's character rather than his technical expertise and, on this occasion, the captain had allegedly left the ship before many of the passengers escaped. This is not the professional behaviour we expect of someone in charge of a ship.

It is a universal, but unwritten, rule of the sea that when the time comes to abandon ship it has to be 'women and children first'. This has been established as both an ethical principle and a practical policy for many years. It passes the common sense test that an adult man's natural strength probably gives them a greater chance of fending for themselves. However, it also plays to some old-fashioned and deeply ingrained, cultural values of chivalry and decency. Although, when the Titanic sank, class came into it as well; you had more chance of surviving if you were a wealthy passenger. So what values are valid today?

We now live in more politically correct times and the 'women and children first' principle might be seized upon by some women, especially those who can swim better than men, as being based on outmoded and patronizing attitudes. Others might just have an innate belief that the world has moved on and we should place perfect equality above every other consideration. We do not wish to provoke a reaction here, nor raise any more hackles than we have to, and so take no particular position in this debate. However, the HR Professional will have a very pragmatic view in any debate on people management: if you do not accept the present policy you must offer a better alternative.

So, for example, should the new policy be 'all non-swimmers first, regardless of sex'? Then next in line, on the 'abandon ship' list, could be 'remaining women and children' before finally allowing the last group off who might be the best male swimmers. Or should that be the elderly first, swimmer or not, non-swimmers second, remaining women and children third, men fourth, crew members of either sex fifth and the captain last? Or should we keep it simple and say every man, woman and child for him or herself? Would that be the most equal, most politically correct policy? 'Women and children first' might hark back to a golden era that never really existed or it could be telling us that, in the twenty-first century, chivalry is a value that should not have died. Chivalry does not have to be regarded as patronising if it is also common sense that a man should put his wife and child's interests before his own.

The reality on the Costa Concordia was panic with some level heads and isolated incidents of heroism. Regardless of any change in twenty-first century social mores this did not stop the captain of the Costa Concordia being publicly castigated, and possibly eventually prosecuted, for not doing the 'right thing'. The 'women and children first' policy is not enshrined in any law and the captain's 'duty' to be the last person to leave the ship may not be legally enforceable. Nonetheless, many of us would still expect a sea captain to follow this unwritten code, even if the captain were a woman. It would be an expected part of their professional duty regardless of gender, or swimming ability. This line of argument leads us towards the notion that there are many varying degrees of professionalism, at different points in time, that have to match the current expectations of customers, clients, patients and society at large. We all have both a pragmatic and emotional desire to live in a world where high professional standards will protect us in our times of trouble.

But do we expect the same professional duty from a train driver and would we expect more from them if we called them train 'captains'? A train driver may well put their passengers' interests first but they have little influence on where the train is heading and even less room for manoeuvre in the face of impending danger. They cannot steer the train out of trouble so judgement does not come into the equation. A bus driver's job is similar but will involve much smaller numbers of passengers and lower speeds. All of these occupations require that the person nominally responsible for the 'vessel' has a responsibility to their passengers but the size, scale and nature of that professional responsibility varies enormously. Yet we expect that single word, 'professional', to cope with the whole range of expectations. It is time to delineate the differences much more explicitly and accurately, especially when it comes to professional leadership and management. So where should we start this quest for the perfect specification of a true professional? Maybe we can start gauging professionalism by how much professionals get paid?

The difference between amateur and Professional is not payment

When a term is difficult to define it sometimes helps to consider opposites. This is probably how we came to think of professional as 'paid' and amateur as unpaid. Professional actors and footballers can be paid millions; amateurs do it for love. This simple equation could be written as: professionalism $=$ payment.

As a theatre-goer you can choose to see Shakespeare performed by an amateur troupe or a professional company. Your expectations, and willingness to pay, will then be influenced accordingly. The more professional the acting, the stage design and the lighting, the better your experience. The laws of demand and supply determine that if you want to hear the greatest opera singer perform live on stage you will have to pay a very high premium for the privilege that is the rarity of their talent. If the world were full of brilliant tenors or sopranos we could all afford to hear them live. The relationship between Professionalism, value and payment is not always that simple though. When someone is prepared to do something simply out of love it has many implications for the work of the HR Professional. Highly paid lawyers, at the top of their Profession in every sense of the word, may work on a pro bono basis, or choose to take on a case that no one else will touch, simply because they have a social conscience or passionately believe that a good case should always receive a hearing, irrespective of money. How would we ever know what the motivation of each lawyer is though and would their motive colour our thinking about their professionalism? They could be driven by a desire to enhance their public image or sheer ego. Film stars will sometimes accept very low paid roles in independent films or go back to working in live theatre on a minimum wage simply because they want to. So the simplistic equation above must be wrong because the professional training of the lawyer or the actor is then not reflected in payment:

$$\text{professionalism} \neq \text{payment.}$$

Let's face it; being paid money has nothing at all to do with real professionalism. Some of the most talented, and highest paid, footballers and film stars let their fame go to their head and turn into prima donnas. They can behave in a very immature, petulant and unprofessional manner that fails even the most basic, Entry Level test. Conversely, the most respected lawyer does not suddenly discard their Professionalism when working on a pro bono basis.

Just to confuse matters even further there is another category of people we call 'semi-professionals'; those who do receive some payment but not as much as full Professionals. Local, minor league, football clubs will sometimes put cash in the boots of their best players to keep them from joining the opposition. These payments are usually to buy or retain their skills or goal-scoring ability though, not heightened professionalism. Such payments are probably unregulated, even illegal, and would undermine the sense of propriety that one would normally want to associate with professionalism. Rather than call such players semi-professional, it might be more accurate and informative to describe them as 'semi-talented'. This thinking sounds like it fits perfectly into the theory of probability with the relative levels of talent being plotted using our 1 to 10 scale; the least talented on the left and the most talented on the right. If you think about this for a second or two though you will have to conclude that it is a false premise; a contradiction in terms. How can someone, with a 3 or less, have an 'unacceptable' level of talent? What we should be saying is they have no talent; otherwise the word talent becomes nonsense.

To explain the full implications of this insight let us consider whether an Oscar-winning actress would be willing to work with amateurs or semi-professionals, never mind the unacceptables? What would the viewing public think if they paid top dollar for a production only to find the cast were a mixed bunch, including some who had zero acting talent? It doesn't work, does it? Can you mix up a team of professionals, semi-professionals and non-professionals or would their mixed standards, and the audiences' expectations, be totally incompatible? Would the theatre audience walk out and the football fans start booing? Such a state of affairs would be ridiculous would it not? So why is such a ridiculous situation still allowed to happen in the world of management? Why do we put up with managers who have no talent for the job?

How can proper HR Professionals hope to work effectively with management colleagues who are amateurish, unprofessional or cannot kick a ball? What if the board, or their executive colleagues, refuse to learn the official rules of the people management game and have no professional understanding of the wider issues around HR strategy and organizational behaviour? At what point do we blow the whistle for 'offside'? If whole system thinking dictates that everyone in the system has to be working to the same standard then all managers have to follow the same rules of professionalism; and there are rules.

We already have clear evidence that paying some people a lot of money brings no guarantee of even Entry Level behaviour. Likewise, throwing money at the problem of management education is unlikely to transform them into professionals either. Premier league football managers and film directors, who have to manage volatile personalities and prima donnas, probably come to accept this behaviour as the price of stardom. Money might buy you talent but it will not buy you adult behaviour or a Professional frame of mind. So there is a leadership and management tendency to find a trade-off between getting the results they want and tolerating a certain level of bad behaviour. As long as the footballer scores goals and the film star pulls in huge box office receipts, who cares how they behave off the pitch or on the silver screen?

Possessing a talent is obviously a necessary condition for many jobs but that does not make it sufficient. So extra value should be gained from adopting more Professional management methods. Football managers ought to be assessed on their professional management capabilities as much as their results; the results might change but the professional capability will not. The most Professional managers will be those that have the greatest confidence in their ability to manage the people at their disposal; regardless of how much money they can spend in the transfer market. So what indicators should we look for of this heightened professionalism?

Professionalism is intrinsically evidence-based

Payment, and levels of pay, looked like an easy and obvious way to distinguish between levels of professionalism but they turned out to be a very lazy distinction and a red herring. We might even go so far as to suggest that we have recently seen evidence of a negative correlation between money and professionalism in some industries, such as banking. Another distinction we think we can take for granted is that professionals should know what they are doing: we expect professional architects to design buildings that do not collapse. Not only does architecture require a great deal of knowledge it has to be founded on evidence that using certain design principles, construction methods and materials will result in a sound structure. Solid design principles and solid foundations are also a necessary condition for Professional HR.

We live in a world of uncertainty and risk and so crave the reassurance that someone knows better than we do; even if we are sometimes fooled by appearances. Just as your doctor is about to inject you she may well be thinking, 'I think this might help but I cannot be certain.' That is not necessarily the sign of a poor professional. The Professional doctor knows their own limits and will be clear, in their own mind, when they are entering unknown territory. It is being conscious of this uncertainty, and fully acknowledging it, that actually starts to mark out the higher levels of Professionalism. When we reach the boundaries of our own knowledge it does not necessarily mean we have to discard all the skills we have developed along the way. The doctor still has their highly-developed diagnostic skills and can apply them even when they encounter rare or unknown symptoms. When in doubt, what else can they do but stick to a professional discipline they have learned to trust? This includes:

- undertaking a thorough diagnostic analysis that takes into account all observable symptoms;
- attempting to specify the illness;
- identifying the most probable causes;
- choosing the most appropriate treatment; and
- basing their decisions on the best medical research evidence available.

Doctors are not infallible, we should not expect them to perform miracles, and sometimes they have to admit they do not have a cure. We have come to trust our doctors precisely because their diagnostic skills have worked for us on so many occasions in the past. Maybe we trust them too much? Perhaps we should question their methods more closely but that would require us to have a greater understanding of their science. How much we continue to trust our own doctor, as opposed to the whole of the medical profession, will be influenced by how well their treatment seems to work for us; our perception is our reality. However, at the macro level, at the level of the medical profession as a whole, someone needs to be checking the weight of all the statistical evidence available from all the doctors; such as a bell curve of comparative cancer survival rates. It is at this point that we come face-to-face with another worrying dilemma. If the normal bell curve is a truism then some of us will be unlucky enough to be treated by the worst oncologists, relatively speaking. The UK has been trying to address this issue for some years, not only by ensuring minimum standards but by offering patients the chance to view the success rates of different surgeons.[7] In effect, the top surgeons have not only become the benchmark for successful surgery, they set the pace for innovation and change. Hopefully their higher standards will attract future generations of surgeons with similarly high standards. This is the seductive allure of wanting to join an exclusive club.

What makes a profession a Profession?

Groucho Marx was joking when he said 'I don't want to belong to any club that will accept me as a member' but who would want to join a club with sub-standard membership? For a real professional, the tougher the standard the greater the attraction: the highest mountains offer the most exciting climbs. High standards take more maintaining though and necessitate the establishment of a governing body with the power to remove members that are not of the right calibre; we do not want to spend too much time rescuing idiots who tried to climb Everest. The only guarantee of professionalism is a general council, but what if the professional body itself, and those paid to manage club membership, do not have very high standards?

In an article in the UK's *Daily Mail* on 30 December 2011[8] the UK Minister for Schools revealed that in the period from 2001 to 2011 just 17 of England's 400,000 teachers were struck off for 'professional incompetence' and a further 211 for misconduct. In the same article Professor Alan Smithers, from the Centre for Education and Employment Research at Buckingham University, said it was 'nearly impossible' to prove a teacher was incompetent under the current performance management system. Is this why the UK continues to slip down the international league tables for education despite significant increases in education spending and the introduction of performance management (sic) methods borrowed from the private sector?

In January 2012 Nigel Leat, a teacher in a UK primary school, was jailed after systematically abusing the young children in his care. According to court reports[9] a total of 30 'inappropriate' incidents were witnessed by other staff at the school. Of these, eleven were officially reported to the head teacher but not one was passed on to the board of governors or the local education authority. Presumably the teachers who reported these incidents believed their professional duty of care, *loco in parentis,* only extended as far as reporting the problem rather than actively intervening. Did none of them have the courage to stop Leat in his tracks? Would they not have done so immediately if their own children were in his class? All of this paints a very grim picture of the teaching profession as a whole, not just a small group of teachers in a single school. The majority of teachers are professional but this is evidence of what can happen when the rot sets in at the bottom end of the bell curve. The only way to stop the rot is to eradicate it completely.

Hopefully, the standards in medicine and law are enforced more effectively in practice. If you want to be a doctor or lawyer in the UK you will have to meet much more stringent tests. These are set, respectively, by the General Medical Council and the Solicitors Regulation Authority; both of which have powers to prevent you from practising. As we have already seen in teaching, having these powers is not the same as using them and, first and foremost, a profession should always be self-regulating. Levels of Professionalism are determined by the behaviour of each individual and any hint of malpractice has to be brought to the attention of the authorities by vigilant and courageous peers. The regulatory body is a tribunal; it cannot be a police force as well. If a profession needs a police force to enforce its own standards then all its professional credentials are lost. All professionals should be asking themselves how professional they are when the chips are down; when it really matters. To what extent are you prepared to stand up and be counted?

Would the real Professionals please stand up?

One way to find real professionalism is just to ask. Try this question out the next time you are in a management meeting – 'who are the real professionals here?' It will not make you the most popular person in the room but, if you dare, these are some of the reactions you should expect:

- Jokers will just make a joke of it; partly to offset the embarrassing silence that has just descended on the room.
- The dismissive will, true to form, dismiss it as a cheap, trick question.
- The professionals might want to put their hands up but may not have enough confidence in their own professionalism just yet.
- One or two might stall for time by asking you to be more specific or to define your terms.
- The most politically astute will be suspicious and wait for others to declare their hand first.
- The insecure, with hunted looks, will be feeling vulnerable and exposed.
- Those with a professional qualification might be affronted by your audacity in not acknowledging their professional status.

It is the *managers* at the meeting who will have the greatest difficulty in convincing anyone they are professional because there is no single standard available and the conventional measures of share price, profit and market share, on their own, reveal nothing. So this is an extremely sensitive subject for them. Probe too deeply and you could lose some good friends very quickly. So keep it simple, and relatively innocent, by asking whether any of them would be interested in improving their level of professionalism? If there is a trick question here this is it.

A true Professional will always be totally committed to their own continuing, Professional development (CPD) because they accept that they will never have 'arrived'. That is not a tragedy, it is a boon. They will genuinely want to learn how to improve their art and craft and will always be up to speed with the latest thinking. If your doctor does not know which of the latest drugs are the most effective it seriously undermines their professionalism. They would also be paying you a personal disservice, as well as the drugs researchers who dedicated their lives to develop the latest drugs. An absence of Professionalism has a long-lasting, ripple effect. For example, what should we expect from our CFOs? Does their professional status guarantee that the company will be solvent and sustainable, or just that the books will balance and pass the auditors' test? Maybe their professional, financial management is no more than a pretence to help anxious investors sleep at night? There have certainly been enough well-documented cases in recent years to show that a professional veil can mask serious problems.

How professional were the Arthur Andersen auditors at Enron? How professional were the staff at the Securities and Exchange Commission in the US, and the equivalent Financial Services Authority (FSA) in the UK, when it came to regulating large financial institutions leading up to the crash of 2008? Management credibility and trustworthiness are paramount but to what extent are the smart suits and slick presentations glossing over serious professional flaws? Anyone who has worked at executive level will know only too well the elaborate games of bluff and double bluff being played out in boardrooms around the world as barely solvent companies, with dysfunctional management teams, do their best to portray an image of unity and solidity.

Asking someone if they are a professional should not be seen as a trick question, it should be welcomed by anyone who is confident in their own professional standards. If you are supposed to be holding down a professional, management job then you need to be able to answer it convincingly – 'yes, I am a true professional' – otherwise who is going to have faith in you? To do so you need the reassurance that you have a sound and robust working methodology, preferably on a par with the doctor's diagnostic discipline. You also need objective criteria to gauge and assure your professional standards. You need to know exactly where you are on a scale of professionalism.

A cumulative scale of Professionalism

The definition of the word 'professional' must be very elastic because it is regularly applied to everyone from your local hairdresser to top neurosurgeons. We do not wish to decry the hairdresser's skills, nor the pride they take in their work, but surely there are different levels of professionalism at play here? The level of accountability and responsibility will be different, as will the moral and ethical dilemmas that the two are likely to face. There is professionalism and then there is Professionalism; it is the magnitude of implication that really sets the two apart. Mrs Postlethwaite might rightly regard her new perm, from her local hairdresser, as a disaster if she has just come out of the salon looking like an electrified hedgehog. However, her personal calamity would not be on the same scale as someone whose brain surgery has been unsuccessful: at least her perm will grow out naturally.

This issue of scale is particularly relevant to HR and L&D practitioners because they can choose to focus on relatively trivial matters (e.g. resolving the salesperson's grievance about the colour of their new company car, or teaching customer facing staff how to smile) or much weightier fare (e.g. restructuring the entire salesforce, building a brand). The 'grievance handler' and the 'organization re-structurer' could both be working in the same HR department, and both types of work might

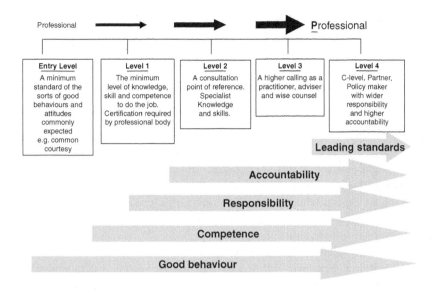

FIGURE 1.4 A Scale of relative Professionalism

be necessary, but there is a world of difference between the two. So we have to be able to delineate professionalism in terms of its potential impact. The Scale of Professionalism in Figure 1.4 is one diagrammatic way to represent these relative levels of professionalism. Let us look at each point on the Scale in more detail.

Taking a wide angle perspective for one moment, we can see that the whole edifice of professionalism is underpinned by the foundations we have already established up to Level 1; in terms of minimum standards of behaviour and basic competence. If a good bedside manner is deemed to be a necessary condition for becoming a GP (general practitioner) then anyone applying to medical school should be assessed against this minimum criterion. This might result in deselecting some, otherwise highly talented, medical students but minimum standards are minimum standards; no trade off is allowed. Nevertheless, there are likely to be different schools of thought as to which conditions are necessary. One might believe that medical knowledge and technical competence are the only criteria necessary to qualify as a doctor. Yet we all know what it is like to be treated by a physician without a bedside manner or respect for the patient. So this Scale is based on a broader philosophy of what constitutes professionalism and comprises two, key criteria:

- All the necessary and sufficient conditions for professional status should be clearly defined and assessed.
- Professional standards have to be validated against our original statement of professional purpose which is to provide 'the highest probability of the highest value solution to the customer's (patient's) needs.'

We can immediately put these two criteria to the test. Can a doctor achieve that 'highest probability' without satisfying an Entry Level condition of always 'listening to their patient's needs'? Doctors are already taught to listen to what their patient is telling them, even if that appears to contradict their visible symptoms. Only the patient really knows how they *feel* and how they feel could be a very important part of the diagnosis and treatment. If those who regulate the medical profession were ever to decide, after extensive evidence-based research, that the patient's feelings are immaterial to their eventual health outcome, then taking those feelings into account would no longer be a necessary condition. The patient might not see it that way though and it could result in a conflict of expectations between doctor and patient. So it is incumbent on the medical profession to explain where it stands on this. Either the evidence supports their professional practice or it does not. Once the position is made clear it has to follow through in both principle and practice.

Where there might be some grey areas or overlap is between the various levels of professionalism. For example, where does responsibility become accountability? We have identified four layers of professional sub-strate that together build the complete picture:

(1) **Competence** – for decision making based on professional knowledge.
(2) **Responsibility** – taking ownership of decisions made.
(3) **Accountability** – living with the consequences of those decisions.
(4) **Leadership** – setting the Professional standards for the future.

Rather than work our way along the Scale from the bottom upwards though, should we not start at the very top? Being a 'Leader of the Profession' is the highest Level attainable, Level 4, and will dictate all the other levels. So what does Level 4 look like in practice? How about the leading surgeons who developed keyhole surgery techniques in order to reduce the pain, suffering and recuperation time of their patients; as well as the cost of surgery? This was a truly valuable innovation, in every sense. Yet even when such innovations are so beneficial the surgeons who pioneered keyhole techniques faced stiff resistance from their more conventional colleagues who had a vested interest in maintaining the status quo. HR Professionals always anticipate that the 'fear of the new' and 'teaching old dogs new tricks' will not only incur resistance but possibly wrath as well.

This is why many ordinary professionals will never achieve the extraordinarily high level of Professionalism that is Level 4. They simply cannot progress beyond their most basic, human instincts. We can only hope to bring them up a notch or two on the Scale so let us now look at each notch in turn.

Entry Level

We have already listed the Entry Level indicators above. This is just a ticket to the professional game. It applies to everyone from the bus driver and hairdresser to the HR practitioner and neurosurgeon; they should all observe common courtesy and decency to other human beings. There is no guarantee of technical competence at this level though.

Level 1

At Level 1 you know how to do the job you are paid to do and your competence is certified to this effect by a recognized body. This could be a bus driver's licence, a pilot's licence or a GP's license to practice. At Level 1 there are immediate responsibilities that go with the job; such as ensuring the passenger arrives at the right stop and the patient receives the right prescription. A very limited amount of accountability also starts to come into play. The bus driver does not pull away until the passenger is safely on the bus. The GP will be responsible for the initial diagnosis and accountable for the treatment up to that point. However, if they have to refer the patient to a consultant they are, in effect, passing further accountability up to a higher, more specialized, authority. There is a limit on what a professional can do at Level 1.

Level 2

The grey and over-lapping areas really start here because Level 2 not only involves specialist knowledge and skills it denotes a greater degree of accountability for eventual outcomes. Not only has the medical consultant had to study for longer than the ordinary GP, and maybe worked harder to gain those higher levels of knowledge and skill, they might also be the patient's last hope of a cure. This imposes a much greater burden on them. A patient does not expect their GP to cure them of cancer but desperately hopes that their oncologist might.

Level 3

Between Level 2 and Level 3 something inexplicable starts to happen. The highly competent professional feels an urge to look outside of their immediate role and the imposed boundaries of conventional practice; this is the phase of the nascent keyhole surgeon. Where this urge comes from we may never know. The motivational drivers could be personal greed, making a name for themselves or an altruistic desire to help mankind. It is more likely to be a highly complex cocktail though. This is not a simplistic game of goodies and baddies.

The surgeons who developed keyhole surgery introduced a radical shift away from more invasive methods. Suddenly, invasive surgery techniques were made to look very primitive and this was bound to make the surgeons themselves look primitive by comparison. This is why innovation often initiates a crisis of conscience and only those who resolve this crisis will move up to the large 'P' version of Professionalism. The liver transplant surgeon knows that a key cause of liver failure can be alcoholism. They make their living out of medicine, not sociology or psychology. The Professional surgeon therefore steps outside of their own comfort zone because they accept they can no longer compartmentalize their Professional calling. So they spend more of their precious time dealing with the root causes of alcoholism; knowing this work is potentially much more valuable to future generations than the surgery for which they have trained long and hard.

Putting society's interests before one's own job security is where Professionalism takes on a completely different hue. For the HR Professional this involves telling some painful home truths, at board level, about the way people in the organization are being under-valued, under-utilized and sometimes even abused. This lifts the lid on organizational dysfunction. A blind eye can no longer be turned and potential whistle blowers have to be allowed to voice their concerns openly. Only a Level 3, Professional HR director will accept all of this as their problem; within their remit. The first real signs of Professional, HR leadership start to emerge at this point.

Level 4

By the time we reach Level 4 there are no boundaries as this is virgin territory. It demands real leadership with a pioneering spirit. A Level 4 Professional consciously anticipates a need for change and actively foresees issues arising. Their innate, higher calling demands that they take action to improve the way the world works. Anyone moving to Level 4 accepts that there will be strong and potentially belligerent resistance to change. Professional pioneers have already learned that they have to watch out for the arrows being trained on their backs but it is also their Professional drive that enables them to conquer any fear of what might happen to them.

At Level 4 you have already put personal ambitions to one side because your overriding dedication and loyalty to your Professionalism is all that matters to you. It is more important than life itself. Your less professional opponents will still be dictated to by their own, narrower, personal and possibly vested interests rather than long-term, societal value. One partner in a law firm might view the family law department as a real money-spinner while their Level 4 colleague sees mediation as a much better way to settle divorce proceedings and family matters. Call this more ethical if you wish but couples who want to still like each other after their divorce will value the integrity and advice of the Level 4 partner much more.

Level 4 Professionalism is a constant, unassailable, unswerving force for good. It will not be influenced or deflected by any changes in technology, legislation or company ownership. Level 4 doctors, despite the risk of endangering their own careers, will stand up to politicians and bureaucrats who want to undermine healthcare standards with ill-conceived change. Level 4 judges fight attempts to remove trial by jury or hold hearings in secret. They fight anything that goes against their Professional grain, their most deep-seated values. Nothing will stand in their way because they answer to no authority other than their own, highest, Professional calling. Level 4 Professionals pursue only the truth; that is why it is a perfect definition of leadership. It is also often perceived, rather unfortunately, as the land of the idealist. To avoid this accusation we need to leave the Scale here for now and retrace our steps. However idealistic a Level 4 Professional might seem to be, above everything else, they will have both feet planted very firmly on the ground. Any cynical board director who reads Level 4 as naïveté or weakness should heed this warning: in any boardroom battle that is decided on evidence alone the Level 4 Professional will always win. Let battle commence.

2

PROFESSIONALIZING THE MANAGEMENT OF PEOPLE

Evidence-based management is already well past the hypothetical stage

According to Wikipedia, the lazy learner's first and only resort:

> EBMgt today is only hypothetical ... Efforts to promote EBMgt face greater challenges than have other evidence-based initiatives. Unlike medicine, nursing, education and law enforcement, 'Management' is not a profession.[1]

Do you trust the evidence presented on Wikipedia? It is certainly not the most rigorously academic reference available but this entry on the whole subject of evidence-based management (EBM) appears decidedly odd and ill-conceived. First, it implies that the professions of medicine, education and law exist in a vacuum from 'management'. Go and tell that to the UK's NHS, which is currently trying to save £20 billion in the face of rising demand. Or tell every UK Chief Constable who is trying to enforce as much law as before with 20 per cent less money. Or even the Crown Prosecution Service who have to do their job within much tighter budgets. All professionals have to work within management constraints.

Second, and even more perversely, it appears to be saying that evidence-based managers do not already exist; they are hypothetical. If that is true then how did we get to where we are today? The first canal builders and railway engineers gathered evidence and surveyed the route before they started building. Anyone planning to build a railway today would have better evidence, based on better technology and better research, but EBM is exactly the same as Professionalism, it is determined more by an attitude of mind than the data available or the technology. Gathering evidence has always been a very natural, human activity and the best managers always used the best evidence they could find. This Wikipedia entry has missed the whole point of EBM which is to find even better evidence and evidence that is difficult to collect, like evidence on how people behave in organizations and how organizations can make people behave in perverse ways.

Third, managers who use the best evidence at their disposal, in the best way possible, should already be described as professionals. The best use of evidence defines management as a proper profession and that goal is not hypothetical, it is already attainable. The key ingredient holding back further progress, the bit that is stuck at the hypothetical stage, is a universal consensus on what constitutes evidence of effective people management. For example, would today's railway engineers manage the people management aspects of their projects any better? Would they subscribe to a new and better theory of people management? That is a good question in itself: what is the theory of people management? In the following list we set out the fundamental tenets of our general theory:

- The theory subscribes to the Utilitarian view of the world – creating as much value as possible to improve the lives of as many people as possible.
- Organizations have a moral imperative to create as much value from their human resources as possible.
- Organizations are born, and continue to exist, only to create value and wealth. They are not for producing jobs, or careers, or a more diverse society but hopefully all these will be the beneficial by-products.
- Value creation is the single arbiter of performance and organizational success.
- The sole purpose of Professional people management is to ensure the highest probability of the highest value from people.
- Organizations are not strictly democracies, and might never be, but dictatorships do not maximise the value from people.
- The performance of people should always be judged by their output in terms of their contribution to the value creation process; not their inputs of intellect, talent, capability or effort.
- People and talent have to be managed if we are to maximize the value of their potential; it will not happen by chance.
- Every employee is a unique human being and the best value is likely to come from treating them as such and working to each of their strengths.
- Professional people management makes allowances for people to grow, develop and improve but it also has to impose clear boundaries and limits on both competence and behaviour.

This might not look like much of a theory, it might not even pass any theoretical test, but it is the foundation for the sort of Professionalism we espouse here. It is a set of principles that have been developed from a clear set of values which, most important of all, can be put into practice. However, our theory can only be as good as the whole system theory within which it has to operate.

Towards a whole system, general theory of Professional management

We produced a much tighter definition of 'professional' in Chapter 1 but we have not yet defined 'management' and we cannot begin to address the issues of management practice or management education until we do. It is not the detail of what a manager does that is our main concern, there are already more than enough books out there dealing with the minutiae of management, but rather the bigger, holistic picture. If we read every book, ever written, on the subject of management would we find they all at least agree on one, common, over-arching, general theory of management? No, of course not. That is why we still keep producing so many management books, often with conflicting advice, because the ground rules were never agreed at the beginning. For example, do you subscribe to the core competence theory of management or do you see validity in the conglomerate model? Even if both schools of thought have some validity do they each require their own separate theory of people management?

One advantage of the online age is that students of management can access all schools of thought almost instantaneously but, as we saw with Wikipedia, they cannot guarantee they will find the correct answer. They could start from the time of Sun Tzu, through Machiavelli, to Adam Smith, Henri Fayol, the twentieth century's Frederick Taylor, Peter Drucker and further on to ...? Yes, on to where exactly? Where in that long and illustrious line is the definitive source on effective people management? Choose whatever timeline you wish, and whichever management theorists you prefer, and you will eventually come to the same conclusion: the basics of management are relatively straightforward (i.e. planning, organising etc.) and although we can still get the basics wrong (like bankers not checking mortgage books) the more complex the management problem becomes the more likely we are to get it wrong, more often. This is the challenge facing the twenty-first century executive: greater complexity means greater risk and greater scale means much more damage can be done. So it is worth our while putting more effort into getting the biggest, most complex issues resolved more efficiently.

As soon as we start to talk about complexity we have to talk about strategy because strategy is meant to be the answer to complexity. Strategy addresses every facet of a complex and intractable issue, simultaneously, in a planned way. The Professional manager admits to himself that the whole organizational system has to be addressed, all at once, he cannot approach it in a piecemeal fashion. So when he talks about strategy he has to mean whole system thinking. Maybe someone like Peter Senge, with his Fifth Discipline, was a name we might have added to that list of management thinkers and theorists? Without a whole system approach gaps, weaknesses and huge holes will appear that can bring the whole system crashing down. We came very close in 2008.

If we could identify a single root cause of the banking crash of 2008 it would be the absence of a whole, banking and financial management system. The reason some bankers did not check the mortgage book derivative products they were buying was simply that there was no system in place to guarantee that they did. The banks themselves did not have adequate systems in place but neither did the bodies that exist to regulate them. The banking industry is a global industry and global industries need global systems to work efficiently and effectively. They also have to deal with the people willing to exploit the system's weaknesses. This is a statement of fact, not cynical opinion, and it can be supported by the bell curve of integrity. It is a fundamental truth about mankind. We need to tighten up regulation even further to outlaw bad behaviour, we need more professional regulators and we need to incentivize bankers to produce value, not short-term profits. Such a system has yet to be devised that can achieve all of these objectives. Designing such a system might prove to be the most difficult, human balancing act that society has ever had to pull off but we have no chance of pulling it off without Professional people management of the very highest order.

Managing wicked problems Professionally

We should not become distracted by focusing only on the banking sector. It might be a particularly important sector today but our primary concern here is the nature of general management in the twenty-first century and beyond. One simple, management lesson we should certainly have learned by now is that many societal and organizational problems are just so darned complex that there is no single, 'best', theoretical solution; never mind a practical answer. In academia they refer to this phenomenon as 'wicked' problems: not to be confused with a wicked sense of humour, although it helps. Wikipedia attributes the origin of this term to C. West Churchman in a 'Guest Editorial' of *Management Science* (Vol. 14, No. 4, December 1967), defining 'wicked problem' as:

> a phrase originally used in social planning to describe a problem that is difficult or impossible to solve because of incomplete, contradictory, and changing requirements that are often difficult to recognize. The term 'wicked' is used, not in the sense of evil, but rather its resistance to resolution. Moreover, because of complex interdependencies, the effort to solve one aspect of a wicked problem may reveal or create other problems.

One famous, classic, wicked problem was the Cuban missile crisis of 1962. Nothing like it had ever happened before so there was no frame of reference available. Whichever course of action the Americans took would have potentially catastrophic consequences. A contemporary, and equally wicked, problem is how should we manage the future of the EU while the Eurozone is in crisis (as at September 2012). There are just too many variables, too many unfathomables and too many uncontrollable factors to be able to say, with foresight, the 'best' way to manage this situation. Of course many historians, commentators and writers are already offering their opinions, whether we want them or not, knowing full well they will never be held to account for their free advice. As any management writer knows, the easiest advice to give is the unaccountable variety.

Other 'advisers' wait until the crisis is over, when they have the benefit of hindsight, by which time it is too late to change anything and is of little use other than for academic debate. This type of hindsight is unlikely to inform future generations because the very nature of a wicked problem is the uniqueness of its complexity. There is no chance that the exact circumstances of the Cuban Missile Crisis will ever be repeated; although this would not deter Hollywood from producing 'Cuban Missile Crisis 2'. This is the problem with management theorising: there is no way to provide an acid test of the application of leadership and management theory other than in the here and now. The historical view is nothing more than virtual history – 'What would have happened if they had chosen options P, Q or Z instead of A or B?' The Cuban Missile crisis was one where calamity was just around the corner at the flick of a nuclear switch. However, even if the Americans were caught off guard, such crises do not just appear out of nowhere, the gestation of wicked problems can usually be measured in decades, if not centuries.

Historians of management should not be asking 'how is the crisis *being* managed?' so much as 'was it ever managed at all?' The Eurozone crisis of today was instigated long before the Euro was first launched on 1 January 1999. Many economists, with foresight, predicted that it would not make any economic sense without fiscal union. But fiscal union was not the concern of the politicians whose primary goal was political union. Of course you cannot have one without the other; that is not rocket science. Regardless of the opposing debates, once the decision to go ahead was given rules had to be written to ensure that the *system* would not be undermined by weak economies, such as Greece; and Greece's weaknesses were well known at the time. Unfortunately, several countries were allowed to ignore the rules and when rules are ignored the system no longer exists. So at what point did *management* come into this equation? What we have now is called *crisis management* which, paradoxically, would not be necessary if the obvious crisis had been avoided in the first place. The EU's crisis management is the antithesis of Professional management and clear evidence that the EU, with a population of 500 million people, is still not Professionally managed today. This will come as no surprise to anyone who has been monitoring the EU's very basic failure to account for its own spending over the last two decades.[2]

The emergence of more global superpowers and super blocs demands that we improve the probability of finding better solutions; simply because more power brings with it much greater risk. These are our management and leadership challenges and only better education will enable us to rise to the occasion. We already know the technicalities of mass production, double entry book-keeping, supply chain management and all of the other aspects of modern management, at a micro level. We still have a great deal to learn about managing global, wicked problems at the macro level though; especially how to build billions of people into our equation of societal value.

The Greek question

Take one question that arose during the Eurozone crisis in 2011–2012; should Greece leave the Eurozone? One decision considered, Option A, was to unceremoniously kick Greece out. This would have had an immediate impact, including a possible run on Greek banks. An alternative and diametrically opposed decision, Option B, would be *not* to kick them out. Both of these could be viewed as management decisions. Taking Option A could be described as the *active* option; somebody has to actively remove Greece. Option B could be described as the inert or *inactive* option; where no one apparently has to do anything. This, of course, is a management fallacy.

Doing 'nothing' (Option B) is actually *doing* a lot. In fact it involves doing as much as, if not more than, Option A. It's just that we don't gauge the impact in the same way because inactivity is regarded as hypothetical, like virtual history, as though it never actually happened, whereas the pain of Option A would be felt immediately by anyone queuing up to get their money out of a Greek bank. Politicians will never openly admit though that the impact of Option B is just as real, it is not a figment of our imagination, for obvious reasons. Yet someone in Germany is already spending some of their citizens' own, real money supporting Greece while the EU dithers. If President Kennedy had dithered and, by doing so, had encouraged the Russians to launch a missile strike, we would now have history to tell us what the impact of that *inaction* was; if anyone had ever survived to tell the tale.

There is a third option though, Option C, the strategic option. This could include Option A or B. The only difference is that Option C makes those other options part of a longer-term plan. As we do not know exactly what was going through JFK's mind, at the time, we cannot determine for sure whether he had taken Option B or Option C when he did not press the nuclear button. Discerning the difference between plain old vacillation, procrastination and dithering and the real, strategic deal is very difficult. Only when someone reveals to us how their inaction is part of their grand, strategic plan will we understand what is going on in their head.

There used to be a theory that perceived the universe to be in a 'steady state': not growing or shrinking, just being. This was eventually proven, through scientific observation, to be a false view: there was clear evidence that the universe was still expanding. Similarly, there is no such thing as steady-state management because the universe and the world we inhabit are changing every single second. Change at the level of the individual organization can be happening imperceptibly but it is happening nonetheless. For example, foreign exchange rates are changing every split second and can have an adverse or favourable impact on an organization's finances. Professional managers anticipate as many problems as they can. Professional CFOs make decisions as to whether to hedge against sharp exchange rate fluctuations or not.

A Level 4, Professional, leader anticipates the biggest, most wicked crises and ensures that his or her organization is as well-prepared as it can possibly be; ready for anything that is ever likely to be thrown in its way. This level of Professionalism might involve the use of the latest scenario planning technology and complex algorithms but, above all, it should mean that their people do not panic in a crisis. The Level 4 CEO wants to feel confident that his or her people have all been well selected, effectively trained and developed, and placed in the most appropriate roles in the most adaptable organization designed to deal with anything. Surely, this people dimension is the essential ingredient in any General Theory of Management. Whole system, people management thinking has to be an inseparable and indivisible part of that theory. So this is the ultimate standard by which we should be judging our present and future leaders.

Defining Professional leadership standards

The benchmark we have just established is not that distinct yet, but you can at least start to look around you and count the number of senior executives who might come even close to matching this profile. There are not likely to be many of them, according to the bell curve of leadership. As there is an acute shortage, and no one admits to poor leadership, some of our executives will already have been self-anointed as 'leaders' simply by re-naming themselves as the 'leadership team'. They have probably never exhibited any leadership behaviour before and have no willing followers either, but that does not matter if no one is measuring their leadership. Even if some of them are supposed to be accredited 'professionals', how many are subject to a general council that has the authority to strike them off?

If any of them are already members of a professional institute, like engineers, it is more likely to testify to their specialist, technical knowledge than to their leadership or management prowess. In the UK, their professional body could even have been awarded chartered status[3] or a similar seal of approval. But Level 4 Professionalism does not relate to technical competence alone so what stance do professional institutions take on standards of leadership and managerial competence? How do they incorporate these standards into their complete assessment of the professional status of their members? In order to find out let us look at the specific example of the engineering profession in some detail.

Visit the UK Engineering Council[4] website and it will tell you that it:

> ... is the UK regulatory body for the engineering profession. We hold the national registers of 235,000 Engineering Technicians (EngTech), Information and Communications Technology Technicians (ICTTech), Incorporated Engineers (IEng) and Chartered Engineers (CEng).

Part of their role is to set, monitor and maintain professional standards of which the highest is 'The Chartered Engineer Standard',[5] which includes several references to specific areas of management ability. We have not chosen these particular items at random. They were carefully selected to highlight what the Engineering Council deems to be the particular management capabilities that necessarily sit alongside technical ability. Including:

C. Provide technical and commercial leadership.

Plan, budget, organize, direct and control tasks, people and resources. This could include an ability to:

- Set up appropriate management systems

- Organize and lead work teams, coordinating project activities
- Gather and evaluate feedback, and recommend improvements.

Manage product improvement. Interpret and analyse performance. Determine critical success factors.

- Lead teams and develop staff to meet changing technical and managerial needs.
- Agree objectives and work plans with teams and individuals
- Identify team and individual needs, and plan for their development
- Lead and support team and individual development
- Assess team and individual performance, and provide feedback.
- Promote quality throughout the organization and its customer and supplier networks.

One of the UK's most famously talented, and workaholic, engineers from the nineteenth century was Isambard Kingdom Brunel (celebrated again during the London Olympics opening ceremony in 2012). Some regard him as an engineering genius and many of his impressive structures are still standing and operational today. That same genius and drive also instigated several major projects that bankrupted his backers: he did not score so highly on the bell curve of financial management. So while a professional engineer will admire his engineering genius they also know that sound project management has to be part of a complete repertoire. The 'success' of a project can never be gauged on technical excellence alone but assessing project management skills is not as straightforward as checking whether a bridge is likely to collapse or not. Nevertheless, we have to assess the leadership and management capabilities of engineers, just as much as any other manager, regardless of how difficult a task this may be prove to be. If we do not, then we are not assessing the whole of their professionalism. So let us make a determined effort to do just that.

Defining management

What does 'management' actually mean? One of the greatest management thinkers of the twentieth century, Peter Drucker, always regarded management as a profession despite what we read on Wikipedia. In his book *On the Profession of Management* (Harvard Business School Press, 1998) he spelled out the purpose of management in one sentence:

What is the first duty – and the continuing responsibility – of the business manager? To strive for the best possible economic results from the resources currently employed or available.

(Chapter 6. 'Managing for Business Effectiveness', page 65.)

Now, before you ask what his take on people management was, you might be pleased to know that he had already covered this earlier. In the first line of Chapter 3, 'How to make people decisions' he declares:

> Executives spend more time on managing people and making people decisions than on anything else – and they should. No other decisions are so long lasting in their consequences or so difficult to make.

So, with this advice in mind, let us review the Engineering Council's professional standards, line by line, from this 'people decisions' perspective. Their standard requires that engineers 'Set up appropriate management systems' but does not define what a management system is nor does it impose a specific requirement for the introduction of a people management system. So we need to offer them a definition of a system that will serve both purposes. Our working definition of the term 'system' is 'Setting up the means to ensure that what you plan to happen actually happens'.

If you plan to build a bridge, a project management system should ensure you build a bridge. Part of that project management system has to be a system that ensures you not only have the right people on the project but that they work together well enough to complete the task, on time and to budget: that is assuming the budgeting system is working effectively. We then only need to add Drucker's condition that the whole project management system should achieve the 'best possible economic results'. We prefer our own, more precise, terminology to Drucker's and would replace his words with 'best possible value', having defined value very precisely in Chapter 1. So how does the complete project management system ensure that the people involved create as much value as possible?

The engineers' standard already acknowledges that this will involve the abilities of 'organising and leading work teams' and 'coordinating project activities'. But what if the members of those work teams, from a range of disciplines, are not as capable as the project requires? What if the culture of the organization does not lend itself to cooperation and harmonious working relationships? What if the project manager does not have the ultimate authority over the project? Even if they do there is the further requirement to 'Gather and evaluate feedback, and recommend improvements.' Getting honest and valid feedback is essential to organizational value but does this happen naturally in most organizations, or does someone have to consciously create the right environment? What if there is a pervading culture of fear? How do you recommend improvements that seem to 'point the finger' at another senior manager's apparent incompetence? Can everyone's performance always remain open to question or is that level of transparency not encouraged? The engineers' standard recognises all of these management issues when it stipulates 'Manage product improvement. Interpret and analyse performance. Determine critical success factors'.

We have already seen in Chapter 1 that performance measurement for the management of people is highly problematic. What new or extra management insights, therefore, does the engineering standard bring to bear on this perpetual debate? Or is this standard nothing more than a bland and superficial statement; a mere nod in the direction of conventional management dogma, rather than signifying any serious intent to move the engineering profession forward to a much more solid evidence-base? Is their language just too vague for the purpose of setting a proper, measurable, professional, management standard? Do engineers, who measure everything, have any idea how to measure people? Maybe we get an answer by looking at another of their requirements to 'Lead teams and develop staff to meet changing technical and managerial needs'.

What is the distinction between 'leading' a team and 'managing' it and would greater precision in our choice of terms add value? What does 'development' mean and how will you know that development is not only happening but adding value to the project at the same time? None of the answers to these questions are to be found in the engineers' standard but it does not stop them talking about it. Apparently a professional engineer should also 'Promote quality throughout the organization and its customer and supplier networks'. Can any individual engineer, or indeed the whole of the engineering department, promote quality in this way unless the whole organization is doing that strategically and holistically? It is amazing how soon the engineer's own discipline of precise language gives way to imprecision as soon as the conversation turns to the topic of people.

Reading between the lines one senses that the writers of the standard do not really believe what they are saying and show no real commitment. The cynical observer might receive the distinct impression that these engineers do not believe that management can be as precise a discipline as their first love, engineering. Yet if engineers want to produce a credible, professional, management *system* they cannot afford to leave this huge cog out of the machine. They need to indicate very clearly where the level of engineering professionalism is set. Is it set at Entry Level or does it aspire to Level 3 and beyond? More importantly, assuming we get a clear answer, do they have the will to make those standards really stick? Or will someone else have to police their engineering standards for them?

Regulations do not produce the best Professionals

One industry that has been through several major shake-ups over the last 30 years or so is the finance sector, but there is still a need for further reform. The Sarbanes-Oxley Act of 2002 was a response to several high-profile company collapses (Enron, Tyco, WorldCom *et al.*). On its way through the US legislature it acquired two titles: the Public Company Accounting Reform and Investor Protection Act and the Corporate and Auditing Accountability and Responsibility Act. The words make the need for change and the intent very clear but the evidence shows that none of this legislation prevented the subsequent crash of 2008.

As recently as December 2012 the UK's Financial Services Authority (FSA), the same body that failed to deal with issues raised at the Royal Bank of Scotland, instigated a Retail Distribution Review,[6] which set out to introduce new professional standards in the financial advice industry, declaring 'The new professionalism requirements will improve the level of consumer confidence and build general levels of trust in the retail investment sector'.

The new regulations place a specific requirement on retail, financial advisers to:

- subscribe to a code of ethics;
- hold an appropriate qualification, including filling in any gaps in their qualifications;
- carry out at least 35 hours of CPD a year; and
- hold a Statement of Professional Standing (SPS) from an accredited body.

There must have been a perceived need for these new regulations (presumably from customer complaints) but the inexact language and indeterminate 'standards' are a classic example of light regulation and, by dint of that fact, light-professionalism. One could reasonably ask how they define 'ethics'; what evidence they have that there will be a connection between 'appropriate qualifications' and sound financial advice; what constitutes valid CPD and which body has the credibility and gravitas to offer a weighty 'Statement of Professional Standing'?

The FSA had already, itself, been accused of 'light touch regulation' after the crash of 2008 and does not seem to have listened to its critics or learned how to do its job more heavily. The lightness of any regulation is usually to be found in the regulation itself, in its enforcement or, in the case of the FSA, both at the same time. Strong regulations with strong enforcement are necessary conditions for a strong, watertight system. We do not have to be too cynical to conclude that these new regulations are already watered down and might turn out to be no more than an extra, costly layer of bureaucracy without any corresponding improvement in the actual standards of professional advice from financial advisers.

Level 4 Professionalism is not about regulations though, or codes, or standards imposed by an external arbiter. The ordinary customer, of often complex financial products, is at the mercy of the professionalism of their own, personal, financial adviser. If the adviser has no intention of showing any mercy, especially when it comes to their sales commission, they will follow their own 'moral' code for as long as they can get away with it. If, in their mind, there is a sucker born every minute they will not only take their customer for a sucker but the FSA as well. Regulatory bodies have to show they mean business and be much more specific about where they draw the line on bad behaviour. They then have to follow through with very strict discipline that prevents the unscrupulous, financial adviser from advising anyone.

In a 2012 article in the *Sunday Times* headed 'Goodwin in FSA pact'[7] it was revealed that a secret pact had been agreed between the FSA and the discredited CEO of RBS, Fred Goodwin. After the biggest and most damaging banking collapse in British history one of the experts 'appointed to review the FSA's work ... said of the (FSA's) report "It was an attack on (Goodwin's) competence. There was no evidence of incompetence."' Presumably this was a reference only to

Goodwin's technical competence. Surely this 'expert' cannot possibly be suggesting, from a leadership and managerial perspective, that Goodwin was not incompetent? If anything, Goodwin is much more competent technically than he ever is likely to be from a leadership perspective.

Any financial advisers reading this expert's view will take it as a reassuring signal that any line drawn by the FSA is in shifting sand. Apologists for poor financial regulators and their political masters, who apply light touch regulation to non-existent financial 'systems', have missed the whole point about Level 4 Professionalism. Using the criteria suggested here, with indicators of performance, could very easily be used to test the Professionalism of business 'leaders' like Goodwin. They might not be perfectly scientific but then neither is the FSA. More importantly, the FSA, by its own admission, had already identified what was going wrong under Goodwin's governance long before the collapse of RBS. A CEO who exhibits a clearly tyrannical style of management and shows no hint of leadership capability should be replaced by someone who does. Otherwise we all suffer the cataclysmic consequences. If the FSA are not going to do their job why bother having an FSA?

Imposing regulations rarely, if ever, changes intrinsic behaviours or mindsets and will not bring anyone up to Level 4 Professionalism: diversity laws do not turn racists into lovers of mankind. What we can do though, if we have any political will at all, is to make these tough questions a standard part of the selection criteria not only for the senior level appointments but for the headhunters that find the candidates as well. So do headhunters have their own professional code? The 30 per cent Club is an organization that is 'Motivating and supporting Chairmen to appoint more women to their boards' and a visit to their website[8] reveals the existence of a 'Voluntary code of conduct for executive search firms' that was recommended 'to address gender diversity on corporate boards and best practice for the related search processes.' Presumably 'success' to the 30 per cent Club is when the number of women on boards hits 30 per cent? Why would that be a success and what evidence would make it best practice? Quotas are not an evidence-based solution, unless there is causal evidence that a quota has improved the value of the organization. Shareholders and societal stakeholders need to have much greater confidence in the questions they can use to hold boards of directors to account. Until governments and regulators acknowledge this fact of life we will continue to produce ineffective legislation and whole boardrooms of 'leaders' who do not lead and certainly do not have societal value as their goal.

Professionalism does not change with the wind

There is nothing new in this analysis, which is based on the very clear evidence of corporate skulduggery and borderline corruption that fills TV screens, newspapers and blogs every day. There is also ample, psychological, research evidence to support the fact that an individual's values do not change much, if at all, over time. This psychology cuts both ways though. Once a crook always a crook. Once a

Professional always a Professional. In the medical world, the cosmetic surgeon who offers a discount boob job, to a psychologically vulnerable woman, must either see no contradiction in their Hippocratic Oath or just does not care. Similarly, the CEO who thinks business is all about sailing as close to the wind as possible will have no compunction in sanctioning behaviour that crosses that fine line between legality and illegality.

In May 2012 the British ex-CEO of Japanese electronics company Olympus finally settled an unfair dismissal claim against the company.[9] Michael Woodford had been fired for unearthing one of the biggest corporate scandals of recent times. He had only just taken over the reins at Olympus, after twenty years of service, when he investigated serious accounting discrepancies. At a press conference in January 2012 he remarked that one of the most disappointing features of the whole debacle was that 'Japanese shareholders have not spoken one single word of criticism about the directors who had presided over this situation.' Why was he so surprised? Had he not already sensed the culture at Olympus after 20 years there? Perhaps this reveals just how tightly-knit and inscrutable boards of directors can become. They want to feel confident they are only surrounded by other equally compliant directors, including their HR director, who will in turn be expected to make sure that no one will rock the boat.

This is the dark side; the evil, mirror image of whole system thinking that Machiavelli explained five hundred years ago, before the phrase 'corporate social responsibility' was ever invented. Contrary to what his many detractors might say, Machiavelli was never evil, he just understood better than anyone else why leaders do what they do. If he were to produce a belated second edition of *The Prince* today the catchy subtitle might be 'The Dark Side of the 5th Discipline'. Olympus is just one more example of old-fashioned, organizational 'terror' tactics used by many despots throughout the ages. Things are a bit more subtle these days but the effect is the same. The cycle of decay starts with the selection criteria for promotion to the upper echelons. Then it quickly degenerates into a vicious circle as those with any integrity left finally decide they can no longer stomach what they have to preside over. The only difference between Machiavelli's time and boardrooms today is that they employ smarter PR people, whose talents are ideally suited to making malign systems and catastrophes appear slightly less malign and a bit less catastrophic. So can we do what Machiavelli always hoped we would, which is to produce much more benign, organizational governance?

Designing a whole management system of a much higher order

True HR Professionals know how to break out of this downward spiral of incompetence. They only read the best management books, Machiavelli being mandatory reading, and know how to design watertight selection and promotion procedures to ward off any risk of the system being undermined or corrupted. The world has never really witnessed this level of Professionalism before though; partly because of history and partly because the 'science' has not been sufficiently well developed. Rather than ask the Engineering Council to set tough management standards, or any other professional registration body for that matter, we will not see any real progress until we have a universally agreed, Professional Management Standard. Accepting this, in principle at least, would be a huge step in the right direction because there is probably still an insidious, but widespread, suspicion and misapprehension that management cannot be condensed into a single, common set of standards. Now is the time to look at what sort of standards are already being set in the very institutions that exist to teach management and leadership.

Would an obvious first port of call be Harvard Business School? This might be viewed as a very 'American' view of management, if such a view exists, and some readers might wonder why we have not chosen somewhere in the Far East for a more contemporary perspective? Why not the Asian Institute of Management (AIM) in the Phillipines for instance (selected entirely at random)? Well, according to their website 'AIM was established in 1968 in partnership with Harvard Business School, the Ford Foundation, and visionaries of the Asian academic and business communities.' So setting our compass for a journey eastwards does not necessarily bring any different perspective. Also, if we had to justify our approach, it would be hard to deny that American management has been the primary influence on management thinking and education throughout the last century, for better or worse, even though recent financial calamities might have cast a shadow over former reputations.

When the Dean of Harvard Business School, Jay Light, was asked why Harvard had not predicted the financial crash of 2008[10] he replied:

> academics did pick up on the individual pieces ... but nobody had put all the pieces together. We just didn't understand how interwoven the different elements were and how we would get this conflagration. None of us really realized that this course of events would expose such a fragile structure.

There are several unnerving aspects to this rather relaxed and possibly complacent attitude from the head of one of the world's supposedly leading business schools. The interview did not portray a picture of a Harvard Dean desperate to protect Harvard's future reputation and credibility. Only seven days later he was made to appear even more out of touch and seemingly unaware of the significant developments that were already taking place within his own faculty. Two of his academic colleagues, Nitin Nohria and Rakesh Khurana, had already openly declared a need for greater managerial professionalism. In a Soapbox article in the *Financial Times*, they argued it was 'time to make management a true profession' adding that when the present financial crisis was over 'it is essential to restore legitimacy to and trust in the practice and profession of management'. They also suggested a code which would enhance 'the value of the enterprise to create wealth for society in the long term', with 'judgements based on the best knowledge available' and presenting 'the company's performance accurately and transparently'.

The fact that Nohria has now taken over as Dean of Harvard Business School could be taken as a signal that the world of management education is undergoing radical change. One clear sign is Nohria's determination to shake up HBS's convention of classroom-based, 'case method' teaching by injecting the principle of 'Learning by doing' into the curriculum. An *Economist* article[11] reviewed his FIELD experiment (Field Immersion Experiences for Leadership Development) and highlighted the fact that its academics have not entirely welcomed efforts to help MBA students 'with the practical application of management studies'. Giving one of the oldest ideas in the world, 'learning by doing', a Harvard makeover might not make up for the failings of the case method but it has certainly undermined a very long and established tradition in management education. If that was Nohria's intention then we should loudly applaud him.

If we need to add any weight to the significance of this shift in American management education, a very recent, but seminal, paper by former American Academy of Management President, Denise Rousseau (the Carnegie Mellon University; H.J. Heinz II, Professorship in Organizational Behavior and Public Policy, Heinz College and Tepper School of Business) entitled 'Designing a Better Business School'[12] sets out to explore what elements might be necessary. In tracing the history of business school design Rousseau goes back to a paper from 1967 by her former professor, Herbert Simon – 'The business school: a problem in organizational design' and in so doing cites one of Khurana's own earlier references to a 1910 critique by Abraham Flexner (Khurana, 2007, p.132):

> Modern business does not satisfy the criteria of a profession; it is shrewd, energetic, and clever, rather than intellectual in character; its aims ... at its own advantage, rather than a noble purpose within itself.

Flexner originally criticised the way medical schools were run and helped to reorganize them before turning his gaze to business education. His medical background might help to explain why he was so keen to apply the idea of a 'noble purpose within itself' to business management. His words could be still be applied to the business world today, without any alteration, and will have even greater resonance at a time of heightened suspicions and cynicism as to the motives of private equity partners, hedge funds, executives seeking to maximize their compensation in the short term and bankers who seem to have forgotten some of the first principles of sound finance.

A business school today can still make a legitimate attempt to teach professional managers how to maximize profits, even for maximum personal reward, but that would hardly qualify as the sort of 'noble purpose' that Flexner had in mind. Our Level 4 Professionalism is certainly designed for just such a higher purpose – maximum societal value – but its absolute legitimacy is in offering the best option for the highest profits at the same time. The two aims of maximizing profit and societal value are not just compatible they are mutually inclusive and our recommendation for raising the level of management Professionalism and education incorporates both.

Value is the higher purpose version of profit

The Nobel prize-winning economist, Milton Friedman, always argued that profit was a perfectly noble cause in and of itself. He had many critics who seemed to miss the essential morality in his message. He used his economist's logic to support a moral case for the perfect allocation of the world's resources as being best served by perfect competition. This model relies on customers being perfectly free to exercise their perfectly democratic purchasing choices. It is intended to be a perfectly virtuous cycle where bad business gets its comeuppance and the best businesses in society survive; simply by providing the best response to the free choices of citizens. Anyone who ever hears Friedman speak[13] will be struck by his absolute confidence, his certainty and the power of his conviction. This can come across as sheer arrogance but he realized that such total coherence is a necessary condition for the validity of any conceptual model. An incoherent economic or management philosophy would be a non-starter: the current version of capitalism is incoherent and contradictory. A coherent, conceptual model is not a sufficient condition though.

Friedman's classic text *Capitalism and Freedom* (Friedman, 1962) spells out his moral capitalism, with freedom at its core. We could go much farther back than Friedman if we wished and find the same arguments in Adam Smith's 'Theory of Moral Sentiments' in the eighteenth century. Friedman was not naïve; he was well aware that neither markets nor the businesspeople that exploit them are perfect. So the principle of regulation to moderate man's behaviour has been well accepted for many, many years going back to the earliest, American anti-trust laws. This paradigm of moral economics requires moral and efficient management, and that necessitates moral people management, but a perfectly coherent theory does not mean it will be perfectly translated into coherent practice.

The case for such a paradigm is therefore strengthened, rather than weakened, by recent experiences of the failings of the present paradigm. Using cheap finance to sell mortgages to people on low incomes was always questionable ethically and proved to be economically disastrous in the long term. We knew that creating an unsustainable asset bubble was always going to end in someone's tears, with all of the consequent damage done to individuals' lives, the financial system and the world economy as a whole. Neither Friedman the consummate economist, nor anyone else who has the slightest concern for the welfare of society, would ever suggest that this is how markets are supposed to work. If professional politicians, professional regulators and professional bankers had all acted in concert to observe the lessons of history, none of this would have happened. They should also note that our trusty bell curve was always in play at the time: not all banking 'leaders' chose to follow the herd. Some stuck to their higher principles of only allowing themselves to make a profit following the rules that they had come to trust, 'never borrow short to lend long', regardless of the temptation to exploit the short term profits they could have made.

Of course, if political and legislative processes continue to allow businesses to be run according to the sort of dubious moral codes exposed by the crash, with negligible or light-touch state interference and controls, then we will continue to get the business standards we all deserve. Equally, one does not have to be an arch-capitalist or rabid free marketeer to support the idea of minimal intervention: there must be a happy medium somewhere between these two extremes. When some of our most revered, albeit 'hard-nosed', business leaders start coming to the same conclusion maybe we are finally getting onto the right track? Who better to illustrate this point than Jack Welch himself? On 12 March 2009 he gave an interview with Francesco Guerrera of the *Financial Times*[14] and said:

> On the face of it, shareholder value is the dumbest idea in the world. Shareholder value is a result, not a strategy ... your main constituencies are your employees, your customers and your products.

Was this really a Damascene conversion at the end of his career or just a very obvious and natural conclusion that anyone, as logical and business focused as Welch, would be bound to reach eventually? Of course pursuing shareholder value, to the exclusion of everyone else's value and values, is a dumb idea. Why would the majority of rational employees want to give their all for the benefit of shareholders whom they are never likely to meet? Who, other than the shareholders themselves, gets excited by the shareholdings of shareholders? There may be many reasons behind Jack Welch's apparent volte-face, and cynics can make up their own minds as to how he reached this conclusion after making his money, but he did not have to say what he said in the way he said it. It could have been a genuine epiphany that led him to moderate the shareholder value obsession that he himself had espoused at GE and no doubt taught to younger generations at GE's academy. The view taken here is that he realized there was more to the purpose of management than the narrowly defined interests of shareholders. He, more than anyone, would realize what a strong reaction his words would receive and the extent to which he would incur the wrath of those who believe the 'American Way' always was, and always will be, the purest version of market driven capitalism.

Welch still proudly declares himself to be a Republican and fervently believes that he holds a coherent view of the role of business in society. There is certainly no intention here to suggest that Professionalising management in any way diminishes or dilutes the benefits that capitalism brings. It offers the same enlightened version that the best minds in political economy always foresaw. Companies that have value as their goal will create more sustainable profits. Welch's successor, Jeff Immelt, has already received some criticism for offering a less successful formula which might be due, in part, to a less coherent vision of the purpose of his business in society today.[15]

A more enlightened, capitalist model is never just about numbers, finance or profits *in isolation*. There is some staggeringly simple logic here that makes perfect sense. The potentially exploitative aspects of capitalism might naturally appeal to those with entirely monetary or materialistic interests but how, in any organization that employs people, can such motivation possibly hope to maximize the value of the organization, and society, if the majority of those employees only have their wage to gain? What motive force will bring out the best in everyone? In Chapter 9 we will see plenty of evidence of people doing what they are told, without asking too many questions or blowing the whistle, but we have already seen plenty of evidence of the damage to society that this type of mentality and culture causes.

So, having inadvertently called into question the integrity and motives of many entrepreneurs and corporate executives, it might be a good time to make our perspective plain. If we plotted a bell curve for the 'integrity' or 'honesty' of the entire, global population of executives what would it reveal to us? If those executives with the greatest integrity score 10 out of 10, then those scoring 3 or less would be the most corruptible. We know, statistically, that those scoring between 1 and 3 would only account for a meagre 2 per cent of the population and the rest of us, scoring 4 and above, have at least an acceptable level of integrity. That means we heavily outnumber the really corrupt, so why have we not rid the world of corruption thus far? This tiny population of the corrupt seem to be everywhere. How do they manage to punch so much above their combined weight? Machiavelli knew the answer.

Put two bell curves together, the one for integrity (or corruptibility) and the one for whole system thinking (or system design capability). When someone scores low on the former and very high on the latter it is a terrible, frightening combination. It means that this very corrupt but highly intelligent person knows exactly how to build the best corruption system ever. This is why history is so full of very clever corrupt leaders; the ones we usually refer to as evil, but calling someone evil does not solve the problem. When their corruption system takes over it has the gravitational pull of a black hole that sucks in everything within reach. Somehow, Level 4 Professionals manage to resist its grasp. So does that mean they have to be equally superhuman, scoring 10 out of 10 on the ability scale for perfectly benign system design? Yes, and that means they have to be 10 out of 10 on human systems design as well.

Maybe this helps to explain why Africa seems to suffer more corruption than any other continent? Once you reach a critical mass of corrupt leaders a whole continent can become infected. Africa's leaders are so corrupt, according to the evidence, that the Mo Ibrahim African Leadership Index[16] felt it could find no one who deserved their award in 2010. But we do not need to travel to Africa to witness the best examples of corruption systems. Executives like Angelo Mozilo, the infamous head of Countrywide in the US, who made so many millions from the mortgage sales that were ultimately converted into toxic debts, was eventually indicted on a civil, not a criminal, action and settled his case out of court. Yes, a civil action. He had committed no crime so he must have been very talented at what he did. So let us not blame Mozilo for anything, not only did he play the hand he had; he played the whole system. What we need to do with the Mozilos of the world is just stop them practising; remove their name from the professional register. If we have to blame someone, which incidentally goes against everything that an HR Professional believes in, then let us blame everyone else who sent very clear signals that Mozilo's behaviour was acceptable. Perhaps they all regarded Mozilo's behaviour as the same sort of trade-off that a film director accepts from prima donna starlets?

Certainly, from a technical perspective, Mozilo must have known his way around the law and fully exploited the commercial opportunities it made available. So where were the Level 4 legal brains that should have prevented this? How Professional were the managers at Bank of America who eventually bought Countrywide and ended up paying most of Mozilo's settlement? How professional are the legislators who did not outlaw this behaviour in the first place, or the regulators who failed to control it, or the politicians who did not show the necessary leadership to resolve it? All of these 'managers', assuming they accept they have a Professional duty rather than just a technical responsibility, have one thing in common, they all played their part in value destruction on an epic scale and, whatever integrity they might possess, it did not come to the fore when it was needed most. Everyone on the receiving end of their incompetence and lack of due diligence, mortgagees and taxpayers alike, should have been able to expect much better from those who are paid to protect their best interests. Is this not simply a case of a fundamentally flawed system creating a flawed culture and a flawed society?

Is Professional HR culture-dependent?

One country that seemed to develop a reputation for building strong businesses, over time, was Japan but it also has a reputation for its cultural traditions of resisting change. We have already seen how damaging this culture was at Olympus. An *Economist* article entitled 'From summit to plummet'[17] revealed that such cultural issues run very deep in Japan by taking a critical look at the declining market capitalization of Japanese manufacturing companies such as NEC, Panasonic, Fujitsu, Sharp and Sony, pointing out that 'the largest Japanese gadget-makers … expect to lose $17 billion in … 2011'. It paints a rather bleak picture in which NEC's decline, in particular, is attributed to a bureaucratic culture that was too cosily dependent on the state as well as its own 'plodding management' that failed to make the most of its 'technically brilliant' people. Its general conclusion was that all of the Japanese companies listed now produce 'little that other firms don't make as well'.

This is a very stark illustration of the classic, evolutionary cycle of organizational change; or should we say inability to change? What caused the most senior managers in these companies to oversee such a decline? The economist Joseph Schumpeter referred to this natural cycle as the 'creative destruction' that is a vital part of the capitalist system. The worst managed companies, by definition, are more likely to decay and collapse than those with Professional management. So how Professional can management have been if it fails in spite of the 'technical brilliance' at its disposal? Moreover, *whose* job is it to stand back and see this situation for what it is? If NEC and all of these companies could go back in time and re-invest the benefit of their hindsight what might they have done differently? 'Plodding management' has to be the very opposite of Professional people management and if investors and other stakeholders cannot bring about an injection of fresh energy and creativity then who can?

Regardless of the specific details of this Japanese culture example, and the validity of the economist's analysis for different cultural contexts, the notion that management can run out of steam is an odd one. Isn't that what leadership is for: to keep stoking the engine and to ensure the people are fired up? To suggest that someone can be a great manager without including this people dimension is not only nonsense, it could be viewed as criminally negligent: that is, if wasting valuable resources, particularly human capital, were ever to be declared a crime. Brilliant technicians at NEC have probably lost their livelihoods, and those of their families, because of the incompetence or intransigence (they amount to the same thing) of those who are paid to manage their talents to create as much value as possible. Of all the resources at a manager's disposal it is only the people that can be nurtured. We need to take this perspective further. People are capital and we all have a right to demand that a Professional CEO should do everything they can to achieve the best return from that capital. The Japanese electronics companies referred to above now have to rethink their management philosophies; not because they particularly want to but because they have to. So how might we encourage all CEOs to start thinking more positively today; before they have to? One way might simply be to re-phrase the CEO's central, management question.

Re-phrasing the people management question

Are you achieving the best return from each person in your care?

That one, simple word 'care' puts an entirely different complexion on the whole matter doesn't it? Should we expect CEOs and other executives to be motivated by caring for their people and would they be recognized for it if they were? Why isn't Jack Welch fêted for caring for his fellow man, when it is so obvious that he does? Why was he called 'neutron Jack' when he created so much value for shareholders? The answer is in the question. The ordinary man in the street does not read Adam Smith, Milton Friedman or Joseph Schumpeter and does not necessarily see the entire theory behind the system in which they have to live. Shareholder value might make intellectual sense, within the whole scheme of capitalist economics, but that does not necessarily make it feel right to many people who might not see it as such a 'good thing'; even while they enjoy its many benefits. Why should they, if shareholders show no interest in them and do not even put pressure on executives to think about their people?

Even the best paid employees, with the most comfortable living standards, know that capitalism has a sting in its tail. Welch's large scale redundancies at GE can be seen either as the self-renewal inherent in Schumpeter's model or, in the minds of the recently redundant, more evidence of the exploitation of workers to satisfy the greed of shareholders. What the world still seems to struggle with is getting everyone to see it the same way. Self-renewal, shareholder value and job losses are all part and parcel of the same system and you either accept the whole system or you do not. You cannot just pick the parts of a system that suit you best and it is unlikely that anyone is going to change the whole system anytime soon or provide a viable alternative. Welch only admitted his own doubts about the system after he had left GE. If he could travel back in time he could not change the whole capitalist system, he was as much a victim of it as anyone he ever fired, but maybe he could have translated his genuine care for his fellow man into a better prescription. Perhaps he could have done something about the imperfections in the way the system seems to work.

UK legislation already imposes a *duty of care* on all company directors, but imposing a legal duty does nothing to engender an authentic management philosophy based on that innate, human value of wanting to do the right and decent thing. Moreover, a director's sense of relief, in knowing their legal obligations are covered, bears no comparison to the deep satisfaction and approbation that comes from fulfilling one's sense of obligation towards one's fellow man. The working relationships between employer, manager and employee are transformed when CEOs and other senior executives genuinely care about their people. But how can senior executives or managers really care, or show they care, when the only knowledge they have about their people is a divisional headcount, departmental salary bill, employee number or anonymous engagement survey? Why should they care if they have succeeded so far without having to? What might encourage them to change their attitude or behaviour in the future?

You cannot force somebody to care anymore than you can force someone to love you. Even some parents find it hard to actually care about and for their children. Truancy officers might force them to bring their kids to school but that does not make them care any more about their child's education. Forcing the issue is likely to be counter-productive. A much simpler and more obvious recommendation is for someone to help executives understand that the value of caring equals the dollar value they can create. As a simple equation it might look like this:

profit motive + care for your people = the greatest possible value ($)

But simple equations never capture the whole story do they? Any executives reading this could immediately be put off if they think they will have to spend more precious time caring for staff. They might not want to get to know their people that intimately or dirty their hands. So let us put their minds at rest because we are not recommending a one-sided relationship here. The people working for the organization need to care equally about what value they can create for the organization, and society, even at the risk of their own redundancy. This is the most mature, symbiotic relationship possible, where every party to the psychological contract knows exactly what the total deal is. When a point is reached in the collective mindset of the organization, that caring for each other and caring for society equals the greatest value possible, we have the basis for not only a very valuable organization but a morally sound one as well. The circle of profit and people might, just might, finally be squared.

This is bound to leave the HR Professional open to the usual accusation of being a typical, 'pink and fluffy' HR person but that would be to completely misinterpret and under-estimate what we are saying. If Fred Goodwin, the ex-CEO of Royal Bank of Scotland, had cared more about his own executives' feelings, never mind the majority of his employees, would RBS have crashed in 2008? Did he care that he intimidated his own managers to such an extent that they were afraid to challenge some of his more arrogant and inept management decisions? Does he care, even today, that the FSA report condemned his woefully inadequate due diligence during the disastrous takeover of ABN AMRO, costing £49 billion? Do any of the ex-directors of RBS care what damage this has done to literally millions of peoples' lives? Or are they the type of uncaring parents who just do not have it in them?

One former director, interviewed by the FSA, reported an element of 'group-think' in the RBS boardroom. To his knowledge, he added, no board member had ever expressed a worry about the ABN AMRO deal. 'Group-think' is a euphemism for the management phenomenon of mindlessness, a very common, generic, organizational problem. It is the same boardroom mindlessness as gender quotas. Something happens within organizations that causes people to stop thinking intelligently. They then fail to see what is staring them in the face, become oblivious to the risks and don't care what the consequences might be. Any HR Professional who is a board director would be looking for the first signs of any tendency to 'Group think' and would immediately view it as an alarming symptom of an insidious disease; a cancer. Of course, neither the highly paid executives referred to in the report, nor their advisers Merrill Lynch, who were 'largely remunerated on a success (sic) fee basis', nor the FSA team who were supposed to control them, could be described as Professionals because Professionals do care. They care, not because it is nice, but because it is the right and best thing to do from a clear-headed, Professional management perspective. Not caring is sub-optimal.

Managing people is already difficult enough, but made doubly so when both parties to the relationship do not care about each other and have conflicting perspectives on value. None of this is currently monitored in the monthly management meeting or the P&L though, partly because it is deemed intangible, partly because it is imperceptible to the untrained eye and partly because it would be very embarrassing for any executives to admit that they could not care less. Yet this fundamental flaw in the executive/management/employee relationship is, in effect, increasingly undermining the whole of the capitalist system. How can capitalism, which is predicated on being the most efficient way to manage the world's resources, hope to continue to offer the best system if it creates a situation of 'us and them' or forces people to take sides and then only appears to reward one side? If you have never viewed organizations in this way before then prepare yourself for seeing some of your most cherished management beliefs trampled underfoot.

Who should take responsibility for how a company performs? Obviously, the higher up the tree we climb the greater the responsibilities we accept and such responsibility does not appeal to everyone. So here is a very interesting question for anyone working in succession planning, management development, organization design or leadership development. Is it a great deal easier for someone to take on more responsibility when they do not care what the consequences of their actions might be? Do you have even less concern about your responsibilities if you are unlikely to be brought to account for your actions? Have we just stumbled upon one of the most obvious Catch-22's in management? Are the people who we hope will lead us in the right direction the very ones who will lead us only in a direction that suits them? If there is any truth at all in this view then it has enormous implications for the direction in which the world is currently heading.

If we want responsible governance we have to assess the capabilities of CEOs and their senior colleagues against a revised set of criteria that incorporates caring for people alongside caring for shareholders and other vested interest groups. This is what Professional management now has to mean; it would be a travesty to define it in any other way. The absence of management Professionalism has been cruelly exposed by the collapse of the global financial system. Yes, the gestation period for the collapse was decades; yes it collapsed due to a combination of very complex reasons and circumstances and yes, the RBS story alone is much too long to be read in any detail by most people. So how long would the report have to be to explain the failure of the entire global banking and financial system and who would ever have time to read or act on it?

Actually, maybe it would not have to be that wordy after all. Perhaps it could all be summed up in a one page executive summary? Underneath all of the complexity is one very simple, human truth. If you create an environment where people stop using their brains, the world becomes illogical and when the world becomes illogical stupid behaviour will swiftly ensue and calamity is bound to follow. So there is a need for someone, especially in large organizations, with a role and a clear brief to stop this ever happening again. Someone who can Professionally manage the whole situation; not just each disjointed part. That person, for want of a better title, will fulfil the role of the 'Chief Human Governance Officer' (CHGO). It would make perfect sense for it to be the CEO but only if the CEO cared. If not, it will have to be a consummate HR Professional, a people manager who is not only capable of taking a whole system view but is powerful enough to ensure the system keeps working as it should.

Who should be the CHGO?

Even the best CEO in the world needs someone who understands organizational dynamics, culture and behaviour and how these are connected to the long-term, sustainable prospects of the organization. If not the CEO then who? The next best candidate has to be whoever is responsible for the organization's strategic view of people management. On paper that is the HR director but, in reality, the person currently doing that job is unlikely to be of the right calibre and, even if they are, their conventional HR management education does very little to qualify them for the role. Establishing the need for this role is a relatively easy step; filling the vacancy is much more of a challenge.

This is not being presented here as some earth-shattering breakthrough in management thinking; quite the opposite. This has been staring society in the face as far back as slave trading and certainly since the beginning of the industrial revolution. The eighteenth century may not have lent itself to the abolition of slavery, or even the emancipation of the ordinary working man, and it may have taken another two centuries before female equality even came onto the agenda, but only those with a vested interest and a closed mind would attempt to construct a theory that it was the best way to run society in the long term. The fact that the world has changed significantly is clear evidence of the obsolescence of such thinking. It was not the plantation managers who decided slavery was bad for business it was politicians and legislators with a higher purpose who said slavery had to end. Professional, higher purpose management has been a very long time coming but it has always been coming. The need for Professional management that is intrinsically about people is clear but the solution, whilst increasingly urgent, is far from obvious.

All management is about people but they are an infinitely complex resource with their individual motivation patterns, talents, brainpower, skills, knowledge, expertise, dedication, effort, preferences, hopes, fears, greed, anxieties, relationships, health, stresses, strains, loves, and hates. They also vary enormously in terms of their willingness or refusal to accept responsibility and accountability. Managing all of these human forces for the greater good in a modern context where people expect to have their say, regardless of whether they have anything worth saying, requires a level of Professionalism never seen before. This radically new level of management Professionalism inevitably calls for a radically new type of management education. So how are the worlds of academia and management education coping with the changing demands being placed on them?

3

THE DEFINITIVE, PROFESSIONAL MANAGER

The huge gulf between management academia and management practice

Should there be such a thing as 'pure research' by management academics or should their research questions always be relevant to the practising manager? Certainly management research is more likely to be of use to the practitioner if it has already taken the practicalities into account. So at what point should research evidence and operational practice join up and become indistinguishable? We have already determined that the only evidence worth collecting is evidence of value, but academia does not necessarily see it that way. Some academics do not even believe there is such a thing as evidence-based management. Two academic papers published in 2006 asked 'Is there such a thing as EBM?' (Learmonth 2006) and 'Evidence-based Management: The very idea' (Learmonth and Harding 2006).

One of the main academic objections to evidence-based management (EBM) is that management cannot be objectively measured and is therefore not a suitable subject for scientific study. Other academics may not want research and practice to get too close and some will even use the barrier of the peer review system to stop practitioners encroaching. This is rather ironic because the peer review 'system' is intended to assure academic integrity but it might have come at the cost of creating an enclosed and exclusive mentality that lacks integrity and is resistant to change. It only values other academics' views and gives little, if any, credence or weight to the hard-won and very valid experiences of the practising manager.

Occasionally you will come across quasi-academic-practitioners (or should that be quasi-practitioner-academics?) who want to straddle both camps. A good example comes from the Director of the Infosys Leadership Institute whose blog tries to show a connection between leadership, creativity and innovation,[1] stating that:

> Teresa Amabile (Harvard), John Antonakis (Lausanne) and David Day of Western Australia give practical and original evidence-based guidance. For

Infosys leaders, this means helping our teams holistically understand the client's current state, so that our teams can craft consulting and intellectual property-driven solutions to make client aspirations a reality.

Reading this it is difficult to know whether the emphasis is being placed on the academic evidence, the practitioner application or Infosys's marketing. The language is flowery rather than scientific, not a single measurement is mentioned and we are not told what the 'evidence-based guidance' consists of. Also, whether terms such as leadership, creativity and innovation can be defined well enough to be part of a personal development plan, or measured in any meaningful way, is a moot point. One thing we can say for certain is that no causal connection has yet been established between any of the ideas offered and Infosys' hard, market value in dollar's: simply quoting academic studies from one context cannot validate management practice in another.

This principle is supported in a study published in the *Academy of Management Journal* from Indiana University (Baldwin *et al.*, AMLE, 2011) entitled 'The elusiveness of applied management knowledge: a critical challenge for management educators'. The authors note that:

> Scholars in several different professional disciplines are increasingly focusing attention on the distinctions between conceptual knowledge ... and the ability to apply such knowledge in authentic contexts. The general thrust of such work is that conceptual knowledge has traditionally been disproportionately weighted in the selection, development and evaluation of professionals.

Behind their detailed research is a simple notion that 'managers may often lack the ability to apply that knowledge in *context*' and refers to other studies being undertaken into what really makes a lawyer or a doctor *effective*, as opposed to being merely *knowledgeable*. This is very welcome recognition that there needs to be a distinction made between what we know, what we do and, much more importantly, what effect we have. It is this concern for the eventual effect, the ultimate outcome, that lies behind the sort of changes in thinking taking place in business schools such as Harvard and its 'learning by doing' initiative.

The disconnects between thinking, knowing, doing and value

Despite growing recognition of the gap between theory, research and practice there is no sign of the ivory towers of academe being dismantled and rebuilt as temples of evidence-based management anytime soon. There might even still be some validity in the saying 'those that can, do; those that can't teach'. Whatever strengths academics may bring to management debate; practical considerations and causal outcomes still do not seem to loom large on their list of priorities. If this accusation were to be aimed at scientific researchers it would be grossly unfair because there are many examples of valuable applications being developed from pure, scientific, laboratory-based research. The obvious difference, however, between chemistry and human science is that what is replicable in a test tube may not be so replicable in uniquely different human beings in dynamic contexts. Moreover, regardless of the quality of management research, it is only the manager on the ground, in their own particular context, at a particular time, who can make the theory and research findings work. The manager's prime concern, as Drucker pointed out, is always output from efficient resource utilisation. The manager's mindset is one of pragmatism, even expediency, rather than purity. This is the nature of the gulf between these two differing perspectives, and it was ever thus, but the relentless search for greater value, when more value is hard to come by, means it has to be traversed.

We might make a good start by acknowledging the joint nature of the challenge with attitudes on both sides having to change. The academic economist has a notion of perfect competition in a world of perfect knowledge. The manager is having to work with the imperfections and, given a free choice, would prefer a world of monopoly, not competition, because a monopoly would make their life so much easier. The academic is thinking 'if only the manager would read my research' while the manager is thinking 'if only someone could give me a simple answer to my problem'. If this rather simplistic description bears any relation to the present relationship then one might come to the conclusion that the best solution would be to translate academic scholarship and research into more user-friendly formats for practising managers. This sounds as though it makes sense but, in HR management, the worlds of the academic and practising manager are much, much further apart than this would imply.

EBM should be re-named evidence-based human resource management because it is the people management dimension that is suffering most from a lack of credible evidence. One early tenet of economic theory was the notion of the rational consumer making rational choices. More recent studies in behavioural economics have shown what a fallacy the concept of the rational human being really is. In *Thinking Fast and Slow* (Kahneman, 2011) Nobel Prize winner Daniel Kahneman, a psychologist, comments (at p. 412) 'when we observe people acting in ways that seem odd, we should first examine the possibility that they have a good reason to do what they do'.

Kahneman makes a distinction between humans being 'reasonable' and being 'rational'. He defines rational behaviour as that which is based on internally consistent thinking but goes on to point out that 'Although humans are not irrational, they often need help to make more accurate judgements and better decisions, and in some cases policies and institutions can provide that help.'

Institutions and policy makers can only do so if they know how to influence the behaviour of millions of people within complex systems. This realization is taken into the policy making arena in the book *Nudge* (Thaler and Sunstein, 2008) where the authors provide examples of simple ways to make small adjustments to human behaviour. One such idea is to raise the number of organ, or blood, donors by making 'opt in' the default on a medical form and forcing anyone who wants to opt out to make a conscious decision by ticking a box.

Managing the complexity of human 'irrationality' will come as no surprise to an experienced HR manager, who has probably spent their entire working life helping to resolve issues between managers and employees where behaviour can often be unreasonable, irrational, inconsistent and frankly bizarre. Organizational behaviour theorists have explanations as to why this happens. It has been recognised for some considerable time that human beings, who might otherwise be rational most of the time in their private lives, will behave irrationally and erratically in a work setting. One of the key reasons for such behaviour is that it is enforced by having to work in a controlled and organized environment. The rational human being learns how to survive in this context, even if this means behaving against type. For example, they might witness some wrongdoing at work but choose to leave it unreported because they do not want to get anyone into trouble or jeopardize their own employment prospects. Or they accept poor performance from colleagues knowing it could have serious consequences for the organization. This has huge implications for executives. How do you manage people for the greater good if they believe that will conflict with their own, immediate interests? What chance do we have of introducing better, evidence-based, people management when the cold logic of evidence takes second place to the understandable rationality of personal survival?

Measuring the unmeasurable

The manifestation of such problems has become more apparent as organizations have grown in size and complexity but they are incredibly difficult to pin down. In order to resolve them we have to address another issue first; how do you measure the seemingly 'unmeasurable'? This is why the Conference Board, a well-respected, gulf-traversing, quasi-research-practice organization, started to research the new subject of evidence-based human resources in 2009. Traditional HR management has been particularly resistant to measurement, both in theory and practice, and has never properly addressed the question of meaningful evidence. The report[2] tells us clearly (p. 16) where evidence-based HR management fits into the ongoing evolution of management thinking:

> While many of the evolutionary forces (of EBM) are relatively new, Evidence-Based Human Resources also applies long established standards for demonstrating causation using the scientific method. These are not new standards, but they are very new in their application to the field of human resources.

This correctly identifies the direction of travel for academia and management practice but there are no actual examples in this report of the 'standards for demonstrating causation' in an HR context being satisfied by 'using the scientific method'. Instead we are presented with the popular statistical trick, favoured by the less professional academics and HR practitioners, of pretending that correlations demonstrate causation. If respected authorities do not expose this tendency for what it is then the new field of evidence-based HR management will just become another fad, in a very long line of HR fads, to be exploited by unscrupulous consulting firms.

One book published in 2011, *Transformative HR. How Great Companies Use Evidence-Based Change for Sustainable Advantage* by Professor John Boudreau (Center for Effective Organizations at the University of Southern California) and Ravin Jesuthasan (Towers Watson) suggested that it knew something about evidence-based HR. The authors try to convince their readers that the bankrupt, taxpayer-bailed-out, subject of a 450-page FSA report of failure, Royal Bank of Scotland is a 'great company'. If they had waited another year before publication they would have found (as recently as August 2012)[3] that this great company's losses had doubled to £1.5 billion, it had to make mis-selling provisions of £135 million and its 'IT meltdown', when its customers could not access their own accounts for over a week, was going to cost an extra £310 million.

It just so happens that RBS is a client of Towers Watson; a consultancy firm born out of a merger between HR consultancy Towers Perrin and actuarial consultancy Watson Wyatt. In 2001 Watson Wyatt had jumped on an earlier bandwagon, human capital reporting, and produced their own proprietary product, imaginatively called the Human Capital Index. This, according to their own advertising, suggested they had found a:

> clear relationship between the effectiveness of a company's human capital and shareholder value creation. This relationship we found is so clear that a significant improvement in 30 key HR practices is associated with a 30 per cent increase in market value.

The 'clear relationship' that they had 'associated' was of course a very convenient correlation. It might not say so but we are meant to read 'association' as a lighter version of causation. In this latest book Towers Watson take their perversion of statistical theory and RBS's track record to new depths (page 109):

> The approach to discovering the most important flavors of HR metrics was through thorough research. RBS worked with Nitnin (sic) Nohria (Dean) . . . at Harvard Business school to study the issue . . . and then spent time . . . with the Organization Surveys and Insights team of Towers Watson to do the serious statistics (Cronbach's alphas . . .) needed to prove the measures they intended to use really were valid.

Mysteriously, it continues with a non-attributed quote, which presumably comes from RBS's 'head of human capital strategy' Greg Aitken,[4] who was producing HR metrics under the old regime at RBS over ten years ago:

> We reached the important but not new conclusion that the two lead indicators, in terms of superior sustainable business value in customer service, are great leaders and highly engaged staff.

There is no mention here of the engagement levels of staff who mis-sold RBS products. Is this what Nohria had in mind when promoting HBS's 'new' concept of management as a profession? Can Cronbach's Alpha really turn a very badly performing company like RBS into a 'great company' or is this just all a very cynical case of quackademia trying to blind people with science? An allied question is did Towers Perrin realize what sort of 'used car' they were buying when they merged with Watson Wyatt in 2009 and, if they did, what does that reveal about their own professional values and their due diligence? High standards of Professionalism build brands with integrity; these remarkably low standards put intelligent HR professionals in a very awkward position.

A critical review of Boudreau and Jesuthasan's book, in this same vein, was originally posted on the 'Evidence-Based HR'[5] site. It prompted a practising SHRM member to contact us to explain the predicament in which they had been placed by this sort of thinking.

HR Metric 'hooey'

I enjoyed the book review of Transformative HR and am relieved to find that I'm not going crazy. In the last year I've had to work with what are supposed to be some very respected organizations in regards to HR Metrics and my management seemed to think me a bit of an upstart when I claimed 'The Emperor has no Clothes!' I was beginning to think I was the only one involved with HR who thought the way I did! So many times I've Googled the term 'HR Metrics' with words like 'Fraud' or 'Scam' but I did not get any hits of note. I came across your review only because my management wanted me to look at Towers Watson's HR Metrics database and your article on 'Transformative HR' came up. Isn't there anybody else who recognizes this nonsense? I am perplexed by this 'group think' so prevalent in HR, where intelligent people willingly suspend their disbelief and accept as fact shaky inferences that anyone with a vague memory of Statistics 101 (the beginner college course) would readily reject. I believe Nietzsche said something along the lines of 'Madness is the exception in individuals and the rule in groups'.

As someone who has advocated for years the need to quantify HR activities and initiatives I was thrilled when I heard that we were purchasing access to what I understood was the most respected HR Metrics service for benchmarking. It was a crushing disappointment when I was forced to conclude, after much study and analysis, that it was of no real practical business use. Chastened by this experience, but still looking for benchmarking data, I contacted a rep of a professional Human Resource organization I belong to that was selling benchmarking reports. What ensued were months of 'spirited debate' about the worth and valid application of their data in the context of their promotional claims. I was told that in all the years in his position I was the only one ever to scrutinize data and ask questions the way I did. Despite our jousting, the rep (who I respected for his relative honesty and frankness) still invited me to participate in a metrics standards committee. I agreed and noted that I was looking forward to having a 'chat' with a certain sales rep on the committee who sold the aforementioned HR Metrics database service to my company. Perhaps it was a mistake sharing my enthusiasm because I was actually never contacted to join! Or perhaps it was my criticisms of how they were trying to equate certain Human Resource Metric measurements with actual company performance. I didn't like the idea of them trying to create more dubious correlations and then sell them in reports to HR professionals who didn't have the statistical insight to understand what was hooey.

American PHR member of SHRM, September 2012.

So SHRM does have at least one highly intelligent member who has not been taken in, is willing to 'scrutinize data and ask questions' and prepared to speak out. One brave soul, a Level 4 HR Professional no doubt, is all it takes to produce an irreparable fissure in the dam of collective HR ignorance; especially when that lone voice has logic and the science of statistics firmly on their side. SHRM now has to resolve a very serious, internal conflict: either take their own member's advice, and change their ways, or prove their own professional member is wrong. Similar changes will also be necessary in the professional body that is supposed to be monitoring the behaviour of actuaries.

Who is checking on the statisticians?

While Cronbach is probably turning in his grave, actuaries have a long-held reputation for being one of the highest paid professions. For that sort of money you might expect the very highest professional standards but we demonstrated earlier in Chapter 1 that money has little or nothing to do with levels of professionalism. If you visit the UK site of 'The Actuarial Profession' you will find they have their own Financial Reporting Council[6] which sets and maintains their technical and ethical standards. The ultimate aim of its regulatory regime is to:

> ... enhance the quality of actuarial reporting and promote the integrity, competence and transparency of the Institute and Faculty of Actuaries to the benefit of those who rely on actuarial advice.

As far as we are aware none of the actuaries at Watson Wyatt were ever struck off the Register of Actuaries for any claims they made or the methods they used. Maybe no one cared or perhaps actuarial statistics is just too arcane and impenetrable a subject for any lay observer to notice its failings? It would not be so bad if Watson Wyatt's own actuaries had believed in what they were writing. In a separate Watson Wyatt

Report that preceded their 2001 claims (HCI – European Survey Report 2000) they had already admitted that while their data in North America:

> ... demonstrates a very strong correlation between effective people practices and shareholder value, on its own it does not prove a causal link.

Mixing up the worlds of HR consultancy, actuarial practice and academia can produce a very murky cocktail indeed. Is it too naïve to expect anything else when money is at stake and professional standards are absent? Perhaps the whole intention is to produce such a heady mix that it will confuse and exploit the average HR director. HR directors are not stupid though so they must be complicit in this deceit. While HR does not have much influence in the boardroom this should not worry us unduly but it appears that Towers Watson does. According to the book (at p. 210) RBS's current CEO, the otherwise highly intelligent Stephen Hester, sees nothing wrong in spurious correlations between intangibles such as 'listening' and company performance. In fact: 'A good deal of the communication about results of employee listening comes directly from Hester, the CEO'.

The management consulting industry has already earned itself a rather dubious reputation because it is unregulated. Some academics, like management consultants, could easily fit into the stereotype of borrowing your watch to tell you the time. It now appears that the self-regulating, peer review system is not working as well in academia as it should. Maybe both need their own general councils? Who can testify to Professor Boudreau's bona fides and what does this book tell us about Professional standards at the Center for Effective Organizations and the University of Southern California? How many more of their academics are passing off correlations as causation? How many are quite happy to make themselves look very careless by citing 'great companies' whose performance is so dire? When bandwagons start to roll none of these questions matter because what is popular becomes what is 'right'. Once enough people are on board even the most intelligent consultant or academic is forced into making a choice: do you go with the crowd or do you stick to your Professional principles? Anyone who is not a Level 4 Professional will join the crowd immediately simply because they feel there is safety in numbers. This is that classic defining moment in Professionalism and the majority fall at this hurdle because no one is punishing those promoting such patently abysmal standards.

Professional institutions should be the ones to put a few chocks under the wheels; to slow down the bandwagon's progress and take stock. That is what we might expect from the WFPMA (World Federation of People Management Associations) but in 2012 they teamed up with Boston Consulting Group to produce a report – 'From capability to profitability. People practices and the bottom line' – using exactly the same type of correlative research methodology, again based on HR's view of its own practices. That is like asking homeopaths about their views on homeopathy. Following such methods BCG's report admits (at p. 3) that 'To claim a direct cause-and-effect link here would be over-reaching...' but nevertheless they do claim it is 'a worthwhile exercise if it sheds light on those activities that seem to be particularly beneficial'. This is the movie director's trick of an opening shot claiming 'Based on a true story'; knowing full well that no movie can ever tell the true story and they are unlikely to end up in court for saying so. How can they claim to know that certain HR practices are 'beneficial' if they have not established a cause-and-effect link? Hollywood's feelgood movies have finally arrived in HR in the shape of large consultancy practice reports for professional bodies paying to protect the interests of their members.

One can understand why the WFPMA would sponsor such reports but this type of 'research' (sic) is bound to be self-defeating. If such reports on HR's 'impact' ever convinced anyone, why do they need to keep producing them? The more of these reports commissioned the more they make HR's pleas for credibility seem desperate. Employing a formerly, well-respected consulting group does nothing to improve validity or credibility when the methods are so obviously flawed. If BCG wants to enhance or restore, rather than diminish, its own reputation as a Level 4, Professional consulting firm it would be wise to avoid being caught in the HR trap. It would be better to advise the WFPMA that if its members want to show a connection between their practices and the bottom line, they need to start with that end in mind. If they start from evidence, that is based directly on existing organizational performance data, and then design their HR practices to measurably improve that performance, then their report would have in-built credibility. That sounds so obvious one wonders why the WFPMA and BCG have not already thought of it? What does that say about their management education?

The pillars of management education?

As soon as we ask the question 'how do managers become educated?' we quickly realize just what a vast array of theories, models, methods, tools and techniques are competing for their attention; some more trustworthy than others. In the list below we identify a whole host of management theorists, theories, ideas and practices but hasten to add that this list is impressionistic, imprecise, and slightly tongue-in-cheek. What we are trying to convey here is that much of modern 'management theory', rather than bringing illumination and management enlightenment, has succeeded in spreading fear, contradiction and confusion; especially in the field of people management:

Where do you get your management ideas from?

- What you just heard on the radio, saw on the internet, read in the paper or watched on TV.
- What a friend told you in a bar.
- Management gurus (choose any one from …).
- Charlatans and snake oil merchants (choose any one from …).
- Historical figures who are deemed to have some wisdom for managers today (e.g. Sun Tzu, Confucius, Machiavelli?) even though they wrote for entirely different times, cultures and often military contexts.

- Serious management thinkers and theorists with some practical applications (e.g. F.W. Taylor, Drucker?).
- Management thinkers without an obvious, practical application (e.g. Moss-Kanter, Handy?).
- Human motivation theorists with models that have high face validity but are too simplistic for complex, organizational dynamics (Maslow, Herzberg, McGregor?).
- Management research academies (e.g. Academy of Management,[7] Advanced Institute of Management[8]).
- Academics, quasi-academics or even pseudo-academics trying to prove there is something new under the sun by offering the latest, best-selling, 'big idea' (Hamel and Prahalad on core competence, Chan Kim/Maubourgne on 'Blue Ocean' Strategy, Daniel Goleman on Emotional Intelligence?).
- Management 'educators' and 'trainers' (anyone who says they teach or train managers, irrespective of their qualifications or abilities).
- Academic management educators (PhD's teaching on MBA programmes, regardless of whether their teaching is evidence-based or effective).
- Management entertainers (e.g. conference and after dinner speakers who tell interesting stories, taken from the worlds of celebrity, sports, science etc.) often with little or no obvious relevance to the audience.
- EBM academics (Pfeffer and Sutton, Rousseau, Briner).
- Evidence-based managers (watch this space).
- Biographies and autobiographies of famous entrepreneurs (Donald Trump, Richard Branson) who might have some lessons for managers.
- Billionaire entrepreneurs, who spotted the money-spinning opportunities presented by the natural monopolies associated with computer technology and the internet, (Bill Gates, Larry Page/Sergey Brin of Google) who can teach you everything you need to know about monopolies except where the next one is coming from.
- Successful companies run by billionaire entrepreneurs who we assume know what they are doing when it comes to management (Bill Gates, Larry Page/Sergey Brin) even if they try to convince us people management can be reduced to an algorithm (Google).
- Entrepreneurs and other business leaders who practised their own brand of management philosophy (Henry Ford, Eiji Toyoda, Ratan Tata, John [Spedan] Lewis) whether it has any relevance today or any generic applicability.
- Acclaimed corporate managers who believe they have developed their own management philosophy (Jack Welch with his acquisition strategy and forced ranking policy).
- Business schools who use the 'case method' (but note Harvard's changing methods).
- Corporate and operational management colleagues who practise the conventional management lessons they were taught at conventional business schools.

- Simple but highly effective business models (McDonalds).
- Game-changers – extremely rare but brilliant minds irrespective of management style or control freak tendencies (Steve Jobs).
- Consultancies producing their own, non-validated 'research' to sell their product to managers looking for simplistic solutions to complex problems (Gallup's Q12, Watson Wyatt's Human Capital Index).
- Consultants inventing their own proprietary model around a general management concept but without a proven, core, people management element (Kaplan & Norton's version of the business scorecard without any useful people measures).
- Books that describe what others did successfully without showing you how it could be applied in your own specific, organizational context (Tom Peters, Jim Collins).
- Books that describe successful companies and try to draw out general lessons only to see those same companies ultimately fail (Tom Peters, Jim Collins).
- Popular writers with catchy titles (Malcolm Gladwell).
- What your management institute tells you to do.
- What your professional institute tells you to do.
- Practising managers who you get to know, respect and trust based on the evidence you see with your own eyes.

What a minefield for the unwary, unthinking and unprofessional manager? No wonder the manager's head on our cover is spinning. All of this confusion has brought with it many serious failings.

The consequences of failing to define the Professional manager

This list is not intended to be a particularly rigorous or scientific summary of the state of management thinking today but then that is precisely why it has been presented in this way. Serious-minded readers might consider its compilation to be either frivolous, invidious or both, especially if one of their favourite 'gurus' is on the same list as someone they regard as a snake oil salesman. Therein lies the problem. Without a general council to uphold professional management standards one man's guru is another man's charlatan, yet nobody has taken on the task of condensing management wisdom into a single, professional qualification. If you invited anyone on this list to work with you they would come with no Professional certification or guarantee of success. But then surely that is only the same as the doctor who cannot guarantee a cure and yet still manages to satisfy the General Medical Council's professional standards committee. The proposition for the professional manager is totally analogous: can they specify organizational illnesses, diagnose the causes and be prepared to be held accountable for the outcome of their prescriptions? You could already be that type of professional or at least want to learn how to become one. That has to be better than any concoction an individual might brew from their own uneducated, list of ingredients like those in the above list.

Maybe management is actually not that complex a subject after all and these pillars of the management education establishment are just complicating matters? Even if the causes of management problems are highly complex that does not necessarily mean the solutions have to be complicated. High blood pressure is one of the most common, medical problems in the West and the causes of hypertension are incredibly complex. So complex in fact that there is no chance of treating it through simple cause and effect analysis. So how do doctors treat hypertension sufferers? Partly through sound advice and partly by prescribing a combination of a few tried-and-tested drugs that tend to either work for the patient or not. The doctor uses a professional form of trial and error and professional managers follow exactly the same principle. When it comes to managing people in large organizations can you afford not to? Whatever the complexity involved and whatever the strategic objectives that are set, they all have to be translated into a simple form of treatment that works for each individual; if necessary, through trial and error. That is a very different type of management to conventional HR departments where bottles of the same pills are handed out indiscriminately, without anyone ever bothering to check the outcome.

Many HR practitioners do not actually believe the complex can be made simple and that suits them. They accept a notion that management is intrinsically ambiguous. One organization that appears to have bought into this belief, and has incorporated it into its own competence management, is Microsoft. Competence management itself is based on the very shaky theory of competence (see Prahalad and Hamel in the list above) which re-invented the word competence into 'competency'. It also required the invention of dictionaries of management competencies. Microsoft's own list is shown as a 'Competency Wheel'[9] where, under 'Education Competencies: Dealing with ambiguity', they state: 'This competency is one in a set of complete functional and behavioral qualities that, when fully realized, can help lead to professional success.'

Microsoft also adds its own 'Recommended Readings' list of eleven books but does anyone ever check whether the books have been read? Does it matter if they are not read? What if an intelligent manager at Microsoft, who has their own preferred reading list, says they do not buy into the whole theory of competence or the practice of developing managers according to a rigid wheel? Has Microsoft's wheel enhanced their understanding of the problems of management or has it made the situation worse? Both sides cannot be right if they are so diametrically opposed. Is this wheel being offered on a trial-and-error basis where individual evidence can be fed back? Has anyone suggested this particular notion of managing ambiguity is nonsense and should be removed from the wheel? We can easily test the sanity of any management idea by just trying it out.

What should the ambiguous manager say to their team? – 'Sorry guys, I'm not really sure what to do for the best, it all seems a bit ambiguous to me'? Or does the professional manager consign this concept to the historical bin of bad management theory and confidently declare – 'We don't have all the information that we would want in an ideal world. I'm not even sure that the executives have a coherent answer either. What I do know is that consignment has to go out today; so let us manage what we can as well as we can'.

The really Professional manager would go much further than this, and in doing so, would rarely find themselves in this situation in the first place. If they work in a Professionally managed organization they will not be expected to manage ambiguity at all because they will not be set ambiguous performance objectives (e.g. 'get that consignment to the customer tomorrow but don't go above your budget'). A Professional manager will be acutely aware of the problems that any management ambiguity can cause and will make sure they are not compromised in this way. Being Professional, they will not be afraid to challenge an ambiguous instruction, and speaking out will be respected and welcomed in a Professional organization. Professional organizations employ Professional managers to use their brains, not blindly follow instructions, rules, regulations or competency wheels.

Here is some Professional advice for Microsoft. The concept of 'managing ambiguity' is not at all helpful, it is a perfect oxymoron: it is managerial nonsense. At any specific point in time a manager can only manage what is in front of them. Yes, an employee might be instructed or expected to perform a task with an uncertain outcome (e.g. a firefighter is ordered to enter a burning building) but a Professional manager will never regard this as an ambiguous decision. Look what happens when ambiguity is introduced into the management formula.

A true story headline[10] reads: 'Charity shop worker drowned in lake just 3ft deep after firemen refused to wade in due to health and safety rules.'

This was the story of a charity worker who drowned in a three feet deep boating lake, in an urban park, when a policeman and a paramedic were ordered *not* to try and rescue him. The inquest was told that 'health and safety rules' stopped them going more than ankle deep into the lake and the testimony from the police officer, quoted verbatim in the article, revealed that he was more than willing to enter the water, even going against orders if necessary.

Regardless of the circumstances of this particular case (there have been others) we have got something seriously wrong in management when the enforced behaviour of people at work is of a lower moral standard than they would reasonably expect to apply to their personal lives. Let us not rush to blame the watch manager at the fire station, as tempting as it might be. For all we know his behaviour was entirely consistent with the system he had to obey; he had no ambiguity in his own mind. We might be moving into dangerous waters ourselves here but they are unlikely to be anymore dangerous than a boating lake only three feet deep.

Management and 'ethical' behaviour

We cannot talk about people management without raising the issue of ethics. Professionalism should bring clarity to the situation, not further confusion. The reason we have chosen to put the word ethical in quotation marks is simply a pragmatic recognition that it is impossible to define 'ethics' in management. This should not mean that there is any ambiguity around ethics. The behaviour of the watch manager, and whoever else was in the control room, could be described as ethical in the sense that they believed that a proper chain of command is the most ethical form of management. Without this chain of responsibility we might have chaos and how ethical would that be?

Conversely, we could view the fire station staff as typical jobsworths: a term that comes from the phrase 'it's more than my job is worth' – a real word defined in the Oxford English Dictionary as 'an official who upholds petty rules even at the expense of humanity or common sense'. This story is a perfect example of jobsworthism in its most pejorative sense. While a jobsworth might try to give an impression of doing their job properly they are taking absolutely no personal responsibility whatsoever. Any jobsworth can be easily replaced by a manual because no human, managerial judgement or discretion is being exercised. Society is actually going backwards when it starts lining its management shelves with jobsworth manuals. If we want to halt this phenomenon we have to find out what is causing it. One thing the Professional manager knows for certain is that we can always trace problems in the system back to the overall system that governs, or should we say dictates, human behaviour.

Whole system thinking is the essential tool of the Professional manager, especially those who aspire to being Professional HR managers. Put one to work on this case study and they will undertake a thorough, root cause analysis to find out why this incident happened. Other, less professional, observers will rush to point at least one finger of blame at someone, probably in the direction of the legal profession, who would be cited as the main culprit behind people being too afraid to act independently these days. Let us just check that particular hypothesis out using a 'virtual history' technique.

What would have happened if the police officer had jumped in and then drowned in the process? Would the authorities recognize his bravery and declare him a hero? Would they offer a pension to his widow? Or would they regard his actions as contrary to regulations and discipline his sergeant into the bargain? Would the widow engage a lawyer to sue the authorities and would it all end in a protracted legal battle where justice is determined by a legal profession that has its own bell curve of professional scruples? Would either side's legal team be concerned that somebody had actually died while trying to do good? At what point in this scenario would any ethical questions be brought to bear or resolved satisfactorily? Or would humanity have got lost somewhere in the whole sorry process?

This does indeed sound like dangerous management territory but in fact it is the very opposite. It should all be very straightforward but the concept of 'management ambiguity' has created management monsters and ranks of jobsworths who are happy to work for them. Management is, and always was, meant to be a discipline. Professional people management in the police force should have started long before the police officer in the park ever thought of joining up. The same principle should obviously apply to the fire service as well.

The New York City Fire Department (FDNY) lost 340 firefighters, a chaplain and two paramedics in the attacks on the World Trade Centre on 11 September 2001.[11] If you were thinking of becoming a New York firefighter you will probably want to know what you are letting yourself in for, so take a look at their site; they were recruiting last time we looked. You will see a reference to joining 'New York's Bravest', that means being prepared to sacrifice your own life in the service of others, we think. It does not specifically spell that out; maybe it should? Or maybe the culture and history of the FDNY is enough? If another '9/11' were to happen again today would prospective recruits be expected to behave in exactly the same way as those who gave their lives before?

We have no intention of making light of a very serious subject. Professional HR is about serious matters of human safety, life and death. We are using this extreme case to make governments and policy-makers wake up to the full implications of not having a complete system of Professional people management. What part did the US security services play in the lead up to 9/11? Were they being Professionally managed and preventing any gaps appearing in their part of the complete system? Did the architects who designed the Twin Towers know that their buildings could collapse in this way and, if so, did they tell the FDNY? The problem with referring to 'another 9/11' though is that it will never happen again. If there were ever to be a 'next time' it would never be exactly the same as before because life does not replicate itself exactly: life is not a perfect science or a perfectly controlled laboratory experiment. So what have the security services learned and can we have more confidence in them for the future?

Also, on the ground, FDNY firefighters have to use their own judgement in the specific and unique circumstances they face every time they are called out: they might just make the 'wrong' judgement call. By 'wrong' we mean not the best of all the calls they could have made. They might not choose the option that gives them the highest probability of doing their job and coming out alive. So what should the fundamental management principles of highly dangerous firefighting be? If we get those principles wrong we will get the wrong decisions and the wrong behaviours more often, and more firefighters will lose their lives unnecessarily. What evidence can we gather to give us more confidence that the fire service is getting better at this? Once we can establish these criteria we can start specifying, selecting and training to those standards and let new recruits know what they are letting themselves in for.

Similarly, soldiers know they could get killed and professional soldiers accept that risk. What professional soldiers should not be asked to accept is any unprofessional management of that risk. The US and British military planners have very different views on this. In the US, friendly fire and collateral damage are expected and factored in much more than in British thinking; this is a cultural issue as much as one of military strategy. Anyone thinking of joining the fire service, the police or the army needs to know where they stand, without a scintilla of ambiguity. What they do not want to have to worry about is whether their fate, or the wellbeing of their loved ones, might one day be left in the hands of a jobsworth or an unscrupulous lawyer in a legal wrangle. Now there's the rub: what does the legal profession do to play its part in lowering the probability of us making the wrong decisions?

Going back to the death in the lake briefly, did the possibility of legal implications play any part in the decision-making process? Of course it did. The legal system is part of the whole system but does that mean it should end up controlling the whole system as it seems to? Do the leaders of the legal profession accept that they are accountable for the police officer not going into the lake? Are there any Level 4 Professionals among them who are evidence-based managers? If there are, should they be basing their legal judgements on the evidence of the consequences of their actions? If there were many other bodies left floating in lakes would they start to see their legal framework in a different light? Perhaps one or two Level 4 legal Professionals would start to be a bit more innovative in their thinking. If they are not then the future looks decidedly bleak; especially if any of us should ever have the misfortune to trip over one day and fall unconscious into three feet of water.

We could continue to debate ethics here but that is probably best left to a dry and detached academic class taught in business schools. There is often no time for ethical discussions when a surgeon has to make an instantaneous decision while their patient is already under the knife. The ethical decisions were taken for them a long time ago; when they had to swear an oath on joining the profession as a medical student. Companies are in exactly the same situation because ethics, implicitly or explicitly, should underpin all management decisions. Yet we frequently witness stark examples of management ethics being quickly discarded when no one is watching or governing effectively.

Without ambiguity, ethics and ethos form a very solid foundation for organizational culture. One company that employs thousands of people in public service, Serco, addresses the question of a 'Public service Ethos' in its own, online Resource Centre.[12] While this is laudable it is just one more indication that we do not have a universal ethos of organizational management. Should each company be devising its own ethos or should there not be just a single, organizational ethos for society? We are either all in this system together or we are not. We can only make the best of it by all agreeing what 'best' looks like.

Management Professionalism offers the highest form of ethical certainty

When we are considering how to invest our savings we seek the best financial advice we can afford because the majority of us cannot hope to become experts in financial appraisal. We have to trust our advisers to manage the complexities of investment decisions for us but we also want them to make it simple enough for us to make an informed choice. So they offer us three simple investment choices: do we want to take a high, medium or low risk? Our eventual assessment of the quality of their advice will be dictated, to a very large extent, by the *actual* returns we receive and whether those returns seem to be *directly attributable* to that advice. If we conclude that the returns are more down to luck than judgement, or some other unforeseen quirk of the market, we will attach less value to the advice itself. Over time we build a degree of certainty in our minds that certain financial pundits get it right more often than wrong. That is why Warren Buffett is so revered. Exactly the same principle applies to management in general and people management in particular.

So who can the CEO trust when it comes to advice on people management? If the HR professionals have no general council, if going to a university professor from a reputable university offers no guarantees and if consultancies are so flaky, they need to be very wary indeed. There is a much simpler and more assured alternative though; don't do anything without an evidence base. This is particularly true in the crucial, but currently unmeasured, area of people management because, as the Indiana University paper (Baldwin *et al.* 2011) revealed, there is enormous room for improvement:

> ... roughly 50 per cent of American respondents to workforce surveys reported that they are less than satisfied with their current manager − and many have noted that the very worst aspect of their job is their immediate supervisor (Buckingham & Coffman 1999). Other studies have shown that fewer than 25 per cent of managers regularly manifest the fundamentals of effective management, such as providing clear expectations and goals, involving others in decisions that affect them, and coaching via regular feedback (Tulgan, 2007). Similarly, scholars working with the Center for Creative leadership and others have found that lack of managerial skill is the most frequent derailer of careers and that roughly 50 per cent of people who take management roles essentially fail (Carens, Cottrell, & Layton, 2004; McCall, Lombardo & Morrison, 1988; Shipper & Dillard, 2000).

Can any CEO afford a 50 per cent failure rate in management? That is the equivalent of managing according to the random toss of a coin: you are as likely to lose as to win. However, if we want to improve this situation we cannot jump to the conclusion that the root cause of the problem is the managers themselves. This evidence does suggest that any development managers have had in the past is not working well enough, but that could be because the development activity itself is not evidence-based. Also, managers do not work in a vacuum; they work as part of the system so maybe changing the management system is part of the answer? Perhaps the managers are not really sure in their own mind what the organization is really about; they really have been placed in an ambiguous predicament and their teams are responding accordingly? Is the company only interested in profit or is it more concerned with a wider societal purpose? These questions might not get asked every day but they are regularly passing through everyone's mind. Everyone wants more certainty about the future and how the organization will respond to a crisis or some unforeseen event. What might they then be expected to do; how will they have to respond? The most reassurance their manager can ever give them is that offered by doctors to their patients: 'trust me, I'm a dedicated Professional.'

4

EDUCATING THE PROFESSIONAL, EVIDENCE-BASED MANAGER

Educating the dedicated Professional

Regardless of your own management experience, put yourself in the shoes of a relatively young and inexperienced manager for a moment. This particular manager sees Professional management as a vocation though and their personal dedication is on a par with any medic aspiring to become a top neurosurgeon. It goes without saying that this young Professional has great integrity, a huge appetite for learning and a pathological desire to follow only those management methods that are evidence-based. He takes his work very seriously but also recognizes that the people aspects of management are as much about judgement, art and craft as they are to do with hard facts and figures.

This young manager is also conscious of joining a relatively new profession and so will not expect to meet many fellow Professionals at the same level. He is also smart enough to know he will have to survive in the prevailing culture. This means coping with a process of organizational transition and possibly feeling ostracized by other managers who might close ranks against him. Nevertheless, this young manager has the bit between his teeth and wants to make a determined effort to be evidence-based in everything he does. What better place to start than in building his own team? So how different would evidence-based team building be compared to the conventional variety?

If he asks his conventional learning and development (L&D) manager for help he might be offered a very old idea, Belbin's team roles. This might look evidence-based, because it is actually based on the research of academic Meredith Belbin[1] who identified nine separate roles in teams, but Belbin's research would not qualify as the sort of evidence he needs. If the L&D manager is unprofessional they will already be buying this product off-the-shelf, without any question as to its validity or having made any effort to contextualize it. The young manager does not accept this unquestioning approach and so immediately starts to adopt a critical perspective; even though they might have no experience of training and development.

He would begin by challenging Belbin's underlying thesis with some very searching questions:

- Where is the scientific evidence to validate the concept of 'team roles'?
- Does Belbin's assertion, that people naturally take on roles in teams, contradict any proposition that people can be *put* into specific team roles?
- Does the research methodology of observing individual and team behaviour, in a simulated rather than a real environment, have any relevance to his own specific context?
- What other variables, factors and influences would have an impact on team performance in spite of a specific combination of roles being present?
- How do you deal with the real life practicalities of forming teams with exactly the right mix of roles?
- How do you develop someone for their team role?
- What effect does changing team members have on the dynamics of the whole team?

You might have noticed that while these are all very interesting and valid questions they are all quite academic: they are either theoretical, hypothetical, or concerned with the process of team building and development, not the outcome. Yet it is the outcome question that is the acid test of Professionalism; it is the only question that matters. We are back to the value question but this young manager phrases it differently: 'If I had a magic wand, and was allowed one wish, what value would I wish to get out of my team?'

This also sounds like a hypothetical question but it most definitely is not. It is an output and outcome question but, maybe counter-intuitively, one that must be asked right at the beginning. It is Stephen Covey's 'highly effective' dictum that we must start with the end in mind. The well-trained, Professional manager will not ask any other questions unless and until they have a satisfactory answer to this one. Anyone thinking of using Belbin, or any other proprietary product for that matter, without first considering the value of the expected outcome will fail this very simple test and nullify the whole process. Professional people management does not have to be any more complicated than that. Belbin's methods might generate an interesting discussion, and L&D people love such discussions, but they rarely get any further than discussing the process. The Professional team manager will give short shrift to the typically imprecise language of the L&D manager who wants to discuss 'team building', 'cooperation', 'managing relationships' and other, similarly vague, notions. They will want that translated into the precise language of value.

This value question is at the core of the Professional manager's *discipline*. Once our new Professional manager realizes the power of this question they are likely to become obsessed with it. They will view absolutely everything they and their colleagues are doing in simple terms of either added value or lost value. Their focus on getting the best value means they will want only the best people for their team. If that is not possible then they will fall back on their second best option, which is to manage the team they inherit to the best of their ability. One notion the Professional manager will not subscribe to though is the prevailing school of management thought that people management is somehow intangible.

Making the intangible tangible

We can illustrate, using this scenario of the new Professional, a generic line of reasoning that can be applied again and again until the young professional metamorphoses into the Professional expert who can easily connect the apparently intangible to tangible value. It is an essential part of the Professional's discipline to translate the indefinable into something more concrete and manageable. Consider the implications of applying this discipline to a full range of management theories and studies that exist in the people management arena. Pick any item from the wider range of activities listed below and then ask yourself two, critical questions:

Critical Question 1

How will improving X (*insert item from the list below*) lead to more value, in hard dollar's?

Critical Question 2

What else do I need to do to ensure the highest probability of achieving that value? People management activities include:

- Employee acquisition.
- Employer branding.
- Employee review and appraisal.
- Competence.
- Corporate social responsibility.
- Diversity.
- Engagement.
- Ethics.
- Industrial psychology.
- Leadership.
- Learning (individual and organizational).
- Motivation.
- Organizational culture.
- Organization development.
- Organization design.
- Organizational psychology and organizational behaviour.
- Performance.
- Reward and recognition – including compensation and benefits.
- Systems – human systems and whole system thinking.
- Talent – including management development.

- Training.
- Workforce and succession planning.

Critical questions 1 and 2 adopt a positive stance, hoping for and anticipating success, but the Professional manager will also think of the risks, downside and possibility of failure. So we need to add two further questions:

Critical Question 3

What are the consequences if it does not work?

Critical Question 4

What actual damage could it possibly cause?

These are very obvious questions to ask of any management decision; whether it is investing in new equipment, taking out a loan or moving office. So why is the same discipline not routinely applied to every single people management activity? You should ask your HR director. Take 'employee engagement' as a case in point. Engagement surveys are regularly carried out in many organizations (e.g. Gallup's Q12), and are usually sponsored and administered by the HR department. If you ask the HR team Critical Question 1, the stock answer will be an automatic assumption that better employee engagement leads to better performance without any acknowledgement of the complex relationships involved. It is based on the simplistic, unthinking belief that engagement is unquestionably a 'good thing', applies in any context and has no downside. It has become an article of HR faith that encourages organizations to spend significant amounts of time and money on annual engagement surveys. This is the state of the average, unprofessional, HR mindset and this crime has been compounded by unprofessional 'professional' institutions, unprofessional academics and consultants all espousing the same erroneous belief system. Or at least it was until very recently.

Angela Baron was still the CIPD's Adviser on Engagement and Organization Development when she wrote the following blog post[2] on 13 April 2011 about employee engagement being the Holy Grail of business: '... or so you would think seeing that the topic seems to permeate everything written on HR at the moment.'

One year later, on 24 May 2012, after she had commissioned research in conjunction with Kingston University Business School, she had reached the conclusion that:[3]

> While we definitely encourage organizations to measure engagement, it's not enough for organizations to focus on increasing their engagement scores without considering what type and locus of engagement is being measured ....

Baron left the CIPD three months later in August 2012, after 25 years.

After reading Baron's latest 'insights' you could be swayed against putting any effort into 'engagement' or encouraged to do even more of it in your endless pursuit of a definitive answer. If you are a CIPD member perhaps you are now just more confused than ever because your professional body seems to keep shifting its position? What the CIPD has not done so far is to grab its magic wand and guess how much value engagement might add. So why does it keep spending money on this type of research? How will it ever get a payback? On what basis did the holder of the CIPD's purse strings for research agree to hand over its members' hard-earned cash? Would it be the 'employee-customer profit chain theory'[4] by any chance?

The employee-customer profit chain theory is based on correlations and it suffers the same fate as every other correlative study. If you have not established which way the arrow of causation points then it can point either way. In other words, exactly the same correlative hypothesis and data can be used to support theories that completely contradict each other. Engagement might improve the business but then a great business model might improve engagement: successful companies are probably nicer places to work than those struggling to survive. That has as much face validity and scientific credibility as the Rucci *et al.* study at Sears Roebuck. Even if engagement does contribute to value there are bound to be many other causal factors, such as retail market conditions, so how much weight does one attach to each of these? The CIPD/Kingston University research provides no clear answers. So commissioning research is probably a waste of time and money if you are not absolutely clear what question is being asked, what the criteria of success are and what the basis for the research method should be. Perhaps this whole, conventional approach to people management research is just plain wrong, on every level. Let us break it down into its constituent parts to see where it tends to go wrong, from the very beginning.

Establishing a more effective, evidence-based, research methodology

This research methodology consists of several Elements.

Element 1: A research question relating to a specific context

Critical Question 1 is not really a generic question at all; it can only be asked in a specific context at a specific time. If the company makes car tyres this question is specifically about making car tyres, the cost of the raw materials, the price you can charge and the state of the tyre market, amongst the many, many other considerations around the question of dollar value in a tyre manufacturer.

Element 2: A sound theory and a logical hypothesis

The 'employee-customer-profit chain theory' is not really a theory at all. It is almost a truism: look after your people and they will look after the customer. At its best this is a simplistic hypothesis that would need to be tested again and again because other factors could so easily prove it to be wrong. For example, totally 'engaged' and customer-focused restaurant staff may suddenly find their level of engagement counts for nothing (in $'s) as customers leave in droves simply because a senior manager has just over-priced the menu in a tightening market. Any theory that is this easy to disprove in practice is not robust enough for an HR Professional.

Element 3: Regression analyses never reveal causation

If you think you could ever find proof of a specific, causal relationship between employee engagement and business performance, think again. How could you possibly prove this when there are so many other variables involved? How can you separate them all out and attribute specific effects and impacts directly to different factors? What difference do factors such as product quality, price, exchange rates and competitors make? The simple truth is you cannot deconstruct and separate out effects in this way. Conventional deconstruction methods are just not up to the job now required. The Professional manager and Professional academic researcher will eventually reach a consensus on this. It will be their defining moment when they face up to the truth of the matter, rather than trying to find a way around it.

Some academics still think they found the answer to this problem many years ago by using regression analysis. They believe that the weight of correlation eventually somehow converts, magically, into causation; it doesn't. That is like trying to answer the question 'what makes mayonnaise taste so nice?' by separating out the eggs and the oil. Of course the question is wrong from the start because the whole point of mayonnaise, what makes it taste so nice and the reason it is so popular, is the perfect blend of eggs and oil, together, as one, in perfect harmony. Pragmatic managers do not get bogged down in chemical deconstruction, they just try different blends of mayonnaise out on customers and then produce the ones that sell the best.

Regression is the great academic lie that many academics cannot own up to because so much of their research is based on it. Without regression they have no method. Douglas W. Hubbard in his book *How to Measure Anything – Finding the Value of 'Intangibles' in Business* (2nd ed., 2010) uses quotation marks around 'intangibles' to signify that he does not believe anything is intangible in measurement terms. He offers a very strong reminder though, as any Professional statistician should, about the severe limitations of regression analysis:

> It is important to state 3 caveats about regression models. First, correlation does not mean 'cause'. The fact that one variable is correlated to another does not necessarily mean that one variable causes another.... Generally, you should conclude that one thing causes another only if you have some other good reason besides the correlation itself to suspect a cause-and-effect relationship. Second, keep in mind that these are simple linear regressions ...

Finally, in multiple regression models, you should be careful of independent variables being correlated to each other … regression modelling … is a useful tool, but proceed with caution.

Even in the more scientific, evidence-based world of medicine regression analysis is capable of supporting two apparently contradictory hypotheses: red wine can be both good for you and bad for you, depending on how much you drink and many other personal factors. So it is with every aspect of people management. There is no automatic rule that says HR activity can only be good; it can be bad for you as well. The art of Professional HR is in being able to spot the difference and making the right judgement calls. Regardless of any of the supposed benefits of red wine, Professional managers are at their best when stone cold sober.

Spotting the difference between correlation and causation

It is remarkably easy to demonstrate just how erroneous regression analysis can be in the wrong hands. Or should that be in the wrong heads? Try this quick test. Look at the two graphs in Figures 4.1a and 4.1b and try to draw any quick conclusions you can about a possible relationship between share price and training spend.

If you understand the basics of simple, linear, statistical relationships you could be forgiven for thinking that each graph portrays a correlation between the two variables shown on the x and y axes. But if you try to infer from Figure 4.1a that there is a causal relationship; that spending more money on training causes the share price to rise, you would be making the fallacious assumption that the x-axis is the *causal* axis and the y-axis is the *effect*: you would be wrong in doing so. Even if such a causal relationship existed Figure 4.1a would not provide the proof. Anyone who

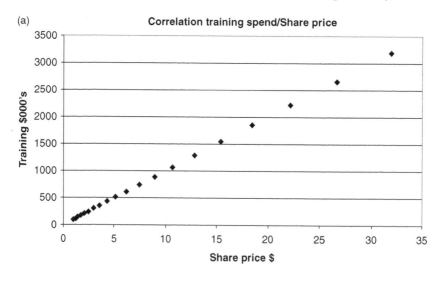

FIGURE 4.1a Correlating share price with training spend

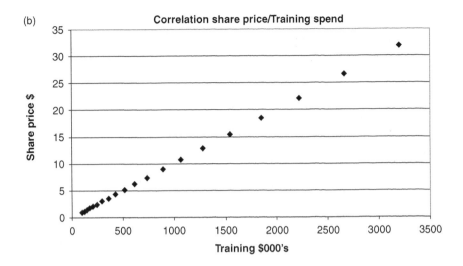

FIGURE 4.1b Correlating training spend with share price

tries to tell you otherwise is, not to put too fine a point on it, either ignorant of statistical facts or just plain lying.

If you are still not convinced and believe your own logic to be sound then look again at Figure 4.1b. Following your own logic this will equally prove that a rising share price causes companies to spend more on training; which is a perfectly contradictory yet equally feasible hypothesis. We should point out that both Figures 4.1a and 4.1b were produced from exactly the same original data, which is shown in Table 4.1. The only difference between Figures 4.1a and 4.1b is that we swapped the x-axis and y-axis around.

This fictitious data was deliberately designed to create an impression of a perfectly linear relationship between share price rises and increases in spending on training. That, in itself, would immediately set an alarm bell ringing in the head of the HR Professional. Such perfect relationships are unlikely to exist due to the influence of the many other contributory factors such as market changes, and even the weather, causing share price volatility. Moreover, if there were a direct, causal link between training spend and share price, ad infinitum, then this company ought to borrow as much money as it can for training. The company's staff could spend so much time on training they would have no time left to serve the customer. That is logic ad absurdum. Anyone even semi-numerate should be able to see through this so why do so many, supposedly intelligent, HR directors and CEOs still set a target for the number of training days per employee per year? Is there such a thing as graph-blindness?

The graph shown in Figure 4.2 shows what happens to misleading correlations in the hands of the unprofessional and unscrupulous. It has been adapted from several similar graphs widely used in marketing campaigns by HR consultancies. Typically they will be found in employer branding, company league tables and the like. One company in particular, a real HR consulting firm, uses such a chart to make claims

TABLE 4.1 Share price and training spend data

Year	Share price $'s	Training spend $000's
1992	1	100
1993	1.20	120
1994	1.44	144
1995	1.73	173
1996	2.07	207
1997	2.49	249
1998	2.99	299
1999	3.58	358
2000	4.30	430
2001	5.16	516
2002	6.19	619
2003	7.43	743
2004	8.92	892
2005	10.70	1070
2006	12.84	1284
2007	15.41	1541
2008	18.49	1849
2009	22.19	2219
2010	26.62	2662
2011	31.95	3195

that its clients (the upper graph) consistently outperform the S&P 500. Even if that statement were true this chart would not support their misleading inference that becoming one of their clients causes superior performance.

This type of marketing is a blatant and shameless attempt to mislead the innumerate and the gullible and to give their wilfully blind clients exactly what they pay for. The BCG/WFPMA report is based on exactly this type of analysis. In any

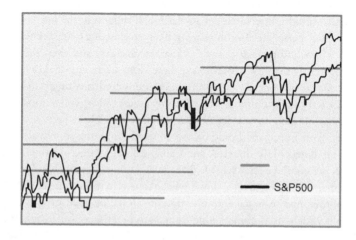

FIGURE 4.2 Painting an intentionally misleading picture with correlations

other walk of life this would be regarded, at best, as sharp practice and, at worst, as fraud. Legal it might be, for now, but Professional it certainly is not and never will be.

So let us just return once more to the Professional HR manager's critical questions, the ones that keep things simple and get right to the heart of the matter from the very beginning. This time we will spell them out in more detail, for an imaginary company called ABC plc, which thinks it needs to have good employee engagement scores.

Critical Question 1 (revised): How will improving employee engagement lead to more value for ABC plc?

This is not an abstract question. The best way in people management to elicit a serious attempt at an answer is to move from the general to the particular; that means making it personal. Imagine one specific ABC employee, Joe, and consider asking Joe this question directly. Very quickly you realize that Joe might not be a representative sample and, even if he were, he will probably have his own, unique views on what engagement means to him. His first thought is likely to be governed by selfish interests and why not, this is our most basic, human instinct. So 'engaging with the customer' is not necessarily going to be uppermost in Joe's mind. Joe might be thinking 'we could do with a new coffee machine'. If nothing else this technique is designed to encourage managers to treat each employee as an individual, rather than as some anonymous respondent to an impersonal questionnaire.

If you think this example is patronising to people like Joe it might surprise you to find that it is actually drawn from recent real life (February 2012), from a very well established HR function, in a very large, successful and well respected global company – Tesco. In *Personnel Today*[5] Tesco's international HR director wrote about 'Listen and Fix – the biggest listening exercise Tesco has ever undertaken.'

So why did Tesco decide to listen and fix?

> Our objectives in undertaking it were to make Tesco a better place to shop and work via a more engaged workforce, and to gain a deeper understanding of what really mattered in all areas of the business: in our stores and distribution; at Tesco.com and Tesco Bank; and at our head office.

None of these objectives were measured specifically for the purposes of demonstrating the value of listening and fixing. So what did they do as a result of the exercise? They:

> ordered 250 coffee machines and 42 dishwashers for staff areas in the stores that needed them most.

An operational manager looking at the people management activities list above for the first time might see it as an HR list; it's what HR people do. If anything, it should be the operational manager's own checklist. Every manager's effectiveness will be enhanced or limited by the organization's ability to get all of these things right. An individual manager can only manage talent if the organization helps them to identify, attract, develop, move around and retain talent. That will be dependent, amongst many other things, on the organization getting its reward policies in tune with the market and managing succession effectively. In other words this is a general management, organization-wide, checklist but one where the HR function tends to instigate and police policies in each of the areas identified. Bringing greater Professionalism to bear therefore has to involve management Professionals and HR Professionals working together; neither can do it on their own.

We should also now consider, in more detail, the third party to this relationship, the one that has been sitting too quietly in the background, the academic researcher. Much of management education stems from academic research. Therefore management Professionalism will only improve if management research improves as well. That can only happen when academics become more Professional.

Professional academics will adapt their scientific method

We have probably all experienced the word 'academic' being used in a derogatory fashion. 'It's all academic' or 'that is only of academic interest' are put-downs suggesting an academic is someone who does not inhabit the real world or has little to say of any practical value. It gets very personal when we hear 'what would he know, he's only an academic'. Yet it is rigorous academic research that is the very cornerstone of a doctor's professionalism. Patients have learned to trust doctors more than quacks because their treatment generally works. Patients do not need to understand all the science behind medicine as long as it looks like the medicine is working. The same should one day be said of managers, but that day will only come when the 'science' of management is more convincing than it is today; especially the science of people management.

Even in the reasonably well-ordered scientific world of medicine the rigorous researchers do not have the field to themselves. The introduction of science did not suddenly rid the world of charlatans and untested, alternative therapies such as homeopathy. Every therapy will have its own advocates and believers. The same goes for managers, they are up against all kinds of therapies and belief systems. So how does the CEO know the difference between a Professional and an unprofessional executive or manager? They ask to see the manager's scientific method.

The illustration in Figure 4.3 is a very simple version of the scientific method but it is worth looking at it in some detail first, so we can fully appreciate the management implications. We need to be clear about the definitions being used, the sequence of steps in the complete process and the part each step plays. Let us look at the definition of the two key words first and then each step in turn.

Scientific: science is the intellectual, practical and systematic study of a subject through observation and experiment.

Method: method is not a haphazard, disjointed or chaotic activity but a particular procedure following a specific series of steps, in sequence.

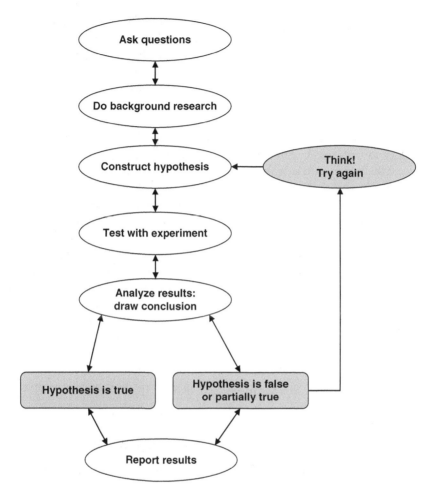

FIGURE 4.3 The scientific method

The scientific method then starts from a question that has to be asked:

- *Ask questions*: the effectiveness of the method is dictated by the quality of the question being asked from the very beginning. The management question should be one where the answer will be of value to mankind. Asking critical, management questions is also challenging the status quo though, so this requires courage.
- *Research*: the scientific method is intrinsically evidence-based with the best research being based on the best evidence available. A manager may call on academic research or have already carried out their own research.
- *Hypothesis*: all questions lead to the positing of a cause and effect hypothesis. For example, here is an effect (cancerous tumour) what are the causes and how could we deal with those causes to produce a cure?
- *Test with experiment*: we develop a prototype drug and use it on rats before carrying out clinical trials.

- *Analyze the results and draw conclusions*: did the drug treatment seem to work?
- *Hypothesis passes or fails*: regardless of any implications (e.g. future research funding) the results of the experiment have to close the loop back to the original hypothesis and be fed back to all interested parties.
- *Think – try again*: if the hypothesis fails we have to go back and construct another hypothesis.

This is a perfectly logical approach when dealing with the physical sciences but if you want to apply the same thinking to management questions it helps to know the Socratic Method (named after the Greek philosopher Socrates). This is also referred to as the Socratic questioning technique, which challenges the accuracy and completeness of someone's thinking in order to help them move towards their own, ultimate goal. You probably noticed that this technique has already been used extensively throughout our text but here is a specific and relevant example.

If a manager starts with the assertion – 'a happy employee must be a productive employee' – the Socratic questioner offers a contradictory assertion to help the manager check their thinking. So you might point out that 'a lazy employee can be a happy employee'. Socrates believed that the first step to knowledge is recognition of one's ignorance. His method encourages us not so much to prove our point but to *disprove* the other person's point of view. Socrates was condemned to death. Nobody likes a smart-ass, especially senior executives who are struggling to convey an impression of intelligence and gravitas. So the cautionary note for the Professional is do not expect perfect logic to work; you will need to do an awful amount of persuading and influencing.

Applying a scientific method to Professional practice

Whether CEOs like it or not, evidence will always speak for itself, eventually. The performance curve in Figure 1.2 should reveal who is a good manager and who is not but that assumes that the managers themselves accept the premise of the bell curve, agree the measures being used and are willing to admit their ignorance: that is a huge call. If we are really serious about Professionalising management we cannot afford to let any of these natural, human objections get in our way. So there is nothing wrong, in principle, with management academics trying to apply a scientific discipline to their management research, including people management, as long as they fully accept these human provisos. Also, human beings will not necessarily believe the most compelling evidence even when it is staring them in the face. They may well follow the 'not invented here' argument (quite rightly) that what worked for someone else, in a different context, will not necessarily work in theirs. So let us bear these considerations in mind when practising 'scientific' people management.

Intuitively, the concept of the happy employee being a productive employee sounds like it makes sense. However, we have already learned, from the fate of Socrates, that asking too many awkward questions is not a great way to win friends and influence people. So, while we should not be deflected by this, we must consciously help executives get used to the idea that they are going to be asked much more searching questions, especially about their people management capabilities, than before. To make this as painless as possible the HR Professional will make sure they only ask their most intelligent questions as politely, respectfully and quickly as possible. They cannot afford to be seen as wasting anyone's precious time.

There is a lot of re-educating to be done. HR practice in most large organizations today is based on very simplistic assumptions about employee happiness and HR people now see employee engagement as a goal. So we have to rewind that mindset back to the beginning, erase old notions, and record some new ones. We need to analyse how HR got itself and its executive team into this situation in the first place. What was the original question that led them to recommend annual employee engagement surveys? If you already run an engagement survey this should help you out of the mess you are in. The technique we will use here is based on a further refinement of the Socratic Method and consists of two more types of question: Type 1 and Type 2.

Type 1: The hypothesis is already accepted

A Type 1 question jumps the gun in the scientific method by moving straight to the 'test' stage, missing out the three preceding steps of 'question', 'research' and 'hypothesis'. The Type 1 question that led to engagement surveys was probably something along the lines of: 'Are our employees engaged?'.

The easy way to spot a Type 1 question is to follow it with a 'so what … if they are engaged? Type 1 questions always lead to a dead end. Type 1's tend to focus on input and process rather than output and outcome. This Type 1 error is compounded by several erroneous assumptions including:

- thinking that you already know what the problem is (e.g. a lack of engagement);
- that a 'proven' hypothesis already has the answer (you accept Gallup's unsubstantiated claims that Q12 proves engagement is linked to performance); and
- that the *activity* (of running a staff survey) is therefore a valid thing to do.

Once the underlying logic has failed it will lead to other nonsensical questions. Here are a couple of very obvious questions that will arise out of such erroneous and unscientific thinking. You will also notice that Type 1 questions tend to lead straight to the door of the consultancy's sales team:

- Are your employees engaged enough?
- How do you compare with Gallup's other Q12 clients?

Even if you believe a high Q12 score provides you with an answer to your Type 1 question, it still reveals nothing about the dollar value of organizational or employee performance. So Type 1 questions are misleading and ultimately pointless. Therefore let us try starting with a Type 2 approach instead.

Type 2: We have not formed a hypothesis yet but think we might have a problem

Type 2 questions follow the scientific method step by step. The best, most intelligent, first questions usually start with 'Why?' and will always be *questioning* rather than making assumptions. Here are a couple of examples of Type 2 questions:

- Customer service data seems to suggest that our staff do not give great customer service: why is that?
- Why is the recent merger not producing the synergies and benefits it was meant to?

Neither of these Type 2 questions has jumped to the conclusion that the organization might need to increase employee engagement or demerge. However, if you find an answer to a Type 2 question it should directly add value. In the examples above this would be extra dollar's through better customer service (and the higher volume business that follows) or cost reductions through economies of scale. Type 2 questions are always focused on value, in dollar's.

The second step is to do enough research to provide a confidence level that you are dealing with the right issues. So, for example, did the customer service survey specifically refer to poor staff attitudes and was there at least a correlation between the survey results and store sales? Correlations do have a bit part in Professional people management but only when used intelligently and within accepted limits. A correlation will not reveal causation but if no correlation exists then you would probably not pursue this line of enquiry any further.

Moving on to Step 3 of the method, we construct a hypothesis of what was *possibly causing* the poor customer service that related to falling sales. We say *possibly* because we do not know at this stage and you are never likely to prove it beyond all doubt anyway. That is why Step 4 is not 'produce a solution' but 'test with an experiment'. Depending on the results of that experiment you will draw your own conclusions as to whether your hypothesis appears to be correct or not. The scientific method starts and ends with evidence: evidence that a problem exists and evidence that the same problem no longer exists (or has at least been alleviated). It is not magic; it is basically common sense turned into a logical, management discipline.

Based on this rudimentary explanation of the scientific method it might appear that there is nothing contentious about using such a simple methodology. This method can and has been applied millions of times to scientific and management problems with great success. The evidence is plain and voluminous: modern drugs and lean manufacturing would not have reached the same level of sophistication achieved in the last 50 years without it. But times change and as we make inexorable progress our well-tried-and-tested methods are stretched beyond breaking point. In terms of people management, that limit was reached once before, over 30 years ago, when organizations started to try and do total quality management (TQM). Unfortunately they did so without the means to make it a total people solution. The time has finally come to complete the total management picture.

Building the pyramids – an advanced, scientific method for Professional people management

The conventional scientific method has serious limitations when applied to the challenge of developing more sophisticated, people management methods. They include:

- Many operational tasks are amenable to the scientific method but they tend to be discrete and one-dimensional in nature; as with measurable quality improvements on a production line.
- More complex organizational issues are wicked, multi-dimensional problems. For example, how to balance patient care with the cost and efficiency during times of rising demand and constantly changing technology?
- 'Laboratory conditions' for people management 'experiments' cannot be held constant and, even if they were, the practical contexts in which they might be applied would be so varied as to make the laboratory experiments invalid.
- Management cannot be as scientific as science, in the sense that human behaviour is less predictable and more difficult to observe and measure than, say, the effect of GM technology on crop yield.
- Many managers still do not accept that management can be a science and are even less inclined to believe that people management can be scientifically studied in the real world, in any meaningful sense.

Having established some good reasons why the scientific method cannot work, it might now sound contradictory to suggest that to cope with all of these potential drawbacks an advanced 'scientific method' is necessary. Sometimes fighting fire with fire works. Let us also add another apparent contradiction for good measure: this advanced method needs to be more sophisticated and at the same time simpler and more pragmatic. Maybe it is time to stop trying to apply the conventional scientific method to general management and design something that is fit for the purpose of twenty-first century management. To do so we will have to incorporate three specific adaptations in the new design:

- An ability to ask very complex questions, in a meaningful way, that can be answered very simply: we will call these Type 3 questions and offer more explanation shortly.
- The organization has to be designed to think: see the feedback loop shown in Figure 4.3.

- The 'results' that need to be analysed and used to 'draw conclusions' have to provide clear, credible and compelling evidence using data that is unconventional: this will include indicators such as the quality of organization design and other human capital management indices.

In principle, these three adaptations are simple but in practice they represent the biggest shift in organizational thinking for over 70 years, when Toyota first introduced the much-imitated Toyota Production System; the original TQM. This necessitates a seismic shift from conventional management paradigms to the paradigm of EBM. However, we need to offer much more clarity and definition to what is currently a rather broad and indistinct concept. It might help readers to view EBM as a three-legged stool on which managers should sit and feel secure. The three legs comprise:

- Relying on evidence rather than intuition.
- Making evidence their first, rather than their last, resort in decision-making.
- Seeking real evidence of what works best in the problematic area of people management, not correlations.

So where does academia fit into this brave new world of EBM? Would a fourth leg add any greater stability?

Academic research and the quality of management evidence

Probably the most comprehensive definition of EBM within the academic community is provided in a paper entitled 'Evidence-Based Management: Concept Cleanup Time?' by Rob B. Briner, David Denyer, and Denise M. Rousseau (Academy of Management, Perspectives, November, 2009):

> EBM is about making decisions through the conscientious, explicit, and judicious use of four sources of information: practitioner expertise and judgment, evidence from the local context, a critical evaluation of the best available research evidence, and the perspectives of those people who might be affected by the decision.

Defining EBM well is a good start but it does not tell us how to do it. Before we move onto the practicalities we need to remind ourselves once more of the gulf between theory and practice. Where will managers have learned about this new EBM paradigm? If anyone completed an MBA before this definition arrived on the scene in 2009 do they now have to go back to business school and update it? Or does EBM actually invalidate any and all management education that preceded it? Management 'education' is currently supported on the crumbling pillars listed in the pillars of management education list in Chapter 3 and no one has yet fully signed up to the rules proposed by Rousseau *et al.*

While they are thinking about it, some of them might be reading comments like these from the well-respected economist in the UK's *Sunday Times*, David Smith.[6] Smith writes every week and enjoys a very wide readership amongst the business community and has something he calls his skip index:

> ... based on the number of skips in my street. For three years it has trundled along ... A few days ago it shot up to five. ... it provides evidence of an economy that is not flat on its back. Not yet, anyway.

(A skip is the big waste container that builders use during renovations.)

Smith has a very dry sense of humour so how does the casual reader know whether he is joking or not? How many CEOs who read Smith's column and live in London, or elsewhere, have now started to gauge their own business prospects using Smith's skip index? Let us not kid ourselves that CEOs are necessarily any more evidence-based than that. EBM is not just a paradigm shift, its whole raison d'être relies entirely on the quality of evidence. So our academic colleagues have to go much further than defining evidence, they have to ensure managers can tell the difference between good and bad indices.

It is worth noting that the medical Profession has not always been as evidence-based as it should have been and it can take many years for evidence to inform and actually change medical practice. It was only in 1972 that the 'father' of evidence-based medicine, Professor Archie Cochrane, published 'Effectiveness and Efficiency: random reflections on health services'[7] which drew attention to 'our collective ignorance about the effects of health care'. This eventually led to the Cochrane Library with the strapline 'Independent high-quality evidence for health care decision making'.

In 1979 Cochrane published a further essay in which he suggested that:

> It is surely a great criticism of our (medical) profession that we have not organized a critical summary, by specialty or subspecialty, adapted periodically, of all relevant randomised controlled trials.

Medicine and HR have much in common because they work with the same raw material: the infinite complexity of the human race. Doctors do their best to make people better. HR Professionals do their best to make us all better off. Even if the doctor already knows the answer ('you would be healthier if you lost some weight Mrs Postlethwaite') he cannot guarantee that Mrs Postlethwaite will follow his advice. Maybe the mark of a truly Professional physician is one who does not walk away at that point; believing they have completed their professional task? They keep doing their level best to make Mrs Postlethwaite see sense and do what is in her own best interests. Exactly the same should apply when the HR Professional sees that a manager is not acting on their best advice.

In 2007 the publisher of the Cochrane Library, Wiley, invited leading proponents of EBM (including Rousseau, Briner, Denyer and your author) to join a project that would explore whether and how a similar 'library' could be designed to provide the same reference base for management academics and managers. This was a very laudable and ambitious attempt to combine rigorous, systematic research with a robust test of what actually works in practice. In the event this proved too much of a challenge, at that time. One reason was the lack of a consensus on EBM thinking. Another was the simple fact that academic management research had yet to be converted into a codifiable, easy-to-search, user-friendly format in the same way as the Cochrane Library.

A further reason is that there is one big difference between the fields of medicine and management. Doctors can accurately be described as 'scientific practitioners' in the sense that they combine their science with their practice every day. Managers might be practitioners but they cannot yet be described as the complete deal because they do not have an effective science of people management. In effect, doctors have already closed many of their knowing-doing gaps whereas this is still the big challenge for evidence-based, Professional managers.

In the meantime, Professor Rob Briner threw down a serious challenge to the whole of the HR profession when interviewed by the CIPD's journal *People Management* (1 November 2007). Under the heading 'Tried and Attested' but with the rather negative subtitle 'Some would say HR is prone to chasing fads – but what's the alternative?' he was reported as saying:

> As HR practitioners we are also consumers of a wide array of practices, techniques, services and products, which consultants and others who sell them claim have positive effects. What kind of consumer do we want to be? The cautious and careful type who thinks through the problem, the possible range of solutions, systematically reviewing the logic behind each and deciding which, if any, is likely to be the best? Or do we want to go on gut feel? As professional purchasers of HR products, it seems clear to me which kind of consumer we must be.

This captures an essential aspect of what an evidence-based, Professional HR mindset has to be. Only the individual can decide if they want to be Professional. Belonging to a professional body does not automatically confer upon them Professional status; only a Professional state of mind can do that. So we need to explore what a proper, Professional institute needs to do to assure both its own Professionalism and that of its members.

Professional assurance and EBM pyramids

Whenever an apparently new idea, or new name, appears on the management scene they are bound to encounter mixed and sometimes extreme reactions ranging from 'born again' advocacy to outright scepticism. EBM has already elicited as many negative reactions as positive and although it might try to mirror evidence-based medicine it is much more problematic. It has to cope with more than one 'patient' (employee) at a time and a much more complex, dynamic mix of circumstances, contexts and environments. Therefore one might reasonably expect that it will take some considerable time before EBM becomes the norm: but it will become the norm.

To become the norm in management it needs to develop its own, alternative methodology for research and practice that can produce better quality evidence than conventional management. No such model currently exists so EBM academics have had to borrow a model that was designed for evidence-based science in conjunction with the conventional scientific method. This is not a perfect fit with EBM's specific needs but it does at least address the specific issue of how to distinguish between high and low quality evidence. It is a hierarchy, or pyramid, as shown in Figure 4.4 with the most reliable evidence supposedly at the apex.

We say 'supposedly' because there are some serious questions that need to be asked about this model, particularly when it is applied to the social science of people management. However, before we ask those questions, let us first look at each level in a little more detail, still using a medical example for illustration, before we consider how well suited it is to the study of management practice. So imagine that we are trying to obtain the best evidence to help us find a cure for stomach ulcers. You will see why we chose this particular ailment shortly.

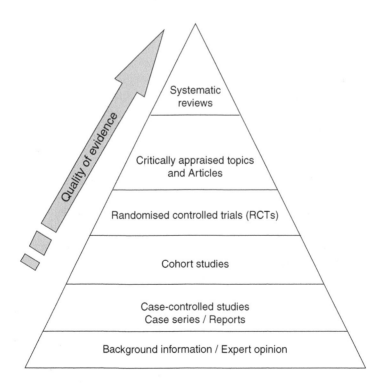

FIGURE 4.4 A pyramid of evidence – one version among many variations

Working from the bottom of the pyramid upwards we envisage a doctor's surgery with a patient presenting with the symptoms of a stomach ulcer. The doctor, historically, would have learned how to deal with ulcers both in medical school and from updating their knowledge through CPD. This knowledge will be reinforced, positively or negatively, by seeing how many patients respond to their treatment. Having the best knowledge available is obviously very important but *experiencing* the application of that knowledge, seeing the evidence with their own eyes, is always likely to be the most convincing test of efficacy for the individual doctor. If the patient is not cured then the doctor will seek further advice on ulcer treatments. So the medical profession strives to improve its Professionalism by moving up through the subsequent levels of the pyramid using case histories, controlled studies and randomized controlled trials (RCTs); always seeking better and better evidence of success.

In the meantime, drug companies use their own evidence to decide there is a market for ulcer drugs and undertake their own research, using case-controlled and cohort studies. Over time, all of the drug trial studies are reviewed together in a systematic review. The reason this is at the apex of the pyramid is that synthesising all of the knowledge and experience across a range of studies reduces the likelihood of errors and improves the probability of high quality evidence. Systematic reviews are regarded as the gold standard. If you are interested enough to find out more about evidence-based medicine you will find there are many versions of this pyramid, all with their own slight variations and adaptations, but the core concept has high face validity. So why did we choose stomach ulcers as our example to illustrate this model? Because the conventional treatment of ulcers, for many years, was predicated on some erroneous assumptions that went unchallenged for far too long.

Until about 30 years ago the major causes of stomach ulcers were considered to be related to stress and lifestyle. In 1982 two Australian scientists, Dr Robin Warren and Dr Barry Marshall, were awarded the Nobel Prize for medicine for their discovery that stomach ulcers can be caused by a bacterial infection (*Helicobacter pylori*). Once this fundamental change in diagnosis was accepted a different combination of antibiotics and new drugs were found to be very effective in curing certain ulcers: 90 per cent of duodenal/intestinal ulcers and up to 80 per cent of gastric/stomach ulcers.[8] Although this is ultimately a story about the successful use of the scientific method, and the pyramid of evidence, what really mattered here was not only the breakthrough insights of the scientists but their courage and resolve in defying conventional thinking in order to pursue a radically different avenue of enquiry. The words 'courage' and 'resolve' are not shown in the standard pyramid diagrams so we now need to specifically include them in our first adaptation. HR Professionalism will be founded on two key principles:

(1) The need for a codified hierarchy of evidence to indicate the relative validity, veracity and weight of evidence.
(2) The need to invite and encourage fresh, often radical, insights to break out of the rut of non-evidence-based convention.

Now we can move on and develop the new, breakthrough, management methodology required for EBM but many executives, behaving like pharaohs, will want to build their own, bespoke pyramids; so a note of caution is needed here. If we apply these two principles to existing studies of management 'excellence' we will expose how much work is still needed to link excellence to evidence. The website of the UK's Advanced Institute of Management Research[9] offers no evidence of any advanced thinking in strategic, human resource management. However, its 'sister' organization, AIM Practice,[10] sells its own 'HRM & Innovation toolkit' that:

> takes up to 15 minutes to complete. When all of your nominated participants have completed the questionnaire you will be notified, and your personalised report will be available online within 24 hours.

What were AIM's aims and were they aiming in the right direction (enough already)? Is this product a response to a Type 1 or a Type 2 question? If a supposedly 'advanced' institute is not advanced enough to answer Type 2 questions (so what if we are innovative?), and offers no evidence of its impact or value, maybe we would all be better off going back to basics rather than trying to be too 'advanced'. How advanced is a management 'method' that can produce a report about a company's readiness for innovation without even visiting the company concerned? This could easily be seen as the very opposite of professional management; it certainly goes against Toyota's principle of genbutsu – go see for yourself. 'Advanced' is rather a meaningless term anyway in the era of EBM. If AIM really does want to demonstrate its 'advanced' status then it should provide evidence of the highest quality, not off-the-shelf products.

Conventional management thinking tends to regard good profits, over a very long period, as evidence of good management. This view, especially since 2008, is now rightly regarded as simplistic and potentially misleading. Long established businesses, with good track records and well-respected management, like HSBC, have come to grief in the face of changing technology and globalization. Other high profile collapses of more recent times, from Enron to Lehman Brothers, highlighted fundamental weaknesses in company reporting, the use of balance sheets and the auditors who are meant to assure their veracity. All of this has added fuel to the fire of academic research into sustainable performance. Thus far, such research has largely been undertaken by academics using the medic's scientific, evidence-based pyramid with only minor adaptations for a management context. This is where the main problems arise in trying to close the academic-practitioner, knowing-doing gap.

If we can generalize for a moment, when academics profess to being interested in EBM they do not mean they are interested in the *management* aspects of EBM so much as the *research evidence* aspects. Academics live to study and research, not to manage. If they are genuinely interested in furthering the whole concept and cause of EBM they have to produce management-friendly, usable research in order for managers to develop into evidence-based managers. To date, they have failed to acknowledge this classic, chicken-and-egg conundrum that is staring them in the face. How can a manager become an evidence-based manager without research evidence and how can researchers produce EBM research without any evidence-based managers?! Fortunately, once this point is accepted by the academics, there is a way out of this apparent impasse. The chicken-and-egg question was always the wrong question, predicated on a fallacy. It assumed that only two mutually exclusive states exist; to be a chicken or an egg. We now know that chickens evolved, just like the rest of us, from a state that was neither quite chicken nor chicken's egg.

Managers are in that state of limbo now; not quite evidence-based but not entirely non-evidence-based either. When managers choose to incorporate better research into their, previously unresearched, decision making they will take their first tentative, but nevertheless conscious, steps out of their cracked egg and into the light of the virtuous circle of value management. They can then be accurately described as evidence-based managers, even if they are not perfect specimens in accordance with the Rousseau *et al.* definition. But a virtuous, management circle is entirely dependent on having virtuous people and yet we know, only too well, that human beings are not always paragons of virtue. So EBM has to incorporate Professional, evidence-based people management to ensure organizations get more virtue than vice out of their people.

For example, if we ask a Type 2 question such as 'Are organizations that introduce SPC (statistical process control techniques) more efficient than those that do not?' there are already plenty of conventional managers out there using such techniques, like Six Sigma, who can take part in the research. So the researcher starts sending out questionnaires and receives a reply from a production line manager who has already been on an SPC training course. This particular manager attended for no other reason than it seemed like a good idea. Nevertheless they used the techniques to good advantage when they returned to work. The manager even sends the researcher a chart clearly showing that production costs have fallen since he came back from the SPC course. This appears to be very convincing evidence of training being applied, value being added and the original Type 2 question being answered. So far so good.

A professional academic will not be satisfied with this. They will want to check this improvement against the costs on other production lines, where managers have received no SPC training, and also those where the training does not appear to have worked. In a perfect experiment they will only be satisfied by including a control group. Let us assume the research covers a thousand such examples, and includes a control group, and the evidence starts to produce a very strong case for the benefits of SPC. This might then be offered as evidence that a conventional management technique, SPC, which has been around for well over 70 years, will produce greater efficiency and extra value. Yet after all of this effort the professional, academic researcher will not have produced an EBM case study. We do not need new research methods or new types of evidence to tell us that SPC can add value or even that SPC training can add value. If that is what EBM is all about then there is nothing new in it. We are already well convinced about the benefits of SPC, and the Toyota

Production System, which is why every professional manufacturer has already tried to emulate it. EBM is not about re-inventing the management wheel it is about a genuinely new paradigm.

The new paradigm of EBM

A professional, evidence-based, organization would only send production managers on SPC training courses if they wanted to reduce their own costs and improve quality. An HR Professional would see it as part of a long term strategy for achieving the highest value possible. They would already have foreseen that the only opportunities left for further improvement, after all other operational improvements have been implemented, are to be found within the capabilities of the workforce. This will open up a whole new world of management possibilities, where the focus shifts away from improving the production process to *improving the people*. It is this shift in emphasis to the *people dimension of management* that starts to transform conventional management into the authentic version of EBM.

If academics keep pretending that EBM can only happen in academic research journals and systematic reviews they will find their research has no greater practical value than the unheeded advice of the doctor who tells Mrs Postlethwaite to lose weight. What is the point in offering dietary advice when all the evidence indicates that she will go to the cake shop on the way home? Excellent academic research will remain firmly on the library shelf, or lost on someone's hard disk, unless and until the academic community as a whole engages more with management practitioners. This is one of the prime causes of the perpetual knowing-doing gap and it can only be resolved by different roles being adopted *on both sides*.

The evidence-based, HR Professional role specification is already a hybrid. It requires someone with a wealth of management experience who has a particular interest in people management and can master academic research. People who can fill such a role must already exist but the role does not. It does not exist in academia, in any business school, any professional institute or management team. Those with the necessary profile are most likely to be found in senior, conventional management positions but they have probably always harboured a desire to push people management to the fore. So one option might be to second them to a project group of like-minded executives that not only has access to academic research but is also given the resources to design new research, based on the new EBM paradigm, to meet their own specific needs.

In the meantime there is no guarantee that senior executives and managers 'know' what they need to know about evidence-based people management and, even if they did, they would not necessarily want to take the medicine it prescribes. So we need to add another iteration to the pyramid of evidence, one that is designed much more with the practicalities in mind rather than any abstract notion of academic purity. Paradoxically, and ironic as it may seem, a determined pursuit of practical evidence will ultimately provide much better academic evidence than anything a systematic review could ever hope for. Our

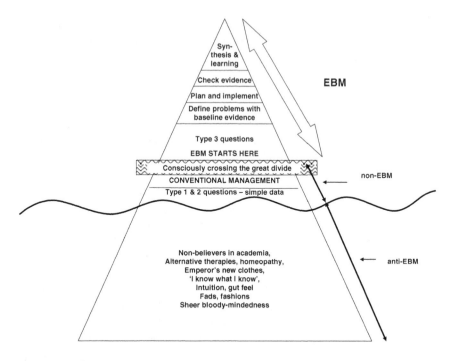

FIGURE 4.5 The complete, practical, EBM pyramid is actually an iceberg

version of this new, people management oriented, EBM pyramid is revealed in Figure 4.5.

The EBM iceberg

What conventional pyramids of evidence fail to show is what lies beneath the surface. Ours is therefore drawn more like an iceberg (but not to scale) with four fifths of conventional management under the surface and EBM at the tip. This EBM paradigm represents a radical departure from conventional management thinking but cannot start from a clean sheet because it co-exists in a world where conventional management still rules. Shifting paradigms is seismic activity and unsettles everyone. Therefore, Professional HR consciously addresses the inevitable resistance of the old order and has to be prepared to re-educate those who are willing to learn. One other advantage of changing the analogy from pyramid to iceberg is that ice eventually melts, pyramids seem to last forever.

There are three broad layers to this iceberg – EBM, non-EBM and anti-EBM – with a dividing line between the top two layers that requires a conscious effort to cross over. It is not just a shift from ignorance, or denial, to acceptance but a blinding revelation that management can actually be so much easier and more effective than you ever imagined. Let us look at each layer in a little more detail:

- Those on the bottom layer are anti-EBM and eschew any notion of using evidence in preference to their gut instinct, common sense or alternative remedies. They actively resist being drawn towards an evidence base by only asking Type 1 questions. They do not recognize the issue of causality and are not even interested in correlations. Their attitudes to people management range from 'they are lucky to have a job' to misguided views on what 'caring about people' means. All of these attitudes amount to the same thing, no focus on the value of people.
- The middle layer, non-EBM, is the main core of conventional management, using common sense and conventional problem solving tools (e.g. cause and effect analysis, process analysis) to answer Type 2 questions. This is still an old paradigm layer where problems have to be deconstructed, regardless of their complexity, and so the most complex area of all, people management, is still subject to simplistic answers. Examples include a 'balanced' scorecard approach that bolts on a separate box of 'people measures', rather than taking an integrated, holistic, whole system approach.
- The uppermost layer is similar to the pyramid in Figure 4.4 except that the questions are now of a different type altogether – Type 3 – requiring the more sophisticated approach we are calling true EBM. Here the level of complexity is such that it has moved the discussion way beyond the bounds of common sense. Here the evidence can often appear counterintuitive with employee satisfaction being seen as the *effect* of a well-designed organization, around a successful business model, and as part of a virtuous cycle of improvement, rather than as a *cause* of performance.

So what exactly are these Type 3 questions?

Type 3, complex questions

They are similar to Type 2 questions, in that they are seeking to add value, but they are not so easy to formulate or frame. They are best described and characterized by their main components. They:

- address issues that are indeterminate or difficult to pin down;
- are intrinsically complex, and multi-dimensional;
- do not respond well to conventional management tools, techniques or measures;
- always contain a strong human element;
- are not so easy to connect to organizational performance or value in dollar's;
- are subject to longer timescales than day-to-day operational problems and tasks;
- require an organization-wide solution, often at a strategic level;
- force us to return to first principles; back to re-thinking 'why are we here?';
- involve problems that remain hidden for some time but, once they surface, can only be resolved with a great deal of time and effort.

Here are some examples of the sorts of issues that Type 3 questions try to address. Note how they are all framed as 'how' questions:

- How can we become more innovative?
- How can we reorganize for the best?
- How do we merge two different companies/cultures to produce greater value through synergy?
- How can we best integrate the people in this takeover?
- How do we get people to accept responsibility around here?
- How do we improve accountability and leadership?
- How can we manage all our talents to best effect?

Obviously, the way we have phrased these questions shows how broad they tend to be, yet they can all easily be seen as having an underlying need to improve the business. They are still in their raw state here though and have not yet been re-framed into a format suitable for the imposition of EBM discipline. That discipline has to take these vague and nebulous questions and check their validity, potential value and relative priority by making simple connections to expected outcomes in value ($'s). This takes us back to the 'magic wand' question: 'if we waved a magic wand and solved our problem what would be different?'

Let us apply it now to the 'how do we improve accountability and leadership?' question. If you improved the leadership of your organization tomorrow, what difference would you expect it to make? That is still too vague isn't it? So how about making it more specific? Why not personalize it by focusing on a small group who you expect to become leaders? What difference would it make to each of them if you waved the wand over their heads? Why not go further and ask each of them, individually, to answer this question? Ask them what outcome they would like to see and ask them to try and put a dollar value on it. You might not have realized it yet but by adopting this questioning process you are already demonstrating the discipline of EBM and it should immediately bring benefits in terms of definition, clarity, focus and value. Sending executives on conventional leadership development programmes, that are not evidence-based, is bound to be an inferior investment when compared to this approach. Look what happens to leadership development when nobody asks the simplest questions.

Here is an extract from an 'External evaluation report', written by the ROI Institute[11] in January 2006, into a £35 million leadership programme that started at the BBC in 2003. It concluded that although one of the objectives of the programme was to:

> address the strategic objectives of the BBC, as well as the specific requirements of each division … no specific and measurable objectives were subsequently required to be met. As one senior manager described it was envisaged as less of a programme in the conventional sense where participants would learn to do certain things to specific standards and more about building a 'community' of

shared leadership values and behaviours … it appears in retrospect that there was less than 100% buy in by all senior management and a number of influential individuals …

It adds that after the programme "'There was no attempt to require participants to demonstrate what they had learned and its impact on business needs.'

This is a perfect example of a vicious circle that starts when Type 3 questions are answered with simplistic, off-the-shelf solutions. It is also an example of an organization not being transparent. The evaluation report was only made available after a formal request was made under the Freedom of Information Act. The BBC, an international broadcaster with a well-earned reputation for reporting the truth, appears to be governed by those who have something to hide. Ashridge management school, which won the contract to provide leadership training for the BBC, is still running similarly non-evidence-based programmes for very large corporations, including the UK's NHS, a body that spends over £100,000,000,000 of taxpayers' money every year, with no evidence base and no evaluation of impact.

The keyword in EBM is 'based'

The keyword in EBM, the one that signifies the seismic shift in management thinking, is the word 'based'. Management decisions that refer to academic research evidence are not necessarily *based* on that evidence. For a management decision to be *based* on evidence it has to relate to specific evidence in a specific context with specific people. For the BBC to have had any chance of running an effective leadership programme it would have had to ensure that everyone going on the programme agreed a *personal baseline* before they attended. After all the theorising, the 'leading edge' thinking behind EBM turns out to be a statement of the blindingly obvious. If you want to get from A to B you need to know where A begins and B ends.

Where the EBM academic community have so far got it wrong is in thinking that EBM is all about the quality of their research evidence: it isn't. All the best research in the world would not have made the BBC leadership development programme effective. The evaluation report showed where the BBC had gone wrong but it did nothing to help the BBC get it right. The role of research in the scientific method is to test a hypothesis and possibly to prompt new theories but the ROI Institute has no evidence-based theory of how to produce better leadership. As strange as it may seem, the ROI Institute had also got it wrong. So what we are witnessing here is one part of a broken system being audited by another broken part of the same system. So where is the ROI Institute going wrong?

The ROI Institute is founded on Jack Phillips' 5-level model of training evaluation, which is itself an extension of the Kirkpatrick 4-Level Model recognized by the majority of L&D professionals around the world. One reason both models are so well known is simply because they have been promoted by the ASTD for many years as the way to address the most crucial question in training – evaluation. How do you know that your training has worked? The evaluation question is particularly important in those areas where outcomes are less easy to determine. A bricklayer does not need to do much evaluation to check that their wall is still standing. That might sound like such an obvious point but it is not so obvious to thousands of ASTD members. So we need to look at these 'levels' of evaluation in more detail.

The 4-level model comprises:

- Reaction to the training (usually a happy or smile sheet).
- Checking what has been learned (usually a test).
- Behavioural transfer (checking to see if they are using the learning in practice, in the workplace).
- Business impact ($'s)

The Phillips version adds an extra, but entirely superfluous, fifth level to produce an ROI calculation that can be adequately calculated at level 4; as long as a Baseline has been established first.

These models might look perfectly innocuous but a properly trained L&D Professional will be able to highlight their flaws. The most glaring error is that the first level, Level 1, starts much too late; *after* the training has already happened. There is no requirement in these standard ASTD models to produce a Baseline of evidence, if there were the BBC would not have spent £35 million on a leadership programme with no Baseline. This very obvious point is the equivalent of a General Medical Council imposing no requirement on doctors to record symptoms, collect data and undertake a thorough diagnosis before prescribing treatment. (For further technical detail on the theory and practice of evaluation see 'Kearns 2005').

So, if you believe you have a problem with leadership, the only evidence-based way to manage that belief is first to translate it into a Baseline, with evidence of what damage or missed opportunities poor leadership is causing. You cannot take another single step until you have a Baseline. There is no point in reaching for the academic journals on research into leadership at this stage. Academics that research leadership, using surveys and case studies in accordance with the conventional pyramid of evidence, might expect to reach the apex of that pyramid with systematic reviews of leadership studies. Yet such systematic reviews can only ever be as good as the Baseline from which they work. If academics have never pinned individual leaders down to a personal baseline it is impossible for their subsequent studies, systematic or otherwise, to produce any causative evidence of performance improvement that is attributable to leadership. Their research would have to fall back on correlations between leadership development and company performance. Any such connection would be tenuous. Using regression analysis and the peer review process cannot improve the quality of such correlations without a solid evidence base. It does not matter how many academic peers review the data, they will not be able to add any weight to this poor quality evidence.

It appears we have stumbled across another alarming fact. The peer review process in social and management science, where the outcomes are difficult to determine, is rather meaningless if your peers are not all, uniformly, evidence-based. We saw earlier that there is certainly no consensus on EBM in academia and how some academics even ridicule 'the very idea'. This is why we have no evidence today of what effective leadership or Professional management looks like. The academic research and peer review system has failed to produce any meaningful evidence. The implications of these findings are very worrying.

The consequences of this fundamental weakness in the academic research system is that effective evidence-based research, and practice, will fail to oust ineffective, alternative therapies and large organizations like the BBC and the NHS will continue to throw hundreds of millions of dollars down the drain of management fads, fashions and homeopathy. But even that huge waste of money is not the biggest issue here. The biggest issue is the number of poor leaders and senior executives who remain in post simply because no one is producing clear evidence of just how poor their leadership and management really is. Instead, business schools and management institutes continue to run programmes that mask the scale of this global problem.

Look at the website of the UK Chartered Institute of Management[12] which claims to be 'Passionate about management and leadership excellence. We are the only chartered professional body dedicated to raising the standards of management and leadership'.

However, like AIM, they have no way of supporting such claims. It has no effective evaluation methodology and cannot show a shred of evidence that they are raising any professional, management standards. If they can why does a similar institution exist called the Management Standards Centre[13] (previously the Management Charter Initiative) with its 'National Occupational Standards for management and leadership (that) are statements of best practice'.

It appears 'best practice' institutions are springing up all over the place, all claiming to set the highest standards. Is this not like having three, or even more, General Medical Councils? Does their joint existence not undermine all of their claims? Who says their practices are best anyway? They are offering no better guarantee of management effectiveness than the UK Engineering Council. Any management institution that makes such empty claims is not ready to make the journey across the great divide in Figure 4.5.

Consciously crossing the great divide between conventional management and EBM

At a talent management and leadership conference in 2012 an L&D speaker from BP revealed that it spends $1 billion per annum on 'staff development' of which 15 per cent is devoted to 'leadership and management development' and 83 per cent to technical training. The speaker, knowing only too well that his audience of trainers have all been taught that evaluation is important, pre-empted any evaluation questions by side-stepping the issue altogether. What he did reveal was that BP still uses the four level, standard model of evaluation. The true L&D Professional takes that to be a clear sign that senior executives at BP are not taking their own development any more seriously than the BBC.

Proper, evidence-based evaluation, based on a proper diagnosis of BP's problems, would have looked for a connection between BP's management failings in the Gulf of Mexico, and elsewhere, and what they need to learn to avoid any recurrence in the future. ASTD members would see no direct, tight, causative connection between evaluation, learning and BP's string of disasters. They would be happy to run menus of courses that bear no relation to serious and urgent business needs. This is precisely what is happening at BP. If senior BP executives see no connection either then what does this tell us about their attitude to such disasters?

We could be forgiven for receiving the distinct impression of a leadership mindset that says working at the bleeding edge of drilling technology means accepting an inevitable and unavoidably high risk of disaster. Investment analysts take note. It is amazing what insights await you by engaging a proper L&D Professional to analyse the subliminal messages behind apparently innocuous conference presentations, in subjects that seem irrelevant to corporate governance. BP, and other large corporation executives, should beware. If you allow your unprofessional heads of L&D to inadvertently portray your company as a non-learning organization then do not be surprised if one day your share price collapses unexpectedly, for no conventional reason that would be apparent to you.

When markets and investment analysts deem a senior management team to be successful there is no impetus to change. Change often requires a burning platform. It appears that when BP had its own platform burning, literally, in the Gulf of Mexico it was still not enough of a jolt to their system to make them fundamentally question their management paradigm. This is why such a conscious effort is required to make the crossing from the conventional paradigm to EBM thinking. However, as with any new development, even the most curious managers will only want to dip their toes in the water first to find out whether it feels nice and warm. Some will find it is just too cold or decide they are not yet ready to be baptized as an evidence-based manager. Others will try and remain agnostic but there is no halfway house in EBM, you are either evidence-based or you are not; it is an attitude of mind. This is why, despite resistance, the EBM movement will continue to gain traction because all managers will have to decide which side they are on. Being on the non-evidence based side of history does not sound like the most comfortable place to be. The Professional, evidence-based manager will definitely be on the winning side of profit and value, if for no other reason than they are more likely to reduce the number of future disasters. EBM has a lot to offer risk management, because all risk can be seen as a people risk, but we would rather that EBM be seen in a much more positive light.

5

HUMAN CAPITAL MANAGEMENT RECOGNIZES THE NEW ORDER

A single, unified theory of Professional management

Management, whether in a capitalist or a mixed economy, is primarily about achieving objectives. The reason we are having to re-think our management models is that our objectives are not as simple as they used to be. We still burn a lot of carbon fuels but at least we feel bad enough about it now to want to balance the commercial considerations with the environmental. The human race seems to have a built-in mechanism for driving change and wanting to challenge its own orthodoxies. This drive helps to explain how we got to where we are and also explains why we are now having to consider alternatives to the orthodoxy of conventional management. Notice that word 'conventional' though, which gives an impression that management evolved through pragmatism as much as ideology or theory. If we are to find a better alternative to convention, maybe we should pull many strands of thinking together in a single, unified theory? One thing we know for certain, the core components of a Professional theory of management will have to be built on a solid frame of whole system theory, comprising:

- A system of political economy that is designed to offer the best value to society – not one interest group or set of stakeholders (or shareholders).
- All organizational entities, profit or not-for-profit, have to subscribe to the same goal of value, based on the same criteria.
- Capitalism is as close as we can get to a natural, whole system because it plays to man's natural inclinations. It is still, therefore, the best method available for value creation through innovation and the most efficient allocation of human resources.
- Best value can only come from effective management of all forms of capital. That has to include human capital with Professional people management recognising each individual as a unique human being with individual capabilities and motivation that need to be optimized.

- So organizational leaders have to commit to a total form of governance that incorporates human governance.
- This means we will have to be able to audit leadership and management effectiveness using evidence, or at least the most meaningful indicators, that the best returns on all forms of capital are being achieved.
- The highest form of management Professionalism is then defined by and assessed against these criteria.
- So Professional management, based on a total quality philosophy of never ending, continuous improvement becomes synonymous with evidence-based management.

You might not agree that this constitutes a theory, or even accept its tenets, but that does not matter too much at this stage. Do you have an alternative that is better than what we have now? What matters is that you have at least put some thought into it and can reconcile your own views with those of the rest of the people who work for your organization. It is a very serious omission to have no single, coherent philosophy on management that incorporates people management. It is even worse to have more than one. There should only be one philosophy, one theory and one Professional practice in operation at any one time. Could this all be described as the single science of management?

A single science of management?

Businesses like formulas, especially cash generation formulas. Microsoft got the right cash generation formula by coming up with *the* universal, computer operating system. Many would argue that it was never the best operating system but that has not stopped Microsoft exploiting the fact that everyone has to pay for the same system. Google invented the best formula for searching the web and it appears Facebook has found the most popular formula for social networking. The beauty of having the right formula is you don't have to think too hard anymore because you can let the formula take over. That is also the biggest problem with successful formulas; people stop thinking. This, as we shall soon see, is the death of good people management because formulas produce formulaic and mechanistic systems, processes, and behaviour.

Jack Welch had his own formula of only staying in markets where you can hold position one or two. Toyota (a company Welch tried to emulate) produced a more complex, more potent formula that involved a revolutionary management philosophy including lean production and extraordinary supply chain relationships. These formulas have worked so well that they become the case studies taught in business schools. That is the same case method now regarded as a weakness by Harvard. Probably because they realized that business success cannot so easily be replicated or reduced to a mechanistic and rigid sequence of scientific steps. Even mainstream scientists have had to go back to asking fundamental questions about what science is because they realized it can no longer be detached from the way the rest of the world works. As recently as 2009 the UK Science Council took a year to produce a new definition of science; and still welcomes comments. Their current definition is:[1] 'Science is the pursuit of knowledge and understanding of the natural and social world following a systematic methodology based on evidence'.

From a management perspective it is reassuring to see that the 'social world' is included in their latest definition and emphasis is placed on a 'systematic methodology based on evidence'. Perhaps the key word here though is 'pursuit', suggesting that this is likely to be an ongoing process, forever. A more pithy definition might simply be that science is a never-ending search for the truth? Why would we not want a beacon of truth to guide our social world? That beacon is called value and science does not have to be pure, perfect or exact for it to be valuable. Think of some of the areas where we already live with inexact science. The weather, climate change, the environment, management, psychology, education and social work are never going to follow a perfectly predictable pattern. It would be a shame for humanity if they were. What these disparate fields have in common is a complex interaction of variables that are not susceptible to laboratory experiments or strict RCTs, but that should not stop us trying to improve outcomes. However, management is already difficult enough; we do not need to confuse it further by having more than one 'science of management' in operation at any one time.

In *Bringing Out the Best in People* Aubrey Daniels (2000 Preface, p. xvi) quotes one of his mentors, Ed Anderson of the Cambridge Center for Behavioural Studies as saying:

> Being a chemist by profession, I often wondered why there is only one chemistry, one biology, one physics, and there are 10,000 psychologies. Of course there can be only one science of behaviour.

Anderson is right. There can be many competing theories, as with theories of the universe, but those theories have to be built on the foundations of the same fundamental *laws* of physics. Ultimately there can only ever be one explanation for a single phenomenon; even if working through the many competing theories takes a long time. So why should the same not apply to the study of human behaviour in organizations? Are there some fundamental laws of organizational behaviour and do organizational theorists agree what they might be? Would one of those fundamental laws be that to get the best out of capitalism we have to aim to give everyone a chance to give their best? Is this the fundamental law that we are still getting wrong and the main reason why capitalism founded on pure profitability does not seem to work as well as we would like? It would certainly help to explain why we are having so many arguments today about accounting practices and organizational governance. If the economic growth of the second half of the twentieth century lulled the West into a false sense of security then events of the first decade of the twenty-first century are doing their best to shake us out of our complacency. The reverberations from this shock to our part of the global system are being felt throughout the rest of the system and there is no bottle of magic pills that will suddenly and miraculously relieve the pain and discomfort. We are going to have to work at this and mere placebos for 'leadership development' will not help.

Managing the placebo effect of HR

Understanding the placebo effect and its implications for HR management is a very, very tricky subject. First, though, we need to be absolutely clear what the placebo effect predicts. The placebo effect, or response, is a real response to a false treatment. If we tell a patient that a sugar or saline solution (without any active ingredients) will improve their condition, they can experience a real improvement. This psychology of expectation can be a remarkably potent force. Before we apply this phenomenon to management let us consider how it can apply in several medical scenarios.

Scenario 1

You go to your GP with an upset stomach and the doctor thinks you have mild indigestion. She prescribes an antacid, not because you really need it but because by writing a prescription she can give the impression she is taking your complaint seriously and looks like she is doing her job properly. This GP knows the importance of patient psychology and expectation. She wants you to leave the surgery satisfied that you have been well looked after. Of course you did not have to visit the doctor for this treatment; the indigestion would probably have disappeared of its own accord or you could have bought the same antacid over the counter. The medical result would be the same but the visit provides you with the psychological reassurance of a doctor's expert opinion. So what is the outcome here? A combined medicinal and placebo effect; you are cured and satisfied.

Scenario 2

The doctor thinks there is nothing at all wrong with you (although they do not say so) but still prescribes a mild antacid on the basis that it will do you no harm and you will feel the benefit of their reassurance. This time the antacid is used entirely for its placebo effect, not its active ingredient. The outcome is an inappropriate, active ingredient, prescription being offered for its placebo, rather than its active, effect. Nevertheless, you go home satisfied.

Scenario 3

Similar to Scenario 2 but this time the doctor gives you a placebo, a fake 'medicine' (in reality just a bottle of coloured water) with a label stating 'For the treatment of stomach upsets'. It produces the same psychological, placebo effect as in Scenario 2 without any active ingredients. Outcome? A placebo prescription but you go home satisfied.

Scenario 4

You really do have excess stomach acid but do not realize it is caused by stress. The doctor diagnoses stress as the main cause and prescribes the coloured water placebo together with a mild tranquiliser for the stress. The active ingredient in the tranquiliser directly reduces your anxiety and stress levels and also, indirectly, produces the *physical* effect of reducing your level of stomach acid. The placebo of coloured water adds extra psychological reassurance, which also helps to reduce stress levels while the active ingredient is given time to work. Outcome? A combination of active ingredients and placebo. You get physically better, and feel better psychologically, but you will have to come off the tranquilisers at some point and resolve any underlying causes of your stress.

Scenario 5

You go to your GP with an upset stomach but after examination she tells you there is nothing wrong and you should go home and stop wasting her valuable time. Outcome? No illness, so no cure, but a dissatisfied patient nevertheless.

Table 5.1 offers a comparative summary of these scenarios.

So what logical conclusions can we draw from this short exercise that might be useful in the context of management placebos?

- Regardless of the patient's perception of their own need the doctor has to produce an accurate diagnosis as the patient might have much more serious problems than indigestion.
- We need to know what the doctor's objectives (success criteria) are before we can judge their performance. Should it be surgery efficiency, medical effectiveness, patient satisfaction, the cost of drugs or what?
- The doctor can achieve the objective of patient satisfaction through inappropriate prescribing, as in Scenario 2.

TABLE 5.1 Isolating the placebo effect

Scenario	Patient's perception of own illness	Doctor's diagnosis	Active ingredient?	Placebo effect?	Patient satisfaction?	Patient cure?
1	Upset stomach	Indigestion	Yes	Yes	Yes	Yes
2	Upset stomach	No illness	Does not activate	Yes	Yes	N/A
3	Upset stomach	No illness	No	Yes	Yes	N/A
4	Upset stomach	Stress induced acid	Yes (tranquiliser only)	Yes	Yes	Yes – for now
5	Upset stomach	No illness	No	No	No	No

- Active ingredients play no part unless they have something suitable to act on: antacid liquid can only act on an acid.
- The most honest scenario (Scenario 5) is the most efficient at matching the treatment to the medical need: a valid diagnosis requiring no treatment and no drug cost, but at the cost of reduced patient satisfaction.
- It is easy to confuse cause and effect where placebos are involved. In Scenario 4 acid is the effect caused by stress. The placebo indirectly reduces the amount of acid, not its acidity.
- Where there is no illness there can be no cure but the patient can still be satisfied.

Each one of these lessons has a direct, parallel application in people management. Imagine that you are the Professional HR director ('doctor') and your CEO ('patient') comes to you thinking that he is suffering from a range of organizational illnesses called 'low engagement', 'blame culture' or 'poor customer focus'. How would you use any of the lessons above to deal with these apparent problems? We will just look at one of them, the 'blame culture'.

- Regardless of the CEO's perception of the problem you have to undertake a thorough diagnosis first (the CEO might have much more serious problems to deal with).
- The HR director needs to have clear objectives and criteria for success. Does the CEO want to see nobody blaming anyone for anything? How would progress towards such a 'no blame' culture be measured and monitored?
- Try to avoid being drawn into offering the CEO a reassuring placebo (as in Scenario 2). The CEO might have a simplistic expectation that an employee survey could just include a question relating to blame, or want everyone to be sent on a 'No blame' training programme.
- Establish any active ingredients that might be needed. A blame culture might need some very strong feedback (medicine) to act on those who keep doing do all the blaming. The CEO might have to take their own medicine, along with everyone else.
- Be honest (Scenario 5) and manage the CEO's expectations by suggesting there might be no problem. What evidence do they have that a blame culture exists? Be prepared for a dissatisfied CEO who thinks you are questioning their judgement and denying they have any illness.
- Is 'blame culture' a cause or an effect? What business problems is it causing? Are there any clear examples that could be analysed (e.g. the failure of an important tender or project?).
- We cannot produce a cure for an illness that does not exist (Scenario 5) and it will only exist when we define it and measure it.

The HR Professional will be well-drilled in adapting this same sequence of questions to any context and sees the whole diagnostic process as a major part of their Professional discipline. It is no less than the basis for their 'science'.

You would think that asking logical questions like these just makes sense; without having to be too scientific about it. So why do so many executives not seem to see it this way? Common sense, never mind science, is often conspicuously absent in questions of people management and we can easily put this assertion to the test. Ask your CFO why they 'sign off' the training and development budget each year, without having any evidence of its value? They are unlikely to be able to answer this question so help them by making it more conceptual – 'what return would you normally expect on any other investment?' That will present an immediate problem. Training is an investment unlike any other and the CFO might not view it as an investment at all but a sunk cost. Either way, they might be reluctant to be drawn on this simply because they have no way of answering the question. Ask them about machinery amortization and depreciation, or even asset appreciation, and they will have no problem at all but the accounting profession has no methodology that accounts for people appreciation.

That means training and development can only be subjected to the most simplistic of accounting processes, a record of income expended with no double entries to balance liability with asset. Such expenditure is therefore a mindless act of faith when it should be as much a clear-headed, conscious, investment decision as any other. When it comes to accounting for people, often a significant proportion of overall expenditure, your average CFO is a complete amateur; but we cannot expect them to admit it. On a much deeper level, CFOs, and the CEOs they serve, struggle to reconcile people expenditure with a notion of people returns. They have not adequately squared the people-profit circle in their own minds. So the first job of the HR Professional is to do exactly that. They have to educate every shareholder, board member and executive that only a business strategy incorporating an intelligent and coherent HR strategy will produce the best value possible. In the same breath, they will also talk about societal value. Surely this is the only virtuous circle that can be fashioned out of combining the interests of profit and people.

The most eye-opening lesson that may yet arise from the present economic turmoil is the realization that many of our erstwhile 'leaders' have no Professional idea how best to follow a much more enlightened form of capitalism that has people management at its heart. Robert Slater collected together '29 Leadership Secrets from Jack Welch' in his book of the same name. We have just found leadership secret number 30 that Welch never mastered. It is called Professional Human Capital Management.

Entering the era of human capital management

If you are now wondering why we have suddenly started using the term 'human capital' to talk about managing people, perhaps we need to provide some background. One might think that choice of language should not make that much difference to practice, but it does. We do not wish to become bogged down in semantics but the highest level of Professionalism requires the highest level of linguistic accuracy, just as a surgeon will have a very specific naming of parts for every part of the body and every instrument they use. We already use quite a long list of different words to describe those ordinary citizens who get paid to come to work every day. An HR Professional knows the importance of only using the most accurate and appropriate. If we cast a critical, Professional eye over the current list of contenders which should we choose?

- People? Rather meaningless but at least it distinguishes human beings from other animals.
- Personnel? Outmoded and gives no sense of regarding people as sentient human beings. It also betrays a rather detached and impersonal perspective.
- Employees? Honest enough and straightforward but suggests that everyone should know their place. Do the executive team see themselves as ordinary employees or masters?
- Staff? A bit old-fashioned and has connotations of the unhelpful distinction made between white collar 'staffers' and blue collar workers.
- Human resources? A reasonably accurate description of what people are to an organization but not the most flattering nor the most popular with employees or managers?
- Associates? Too impersonal and indistinct. Do your people like being associated with you and your company? Are you happy to be associated with them?
- Colleagues? Respectful but fails to define the working relationship accurately enough.
- Human assets? A simple lie even if genuinely well-meaning.
- Human capital? Certainly the most accurate. Wages are the rent for this capital; the interest payment for keeping it at our disposal. It also defines the relationship with the organization perfectly, albeit not to everyone's taste. At least it implies that senior management have to make the very best use of this highly valuable capital.

All of these terms, and more, are still in use today. The CIPD, after 100 years, is still a 'personnel' institute and the WFPMA is a 'people' federation. Maybe this is telling us something:

- Organizations agonize unduly about what to call the human beings that they pay.
- Human beings can be very touchy about what you call them.
- Using the wrong terminology will result in the wrong type of management relationship.

Of all the above choices, only 'human capital' imposes an obligation on organizational leaders to make the most of their people. None of the other descriptions demand the highest possible return and none of them treat human beings with the level of respect that the word 'capital' attracts amongst investment analysts, investors and shareholders. If these constituents regard people as capital it is in their blood to make the most of that capital and that is in the interests of society at large. Human capital is the perfect description and it places a very serious responsibility on the shoulders of the CEO and CFO to account for that capital. That means accountants and auditors have to adopt, or invent, the necessary technology. It is a real pity that most employers and employees do not see it this way. That might have something to do with the education and attitudes of their CEOs and CFOs.

This line of reasoning has been gaining much wider acceptance over the last decade. History will eventually reveal that the beginning of the twenty-first century was more than just a turning point; it was a paradigm shift in political economy and management thinking. An economy cannot be said to be managing its human capital well if it cannot clearly demonstrate this. Let us not stray too far into this virtual world though. One thing we know today, for certain, is that the employment relationship is a very complex human relationship, unlike any other, and as society changes the dynamics of that relationship inevitably change.

Employment is a marriage of sorts but many employees view it as just co-habiting. There might not be any real commitment on either side but there is definitely a legal relationship; one that is constantly being revised by regular iterations to the legal framework of employment rights and responsibilities. There can be love in this relationship too; it does not have to be cynical. But it can so easily turn sour; very quickly. Without wishing to over-state our case this can be a problematic and often fraught relationship with the parties influenced by forces beyond their control (e.g. a merger or takeover). No wonder organizations believe they need help with stress management, counselling, 'divorce' proceedings and constantly checking the mood of the relationship through attitude, engagement and satisfaction surveys. This can become an unholy mess if it is not managed well. What should stop it becoming a mess is a simple question: will we get more value from our human capital by fostering this relationship or not?

On the happy day, when the two parties are joined together, even the most romantic observer knows that the marriage vows are there for a very serious and practical purpose. Our long history of human relationships taught us to cover every eventuality, even in the rosy glow of a new union. There will be 'lovers' tiffs', the honeymoon will come to an end and then the happy couple will really start getting to know and understand each other better. Expectations change but if they learn to appreciate each other's perspective, and cope with the inevitable bad times as well as enjoying the good, it should prove to be a solid marriage. Problems arise if one does not seem to be pulling their weight or if there is a mismatch in terms of effort. In an organizational setting the relationship starts to break up when the remuneration of one party seems unfair or appears to reward poor performance. Sometimes shareholders or private equity partners damage those relationships further by wanting to steal the family silver. Loyalty and fidelity is tested when executives openly look for a better relationship elsewhere. It should not surprise any of us when all of these pressures impede the building of what might have been a beautiful and harmonious relationship.

Humans are good at adapting though. Some people put up with unhappy marriages for the sake of the kids or sheer inertia. How many employees regard that as the best description of their relationship with their employer? The best marriages usually involve people who just enjoy each other's company but it helps if they think their future prospects are better together than apart. Mature relationships are unlikely to survive on lust or money alone because of the reality checks that life throws at us all every day. This is where the reality of a mature, human capital management, relationship comes in: it should be the best deal for all concerned and will be if everyone enters into it with their eyes wide open. In human capital management no one owns anyone else; there are no chattels. Human capital does not belong to a company, no matter what they pay for it. It is not demeaning to regard oneself as human capital because each individual can make up their own mind as to how much their employer can translate their capital into societal value.

Reporting on human capital

While governments and investment analysts have been asking for reports on human capital for some time, the management tools and education required to produce these reports have yet to catch up. HR departments may have changed the name on their door but that does not mean they changed anything else. Behind the wet paint you will find the old HR team trying to give an appearance of new thinking, without any hint as to how this might affect their HR perspective or practices. Regardless of what Jack Welch says, the key constituents for human capital reports are still shareholders and investment analysts. Only HR Professionals will be able to produce the best reports. The HR community is traditionally well behind the curve and is only stung into action when the business community refuses to accept its excuses any longer. So, very late in the day in 2010, SHRM set up its own Taskforce on HR Standards and finally accepted that it had to produce a standard for 'Investor metrics'.

SHRM's proposal for investor metrics (as at 9 April 2012) recommends that spending on 'human capital' should be calculated but then produces a formula that only measures the costs of 'employees'. The formula is shown in section 5.4 of the standard:

> Formula for calculating spending on human capital:
> The number should be reported in $ form.
> (A) Direct cost of employees $_____
> (B) Costs in support of employees
> (C) Costs in lieu of employees $_____
> Human capital expenses (A + B + C) $_____
> (D) Investment in training & development $_____

It offers no explanation as to why or how these two terms have suddenly been used interchangeably and it fails the Professional test of accurate and precise terminology.

Yet we have just seen some very sound, conceptual and practical reasons why human capital is a better term for employees and a better basis for managing the value of people. These omissions are very serious and make SHRM's investor metrics formula look rather crass[2]. So we need to unpick their thinking if we are to suggest a much better alternative.

The switch from 'human capital' to 'employees' is one error. Another is the equally sudden and unexplained switch from referring to 'costs' for A, B and C and then 'investment' for D. Why this switch? Simply because trainers have been taught, by the ASTD's Phillips model, to try and calculate returns on investment (ROI) but the HR community does not think the same way. So what logic is there in this formula? That we are only *investing* in people when we train them? What happened to their salary cost; was that just a sunk cost from which HR expects no return? Rather than grabbing the opportunity to introduce the most important innovation in human capital thinking for decades, SHRM's formula turns out to be a very lopsided and illogical equation. They are using the language of 'capital' but only measuring inputs: concentrating only on the cost, not the value, of people. This is clear evidence that the HR community at large, assuming SHRM genuinely represents the views of its 250,000 members around the world, does not understand the concept of human capital or its potential import. But that is still not SHRM's biggest error.

Human capital is about everyone, not just employees of a particular company. If investment analysts have not been educated to value human capital then they cannot make the best investment decisions. If shareholders do not understand the value of human capital then the company is under-valued, or possibly over-valued, if certain individuals decide to walk out of this relationship tomorrow and take their valuable human capital with them. Companies that are undervalued are vulnerable to predatory speculators. Governments that have no means of valuing human capital cannot manage their populations or their economies effectively. Regulatory bodies, that are designed to control the worst excesses of the markets, cannot do their job properly if no one is reporting on human capital.

This is why the term human capital management has risen to the top of the agenda; not because of HR but in spite of it. It is at the top because it really, really matters and for once HR cannot duck the issue with jargon, hype, imprecise language or crass formulas because we are now asking evidence-based questions and are no longer convinced by meaningless, HR metrics. The era of HCM heralds the era of Professional HR; they are mutually co-dependent. SHRM's Taskforce is proposing that investor metrics are just another form of bean-counting. They have not acknowledged any need for a paradigm shift amongst their membership, or those who employ them. If HCM was about bean counting then thousands of professional, bean-counting accountants around the world would already have stopped us getting into this mess in the first place. But they didn't because they did not know how to. Now that they do, they no longer have an excuse.

The only positive development we can take away from SHRM's current efforts is that they have at least accepted that something has to be done. It is now just a matter of 'what' and 'how' the right change will come about, not 'if'. Governments, regulators, shareholders and the investment community at large have also, already, openly acknowledged that this subject is so important that change is imperative. Whether the sort of HR and L&D professionals that have evolved over recent decades are up to the job or not is no longer a moot point. The evidence is clear; we need an entirely new breed. Yet SHRM, in its efforts to make US standards global standards, has managed to create precisely the opposite effect to the one required. In producing crass 'standards' they are inadvertently crystallising everything that is wrong with HR. SHRM's proposals are serving only to make its 250,000 members a laughing stock and pushing them towards obsolescence. They are also damaging ANSI's reputation as a credible, standards authority because ANSI does not know any better. It is time for the real HR Professionals in SHRM's midst to stand up and be counted. If the Americans, in the joint form of SHRM, ASTD and ANSI, are not prepared to step up to the right plate then someone else will have to.

6

WHAT SHOULD WE DO WITH HR AND L&D?

HR is stuck in the nineteenth century

It is hard to imagine what it must have been like to be ill before medicine became evidence-based and pain free. The History of Anaesthesia Society timeline[1] starts in 1298 with an Italian physician and bishop, who 'used sponges soaked with opium and mandragora for surgical pain relief'. It was another 500 years, in Connecticut in 1844, before a general anaesthetic was used for the first time in dental extraction. It is amazing how long it can take for revolutionary innovations to become the norm. The professionalization of medicine only really started from the mid-nineteenth century onwards, with the adoption of more rigorous standards and the establishment of regulatory bodies. As this short extract from a history of medicine[2] reveals, this was the period that saw the creation of:

> ... new institutions and formal mechanisms for regulating medical practice, and for distinguishing the 'qualified' practitioner from the 'quack'. In Britain, a key development was the Medical Act of 1858 which established the General Medical Council and the Medical Register, a public list of all recognised medical practitioners.

Now, just replace the word medicine with 'HR' and the parallels are stunning. Setting up the General Medical Council and a register of 'recognized practitioners' was obviously a watershed for medicine that the HR profession has yet to reach. The medical profession's subsequent progress and credibility was won by adopting and applying the scientific method to build a much better evidence base. As Stanford Professor, Jeffrey Pfeffer, remarked in his *Harvard Business Review* column entitled 'Management a Profession? Where's the proof?' (September 2011) '... it took more than higher aims to move medicine beyond quackery. It took science and its application to practice.'

Likewise, management will not become a profession without a more scientific and systematic approach to management research and problem solving. HR will not move any further forward until it accepts this. Claiming that HR cannot be a science has allowed many practitioners to get off the hook but it came at the cost of confidence in their methods and credibility. This lack of confidence completely undermines HR's relationship with the line. Managers are expected to accept HR's methods on faith alone and their patience has worn very thin over the years. HR's answer should have been to make its methods more evidence-based, not less, but it chose a different course instead. It started treating line managers as though they were paying customers. Little did HR know at the time just how much of a wrong turning this would prove to be. It has led HR into a cul de sac of its own making.

The HR-internal customer paradigm reinforces the view of HR as a support service rather than a strategically integrated, operational function. This sin is compounded by drawing up SLAs (service level agreements) for the wrong type of services: administrative activities, non-evidence-based policies and placebos, rather than business critical solutions. Moreover, if a customer can accurately be defined as someone who makes an independent purchasing decision, using their own money, then line managers should not be described as HR's customers. They are not making independent decisions and are certainly not paying the bill with their own money. Worse still, the notion of the internal customer entitles them to choose where to spend 'their' money, which can be with any external consultants they might choose (e.g. outsourcing, recruitment firms, training providers).

If HR had any pride in its professionalism that prospect should always have been viewed in exactly the same light as a doctor's legitimate patient deciding to go elsewhere for treatment. 'Elsewhere' being outside of a professionally controlled, legally regulated, approved and accredited healthcare system. Managers might choose totally inappropriate and unproven methods such as homeopathy, herbal medicine or even want to be transformed by Towers Watson, without any greater scientific foundation than their own HR team can offer. In short, in a non-evidence based world, it will always be a case of the blind leading the blind.

Uneducated patients

The default view of the HR Professional is that all executives and line managers are deemed uneducated in matters of people management unless they can prove otherwise. Line managers (HR's 'patients') might think they know what ails them but they have never been taught the HR Professional's diagnostic skills. Like a patient, they might know *how* they feel without knowing *what* is causing their problem. Doctors are taught to always listen to the patient though. It is only when the line manager is allowed to self-diagnose their people problems, on the basis of how they feel, that the relationship between HR and the line breaks down. For example, a manager knows how it feels to have a team where no one in the team ever appears willing to 'take the initiative'. Even if this superficial diagnosis is correct it does not automatically follow that they have a valid prescription. So they then expect HR to help 'incentivize initiative' or L&D to simply run a training course on

'Taking the Initiative'. The more confident managers, the ones who think they know what managing people is all about, do not look to 'HR' to teach them anything. Yet any option based on an incorrect or non-existent diagnosis is the wrong option.

The HR Professional not only has to be better educated than the line, they have to produce evidence that their methods will result in a better performance than the line manager can achieve on their own. Only then will an effective relationship exist. The manager will learn to trust the HR Professional's advice and there will be mutual respect. This is not a relationship where one party knows all the answers or where a standard prescription is appropriate. The only valid prescription is one backed up with evidence.

HR is where it is today because none of these building blocks are in place. HR is not respected as a profession because it does not respect itself enough to have a GHRC. The model of HR as a support function allows internal customers to believe they should always have the final say, irrespective of whether they are educated or not. The free market concept of the customer always being right is only valid where the customer is exercising a free choice on how to spend their own money. It has no validity for managers spending the organization's money if those managers are not prepared to be held accountable for making the wrong purchasing choices. Only an HR professional will be able to tell them when they are making the right, Professional choice.

HR 'doctors', best practice and the halo effect

Private citizens can do what they like with their own hard-earned money. Managers have to be able to justify how they spend the company's money. If they venture outside into the professionally-questionable market for HR and L&D services, they should beware. This is a totally unregulated market and there are no guarantees they will get what they need or what they have been promised. This is a market where the customer will have to be particularly well educated if they are to make wise spending decisions and achieve the best returns possible. In view of this, wary managers will choose to stick with the HR devil they know, albeit a non-evidence-based devil. So the average HR director attracts in-house business, and defends their own policies, by setting out their stall as 'best practice'. That would be OK if best practice were based on best evidence. In HR, best practice just means copying what every other HR director is doing. Those other HR directors are saying and doing exactly the same and so the weird merry-go-round of questionable HR practice continues with no one bothering to stop the music and ask who started it in motion.

The term 'best practice' used to mean something once and became standard terminology when manufacturing companies tried to adopt total quality management (TQM) in the 1980s. It became synonymous with that other well-worn cliché, 'world class'. The original reference point for both was the, now famous, Toyota Production System that every self-respecting manufacturer has been desperately trying to emulate ever since. The foundation of the Toyota Way (of which the production system is only a part) is a total management philosophy that incorporates the utilization of human potential to create maximum value for society. You will not find these words used in the Toyota 'rule book' though. In Toyota's philosophy, managing human potential was never a separate exercise, detached from its long-term business strategy. The vast majority of organizations that tried to copy Toyota, including Jack Welch at GE, never realized this. Even if they had, they would not have found the people elements easy to introduce into their own contexts; especially if they were constantly under short term pressure from shareholders and institutional investors who also failed to understand the long term, value implications of Toyota's people management system.

So, if HR's managerial 'patients' are uneducated, and the HR professionals themselves have no meaningful accreditation, we have a really vicious circle in operation here. CEOs who want their organization to do everything that every other organization is doing ('lean', leadership development, employee engagement), rather than focusing on value, are being encouraged to do so by their 'best practice HR' directors. As with any relationship that fails, neither side can be blamed, it takes two to tango. It probably suits many short-termist CEOs to utter the buzzwords, to keep the market happy, before they move on and leave someone else do all the hard work of people strategy. If there is a number one suspect for starting this vicious merry-go-round it is whoever coined the phrase 'best practice HR' in the first place. It has let CEOs and their HR directors off the accountability hook for far too long.

The other culprits are those who automatically see profits as evidence of management 'best practice'. This is particularly prevalent in, but not exclusive to, the IT sector where extraordinary profits can and have been made. Over the last 30 years or so Microsoft, Yahoo, Cisco and recently Google have all been seen as great shareholder successes. Many in HR have happily jumped to the conclusion this must have something to do with their HR policies and practices. Such superficial diagnoses, of course, are never reached scientifically. In fact there is unlikely to be any insightful or detailed analysis of any causal connection while simplistic and convenient correlations are the only game in town. Why would anyone want to pour cold water on such speculation, what is there to gain; apart from the truth? It is just so easy and tempting to be wilfully blinded by extraordinary success; just as Enron was held out as an exemplar of talent management, before it crashed ignominiously in 2001. The phenomenon at work here is well recognized, it is called the halo effect, although the correct term is halo error.

Google appointed its own, non-HR, analytics 'expert' Prasad Setty, when the latest fad of HR analytics arrived on the scene, because analytics and algorithms are something Google is supposed to be good at. Setty started life as a chemical engineer. Whether he has found a new chemical formula, or any better science, to demonstrate the impact of effective human capital management at Google is questionable. Certainly we should not jump to the conclusion that there is any connection at all between Google's profit performance and any numbers Setty produces. He has to show a direct causal link, just like any other HR Professional, between HR data management and Google's already overflowing coffers. If Setty really is one of the new breed of HR Professionals then he will already know there is no such thing as a quick-fix answer when it comes to shaping and modifying organizational behaviour. If he gets his calculations right he will also help to shatter any illusion of best HR practice and we can all go back to the beginning and build a very different brand of HR.

Why is HR where it is today?

If we trace the origins of any profession, we will find a basic need being satisfied. Patients need doctors, plaintiffs need lawyers, builders need architects, anti-virus software producers need viruses (yes, just what we were thinking) and HR needs people problems. If we judged the practices of yesteryear by the professional standards of today we would have to regard them as relatively amateurish. Professional standards should rise inexorably over time. With the exception of the legal profession, where a UK defendant can still choose to defend themselves in court without any professional qualifications, there are often restrictions on who can and cannot operate as a professional. However, the probability of an unqualified defendant winning their case, compared to a fully trained legal professional, is likely to be significantly lower. So does the same hold true for a CEO employing an HR professional or would they just be better off taking over the case themselves?

There are no specific regulations, in the UK at least, that require senior HR positions to be filled by HR practitioners holding qualifications from the main professional bodies. There is only the same, general duty of care that would apply to any other director. We have already seen plenty of evidence of companies that employ large HR teams making serious mistakes in managing people. So while there is no statutory need for professional HR there is certainly a strong case to be made for boards of directors having better HR advice and guidance than they are receiving today. How would the board articulate their 'needs' though? Do they need help in gaining a competitive advantage and maximising the return on human capital or is their need just administration and keeping themselves out of courts of human rights?

For a very quick picture of HR's perception of its own history you could read the Factsheet produced by the CIPD.[3] This is primarily focused on how things have developed in the UK but it certainly has many parallels with the US experience and elsewhere. A visit to any international HR conference today will quickly confirm the extent to which multi-national companies have spread a uniform brand of HR and L&D around the world. Somewhat paradoxically, this global homogenization of the HR profession is another major cause of its problems. If we take a look at the history of UK industrial relations, for example, the Factsheet switches terminology from 'industrial' relations to 'employee relations' without any clear distinction or explanation. Perhaps we should not read too much into this because academics would certainly highlight several differences. However, if the CIPD is implying that 'employee relations' is a more modern, more positive and progressive form of management, than old-style industrial relations, then it has glossed over some inconvenient truths.

As recently as April 2012, the UK witnessed yet another episode of really bad industrial relations. The public were panic-buying fuel for their cars because fuel tanker drivers[4] were threatening strike action, yet again. These tanker drivers, no more nor less skilled than any other truck driver, reportedly earn about £45,000 per annum. For comparison, that is significantly more than a degree qualified, fully trained nurse[5] or teacher[6] who can expect a salary package up to approximately £32,000. One reason petrol tanker drivers earn this amount is not because of a shortage of capable drivers but because they and their union leaders have always held their rich oil company employers to ransom. These oil companies employ highly paid HR professionals and 'negotiators', who always back down (as does the Government of the day) because we just cannot live without fuel.

On 12 May 2012 the strike action was called off. One headline read[7] 'At last! Fuel strike averted as tanker drivers agree deal. Drivers from seven firms, including BP and Sucklings, narrowly backed a deal securing them better pay and conditions'. Sucklings is not an oil company but a transport company that runs transport contracts for oil companies like Shell. These oil companies thought they could get rid of their industrial relations problems simply through outsourcing. So old fashioned, adversarial IR and conflict have not gone away. Rich companies that can afford to overpay drivers and buy out strike threats will continue to do so simply because that saves them having to manage this tricky people problem professionally. The CIPD cannot airbrush out such disputes from recent history so continues with its pretence that employee relations mentalities have somehow moved on.

Of course relations between employers and employees in the UK, and elsewhere, are probably generally better than they were in the 1960s but this is not because HR professionals have been taught better HR strategies. If they had then the CIPD's many professional members who work in the UK's public sector (i.e. local government, the civil service, NHS etc.) would have developed really good employee relations strategies as well, but they haven't. Instead, the public sector is one of the last bastions of poor performance management and entrenched union attitudes. Of course that is because the executives who run these organizations are themselves very poor at managing employee relations and industrial relations. So when times are tough these sores quickly erupt. This is one reason why many UK public services have been outsourced to the private sector.

One thing that is clear from the historical narrative is how HR has tended to react to, rather than anticipate, developments. This is in keeping with the character of HR which often relegates intractable issues to the 'too difficult' tray while it keeps itself busy with administration. The most obvious examples in recent history are the financial services and banking sector, where mis-selling and lax controls allowed everything to get out of control, and parts of the pharmaceutical industry where in-house research failed to deliver a sufficient pipeline of new drugs. So why were their HR professionals, with their performance management schemes and competence frameworks, not drawing attention to these mismatches between rewards policies and bad debts; between research performance and drug development failures? Whether it is banking, pharmaceuticals or any other industry the problem is the same; ineffective people strategies.

Are employment relationships getting any better?

Life can be harsh and the younger generation in the West are now learning just how harsh with large scale unemployment, even among the highly educated young. Just when we thought we could all relax and feel comfortable with regular increases in GDP it appears that we cannot. This is why we now have to re-visit our relationships with the organizations that employ us. Can they go on expecting more for less? One country that never seems to have forgotten the harsh lessons of its own pioneering history, America, has had a long-standing principle that underpins all employment relationships; the concept of 'at-will'.[8] This principle allows employers to hire and fire 'at-will' in the belief that this provides beneficial flexibility in the labour market. Here is a direct extract from the US National Conference of State Legislatures website that explains the principle.

I. The At-Will Presumption
Employment relationships are presumed to be 'at-will' in all US states except Montana. The US is one of a handful of countries where employment is predominantly at-will. Most countries throughout the world allow employers to dismiss employees only for cause. Some reasons given for our retention of the at-will presumption include respect for freedom of contract, employer deference, and the belief that both employers and employees favor an at-will employment relationship over job security.

A. At-Will Defined
At-will means that an employer can terminate an employee at any time for any reason, except an illegal one, or for no reason without incurring legal liability. Likewise, an employee is free to leave a job at any time for any or no reason with no adverse legal consequences.
At-will also means that an employer can change the terms of the employment relationship with no notice and no consequences. For example, an employer can alter wages, terminate benefits, or reduce paid time off. In its unadulterated form, the US at-will rule leaves employees vulnerable to arbitrary and sudden dismissal, a limited or on-call work schedule depending on the employer's needs, and unannounced cuts in pay and benefits.

There are at least two opposing ways to view this proposition. It is either just a simple reflection on the hard facts of life – no one is owed a living – or it is just there to bolster the fortunes of hard-nosed, capitalists. In practice, it is not as clear cut as it first appears, It continues, under:

> *B. Modification by Contract*
> The at-will presumption is a default rule that can be modified by contract. For example, a contract may provide for a specific term of employment or allow termination for cause only. Typically, US companies negotiate individual employment agreements only with high-level employees. Collective bargaining agreements usually provide that represented employees may only be terminated for cause.
> Cause generally includes reasons such as poor employee performance, employee misconduct, or economic necessity. An employment contract may specifically outline the situations or employee actions that would lead to termination for cause.

America had to learn that what seemed like a sound principle was not necessarily going to be socially acceptable. It is a debate that also rages in the UK today. This was well illustrated recently with the publication of a report, commissioned by the UK's coalition government, to look at freeing up the labour market. The Beecroft report (chaired by Adrian Beecroft – chairman of venture capitalists Dawn Capital and ex-Vice President of Boston Consulting Group Worldwide) – considered allowing businesses to hire and fire staff more easily. The evidence to support this contention is questionable though as the UK is widely regarded as having one of the least regulated labour markets in Europe. It caused enough of a stir for the *London Evening Standard*[9] to produce the headline 'Beecroft report: Letting us sack staff we don't like will be good for the economy, bosses tell Downing Street' after Beecroft himself had written that:

> The downside of the proposal is that some people would be dismissed simply because their employer did not like them. While this is sad I believe it is a price worth paying for all the benefits that would result from the change.

If Beecroft had learned anything about HR while at Boston Consulting Group he should have known that the first step in HR strategy is to have a consensus on the fundamental principles. There is a simple principle that companies should have the freedom to hire and fire alongside an equal and balancing principle that employees can choose who they work for. However, all good principles need good systems to ensure employers and employees do not abuse their freedoms. Changing the law without changing the system is bad policy making and cuts both ways. It is probably as damaging to the UK economy for oil companies to buy off their belligerent workers as it is for disreputable employers to dismiss people they do not like. Both are clear examples of delinquent management and poor value but politicians seem to find it easier to legislate in favour of employers whilst avoiding any legislation that might upset them. The best policy will be the one that works best for everyone. We sorely need more enlightened policy-making, with expertise from HR Professionals, at a national and international level.

Even if HR people are not the first choice for this job, because they cannot see the wood for the trees, those with keener minds and sharper eyes should be. One of the most interesting developments recently is heightened interest in managing the risks associated with human capital. The most glaring examples are the rogue traders like Nick Leeson (Barings, 1995), Jerome Kerviel (Societe Generale, 2008) and Kweku Adoboli (UBS, 2011). These are the people who ended up in court for losing their banks billions, despite the existence of supposedly watertight, foolproof systems. They are also the people who incurred huge extra legal costs for their banking employers, who had to clean up the mess. All these banks had very well paid HR directors. Maybe we would have more respect for HR if it had some high profile successes under its belt. It needs to demonstrate that it brings an extra dimension to organizational governance that ordinary, operational executives seem incapable of.

Fear and self-loathing in Las Vegas

It is well recognized that HR has had to suffer an undercurrent of resentment and barely disguised contempt throughout its history, although this does not feature in the CIPD's Factsheet. Mature managers know that people issues can be intractable and require broader, strategic solutions, but while HR talks about strategy it rarely acts strategically. In August 2005 someone finally had the temerity to call HR's bluff. That person was *Fast Company Magazine* journalist Keith Hammonds. Hammonds attended a conference of 'several hundred midlevel human-resources executives in Las Vegas' on 'strategic HR leadership' and subsequently produced a now infamous diatribe against the whole of the HR profession entitled 'Why We Hate HR'.[10] Although Hammonds is not an HR professional himself he obviously thinks he is qualified to criticize the HR profession. He certainly writes from a common sense perspective and, on that basis alone, succeeds in pricking many of the bubbles of HR hype. In his rant though he missed a rather obvious point. If the 'we', who apparently hate HR so much are ordinary, operational managers, then why do they persist in employing HR people? What does that tell us about their own capabilities?

Can line managers do 'HR' themselves or could they do away with it altogether? We have just seen experienced oil company executives abdicating their managerial responsibilities and the ex-VP of a 'prestigious' consulting group talking about 'a price worth paying' for unethical, illegal and unprofessional employer behaviour. It appears that these highly paid executives really have no idea how to deal with difficult people issues. This is a much better explanation for the blackness of Hammonds' mood. Managers might hate HR but probably hate themselves even more for still having to rely on them. The very existence of HR is a constant reminder of their own inadequacies. The only solution has to be a more mature, intelligent and strategic HR view, rather than Beecroft's recommendation. The new breed of HR Professional will be strong enough to develop an equal and constructive partnership with the line; rather than offer a mere support service for management inadequacy.

It was exactly this type of thinking that had previously given rise to the notion of an 'HR business partner' role and Hammonds advises his readers to follow the advice of one of its main proponents, Dave Ulrich. If he had researched his topic more thoroughly Hammonds would have found that Ulrich's model was flawed from the outset. Ulrich himself finally admitted,[11] three years later, that there was little evidence that his model had worked and put this down to HR people not getting to know their business well enough. He continued to misdiagnose the root cause of the problem though. The problem is ineffective, conventional HR methods and the only solution is to replace them with highly Professional, evidence-based people management.

The greatest irony during the advent of the business partner role was that HR did not follow its own rules. Anyone who knows the first thing about professional recruitment practice would tell you that when a new role is called for you have to produce a new person specification. This specification clearly indicated that HR business partners were never likely to be found within the ranks of conventional HR people. The HR incumbents conveniently ignored this rule though when it was their own job that was on the line. What happened in practice was that conventional HR administrators changed their job title, awarded themselves a new pay grade and then carried on as before because no one had devised the new tools for the job.

The enormous gap between HR hype and reality

It looks like this is a recurring theme in the world of HR. There is still a huge knowing–doing gap but neither general managers nor HR practitioners seem to *know* anything important about the strategic management of people. It is doubtful whether the CIPD sees it this way but they certainly accept that there are some serious challenges ahead. In its Factsheet it expresses a clear aspiration ' … to make a bold contribution towards ensuring that HR is well placed to seize the opportunities thrown up by corporate and wider societal soul-searching on the future of business' and believes it has come up with an answer; a new professional framework, or map[12] and their 'Next Generation HR project' which implies that the skills of the current HR generation are not appropriate for the future. With 140,000 old and existing generation members, who pay substantial sums in subscriptions every year, the CIPD is not keen on spelling out what is wrong with them all. It has managed to get itself into such a contradictory tangle that it has invented a contradictory 'solution' involving a ' … future-focused programme of research to uncover groundbreaking practice today'.

If the old generation are the problem why use them as the architects for 'framing CIPD work'? Has the CIPD not learned anything from the debacle of old HR people failing to metamorphose into new HR business partners? Even more bizarre was the CIPD's decision to seek help by buying into an existing consultancy called Bridge.[13] This is a very strange development indeed, with a very obvious, professional, conflict of interest. It is the equivalent of the Royal College of Physicians buying a private drug company, that sells non-approved and untested drugs, and then using them as a benchmark for the development of the next generation of drugs manufacturers. It beggars belief what was going on in the minds of the CIPD board. It might not have been so bad if the Bridge consultancy was an avowedly evidence-based organization but there is absolutely no evidence of value to be found on their website nor even a nod to any scientific method. One wonders why the CIPD's members, including its highest ranking Fellows, allowed this to happen. In an instant, their professional status had been relegated below that of an untested consultancy and their experience dismissed as irrelevant to future generations of HR professionals.

In the CIPD's monthly journal *People Management* (April 2011) Lee Sears, the co-founder of Bridge and 'Head of Next Generation HR', who has no background in HR, wrote an article entitled 'Insight-led HR', which apparently 'is absolutely central to the role of successful next generation HR leaders'. This is just the sort of jargon that Keith Hammonds had berated back in 2005 and it gets worse. Sears has managed to re-invent a very old idea, being business savvy, and turned it into more unnecessary jargon, namely the three 'savvies': 'Contextual savvy ... organizational savvy ... business savvy'.

This repeats the same trick as those who re-invented the word 'competence' into competency. It is yet another admission that the concept of the HR business partner never worked. So HR now needs to have another go at understanding the business, the organization and the context. Is this amazing insight the 'groundbreaking practice' the CIPD was referring to? Where is this new savvy generation to come from?

Across the Atlantic, the Society for Human Resource Management (SHRM) (the global HR professional organization) also recognizes that the HR profession has serious challenges ahead, declaring that its Mission is to:

> Build and sustain partnerships with human resource professionals, media, governments, non-governmental organizations, businesses and academic institutions to address people management challenges that influence the effectiveness and sustainability of their organizations and communities.

And also to:

> Proactively provide thought leadership, education and research to human resource professionals, media, governments, non-governmental organizations, businesses and academic institutions.

So what answers has SHRM devised? Has it acknowledged the mistakes of its past or admitted that previous generations of HR practitioners are ill-prepared for an evidence-based future? No, they are in exactly the same predicament as the CIPD: having to fundamentally change without being able to admit this to its 250,000 paying members. Instead, it is trying to breathe some new life into its old methods by turning them into international HR standards.

7

ESTABLISHING A UNIVERSAL, EVIDENCE-BASED STANDARD FOR HR

Establishing credible, international standards in HR

As soon as we start asking questions about the quality of HR people we are bound to have to point the finger at individuals. Any decent consultancy firm will tell you that a client buys the consultant, not the consultancy. The same rule applies to in-house HR and L&D appointments. A CEO's expectations of HR will dictate what type of HR person they buy and they will get what they deserve. If HR is perceived as a low-importance, administrative, support function, or a sop to the workforce, or a PR exercise, then you will end up with an HR function that fits the bill. On the other hand, if a CEO wants to take strategic, human capital management seriously, it is not so easy for them to go out into the current market place and find someone. If they did manage to find a suitable candidate what interview questions would they need to ask? What quality assurance mark would they look for?

We took a brief look earlier at the Society for Human Resource Management's (SHRM) efforts on quality standards, with its proposals for investor metrics, pointing out that they did not make much sense. The highest qualification a SHRM member can achieve is Senior HR Professional (SPHR) but what is that worth without any standards? SHRM only appointed its first-ever Director of HR Standards as recently as 2009[1] and it is laudable that it is moving in that direction but, as with the CIPD's 'next generation', it is also alarming that the standards of its present membership are being called into question. It is also confusing when a professional body seems to have two sets of standards: 'HR standards' and 'professional' standards.

SHRM already has its own professional standards[2] under the heading 'Professional Responsibility' and one of its guidelines to members is to 'Measure the effectiveness of HR in contributing to or achieving organizational goals'. So it was no surprise that SHRM's first Standard, officially approved on 8 February 2012 by ANSI, was 'Cost-per-Hire'[3] (CPH). This is a 50-page document on how to measure average recruitment costs. To any operational manager this might seem to be a case of administrative overkill. If the New York Fire Department's head of HR is a SHRM member we would strongly recommend they do not announce that their first foray into HR standards will be measuring the average cost of replacing a firefighter.

SHRM's declared objective is to have its ANSI Standards adopted as global standards under the auspices of the ISO (International Organization for Standardization) and the ISO duly set up a new Technical Committee (ISO/TC260) in pursuit of this goal. TC260's first plenary meeting, attended by national delegations from around the world, was held in Washington in November 2011. At this meeting it was unanimously agreed to establish various working groups, sponsored by individual countries, to look at specific issues that might come within the remit of TC260. One workgroup, looking at human governance, was instigated by the French delegation. Anyone interested in developing Professionalism in HR would want this to be their first standard for it is in the boardroom that HR needs to be at its most convincing. International HR governance standards are an exciting development but any feeling of exhilaration needs to be tempered and qualified.

First, there is already another draft ISO Standard – 'ISO 10018: Quality management – Guidelines on people involvement and competences' that is being developed by another ISO technical committee; TC176 on Quality Management & Quality Assurance.[4] This explains 'the human element in successful management systems' according to the International Register of Certified Auditors. So why is there a need for a separate technical committee in HR? There is probably a very long and convoluted answer to this (which we will not be pursuing here) but SHRM and ANSI have made it perfectly clear that they want to be in the driving seat of international HR standards. ANSI has one of its staff administering TC260 and it is chaired by SHRM's Director of HR Standards.

Second, any disingenuous party might ask another very obvious question; does anyone at ISO, ANSI or SHRM really understand what 'the human element in successful management systems' is? If they do, why has it not shown up so far in their development of investor metrics? Investment analysts have been asking serious human capital questions for some time and are now re-doubling their efforts, having witnessed the financial meltdown in banking and finance. SHRM's first attempt at 'Investor Metrics' indicates that either they still do not understand the questions being asked or they only want to keep providing the answers they already have. We need to take a closer look at both of these 'HR standards' from a 'successful quality management systems' perspective.

The human element in successful management systems

The CPH Standard is exactly what it says it is and looks solely at the costs of hiring people. It does not offer any answers to the question 'what about the quality and performance of the new hires'? These are more important questions than hiring costs but they are also more problematic in terms of measurement. We can understand why SHRM does not want to try and measure the difficult things but that is no excuse. Without answering all three questions, simultaneously, the CPH Standard does not form part of a quality management system. Such a system has to assure that the output from the (hiring) process is fit-for-purpose. In effect, the ANSI CPH Standard will encourage companies to reduce the cost of their recruitment process without measuring any corresponding reduction in the output from those hired. As a direct consequence the net result, from using CPH in isolation, is likely to be a drop in hiring standards.

So how can a national accreditation body like ANSI sign off a sub-standard standard? The answer is as simple as it is prosaic. ANSI does not know how to assure 'the human element in successful management systems' because it has never been done before. SHRM and ANSI would have gained much more respect and credibility if they had just admitted their ignorance. Nobody would criticize them for being at the leading edge of new people system technology. Alternatively, they would have been much better served by visiting Toyota to see how it should be done. They would have to know what they were looking for though and get behind the Toyota Production System to find all of the essential, human ingredients that together create the complete Toyota Way.

Rather than enhance quality management systems, the SHRM proposal for investor metrics is likely to do enormous damage to US industry, and any other country that follows suit, by loading extra bureaucracy costs without adding any extra value. While the CPH Standard is based on the over-simplistic use of the single measure of cost, rather than our definition of value (OCRQ), the Investor Metrics standard goes to the other extreme of trying to cover too many bases. It has sections on employee and human capital costs, talent, leadership and engagement but all its measurement is simplistic. In section 8.6 under 'Sample calculation for leadership quality' it states 'There are many ways of using employee questionnaires to calculate a leadership quality index'.

The example they show is based on how much employees agree, on a 5-point scale, with statements such as 'Our leaders have an authentic purpose that goes beyond short-term profits.' This employee-centric score of leadership might be valid if employees are the best judges but what if they are not?

In 2003, the new Director General of the BBC, Greg Dyke, instigated a staff survey which concluded that 'the corporation is full of management bullies and "Bafta bastards" – badly behaved programme makers who are only interested in winning awards.'[5] A BAFTA is a prestigious award from the British Academy of Film and Television Arts. If that is not the sort of higher purpose that a film and television broadcaster, like the BBC, should be aspiring to then what is? It was that staff survey that led directly to the BBC's disastrous leadership programme.

There are many implicit assumptions in simplistic surveys like the one in the SHRM standard. First, the terminology is imprecise and the question assumes that bosses are 'leaders', rather than just ordinary executives or managers. It further assumes there must be some connection between what employees think about them, the way the organization is likely to perform and whether investors should invest accordingly. This is a very dangerous standard because all of those assumptions can only be traced back to spurious academic research, based on false correlations rather than causative evidence.

SHRM broke one of its own, professional, cardinal rules in 2010 in appointing as its Workgroup Leader, Laurie Bassi, an ex-labour economics professor and former research director for the ASTD, who runs her own investment fund and consulting company. This appears counter to SHRM's own ethical code. Under its core principle 'Conflicts of interest' its guidelines state 'Refrain from using your position for personal, material or financial gain or the appearance of such.' In June 2011 Bassi was interviewed by *CFO* magazine[6] which reported:

> In the mid-1990s, labor economist Laurie Bassi began to notice a strong correlation between public companies' stock prices and how much they invested in training-and-development programs. On average, the more a firm invested in training in a given year, the higher its stock went the following year.

It continues with a quote from Bassi saying 'As companies spend more on training, the benefits to overall financial performance accumulate and the stock price does eventually reward the investment.' To the trained HR Professional what Bassi is doing here is shamelessly passing off her correlations as causation, with no caveats whatsoever. By doing so she should not have been surprised when she found that her 'substantial body of work ... got little reaction from investors ... and was largely ignored.' Serious investors obviously do know the difference between correlations and causation, even if labour economics professors do not appear to.

As Pfeffer and Sutton (2006) point out in *Hard Facts* (at p. 14):

> many practitioners and their advisers are unwilling or unable to observe the world systematically because they are trapped by their beliefs and ideologies. Their observations are contaminated by what they expect to see, or because they aren't logical enough in their thinking. The result is that much conventional wisdom is wrong.

This description must also apply to the 200-plus members of SHRM's Taskforce and Workgroups who are conventional HR professionals, consultants and academics. Many of them work for large global organizations yet none have the expertise or experience necessary for the task in hand of providing meaningful indicators for investors. That will require a much more solid basis of evidence than they have managed to establish in their own work in HR. The reason they have not already done so is simply that no professional HR body, no academic and no national standards institute has yet developed the right measurement technology to answer the investors' valid enquiries.

HR measurement is particularly problematic

If SHRM's members want to make any excuses for their lack of capability it would be better just to admit that HR measurement is very problematic and always will be. An HR Professional will have absolutely no problem admitting their own ignorance; anymore than the GP who has to refer a patient to a specialist consultant. An admission of ignorance is a positive part of the diagnostic process. Failing to admit your ignorance means the final diagnosis will be wrong. Unfortunately, HR is not very good at admitting it is wrong because it is already so insecure and on the defensive. If you ask any HR director today whether they measure what they do you will be amazed just how wide a range of responses this can elicit, including the:

- Dogmatic: 'You cannot measure what HR does'.
- Patronizing: 'Measuring things is too mechanistic for what we do in HR'.
- Complacent: 'Our internal customers are happy with what we do for them'.
- Misguided: 'We benchmark with best practice'.
- Ignorant: 'Why do we need to measure what we do?'.
- Faux-zealous: 'We measure everything' (presumably that includes things that don't matter?).
- Evasive: 'It depends what you mean by measure'.
- Unaccountable: 'We support the business, if they get it wrong it's not HR's fault'.
- Guilt-ridden: 'Why are you asking? Have we done something wrong?'.
- Clueless: 'Sorry, what was the question again?'.

It is this last response that is probably the nearest to the truth of the situation. Measurement is something that has confused the HR profession for many years. This is partly because it is a difficult area in which to apply measurement principles but also because those who are attracted to the HR profession tend not to want to be accountable or measured: and numerical reasoning is not one of their strengths. In short, HR is peculiarly unsuited to the task of measuring itself. It was HR's feeble reputation in measurement that led Google to hire Prasad Setty; the self-proclaimed 'numbers guy'. But hiring a non-HR numbers guy can create its own problems. Engineers have their own discipline of precise measurement designed for engineering. HR is unlikely to be transformed by any discipline that is unable to cope with the uniqueness of individual human beings and the unpredictability of their behaviour. If the solution to the question 'what is wrong with HR?' was as obvious as hiring 'numbers guys' then HR functions around the world would already be full of mathematicians and engineers. There is already a trend in that direction but, as we found in Chapter 1, professional engineers have not yet developed any particularly insightful answers to their own people management problems yet.

Setty was interviewed by *HR Executive Online*[7] in 2010 (four years into Setty's tenure) and it is well worth reading because it revealed the thinking behind his appointment and the mindset of his more conventional HR boss, Google's CHRO, Laszlo Bock. Reading between the lines, a HR Professional will take some convincing that Google are doing anything innovative. Bock declares that 'Prasad has this unique ability to understand data very deeply while understanding what's important to the organization on a people level'. This is a strange admission. In suggesting Prasad has a unique ability to understand 'what's important' Bock is admitting he does not possess this ability himself. So how did he get to become a CHRO in the first place and how would he know whether Setty knows what he's doing? If Bock is right, and this ability of Setty's is unique, what have all the HR people around the world been doing all these years if they cannot see 'what's important'? The ability of senior, high profile HR people to want to shoot themselves in the foot can be astounding. In Bock's case he has managed to shoot every single one of his HR colleagues in the foot as well.

One very positive sign, in Setty's fresh perspective, is his dismissal of the notion of 'best practice' reportedly saying 'Google is not a place where I can go and say, "GE is doing this and so is IBM, so let's try it here, too." This is an organization where people prefer to rely on internal data and want to see what works here.' This insight apparently makes him, according to his interviewer, 'a shoo-in as one of HR *Executive Online*'s 2010 HR's Rising Stars'. It is just as well the study of astronomy and the universe is not run along the same lines as *HR Executive Online*. Would an astronomy magazine journalist be able to announce the discovery of a brand new star, one that has suddenly appeared out of the blue, without a shred of evidence that it actually exists?

So, after four years, what had Setty and Bock achieved from this new, data-driven philosophy of people management? There is no evidence of value in the article. All analysis, regardless of the data on which it is based, has to boil down to practice at some point. It appears that Google's HR practices are no different to any other HR function. It is developing quarterly performance evaluations to find out who the company's lowest performers are (see Chapter 1, Figure 1.2) and provides coaching and training where necessary, or assists people in leaving. This is exactly what organizations like GE and IBM still do. On the evidence presented in this article it seems that HR analytics do not suddenly make HR evidence-based, neither do they transform HR practice. Google will only make progress in evidence-based HR when it asks itself the value question.

The only right question for HR is does it add value?

HR people should only be employed by profit making companies if they can make a contribution to profit. In not-for-profit organizations they should only be employed for exactly the same reason; to maximize the surplus the organization creates to serve as many customers (service users) as possible. This does not need to be turned into some new form of engineering or rocket science. All organizations should have exactly the same raison d'être; to provide as much value as possible for every dollar spent. That means HR should be asking itself the same question, 'does every dollar we spend on HR create more value from every person we employ?' Bock's question of 'what's important to the organization on a people level' should be re-phrased to 'How much more value does Google need from its people?'

This will always maintain the correct focus. The reason HR has a long history of misguided measurement, particularly in the US, is that a whole generation failed to measure value. In hiring Setty, Bock was not openly admitting that he had got anything wrong himself; yet what other conclusion should we reach? If he had read the Conference Board's 'Evidence-based Human Resources' report (R-1427-09-KF) it would have reminded him that the computing systems dictum on data input, 'garbage in, garbage out', applies equally to HR today:

> For decades, experts working on the principle that 'a business is only as good as its people' have pursued the application of analytic methods to everyday HR functions. What they have found is a second principle: a human capital analytics system is only as good as its metrics.

The report also reveals just how wrong HR measurement has been when it re-visits the work of US measurement 'guru' Jac Fitz-enz, stating:

> Since Fitz-enz introduced measurement to the HR function in the 1980s most of the focus has been primarily on measuring the efficiency of HR functions. This focus **fails to address the more meaningful issues of how human capital creates value** (Paul Kearns' emphasis) and how HR interventions serve as catalysts for improving business outcomes.

The Conference Board could not have made its advice any clearer and has earned respect precisely because of this type of insight. However, identifying the problem only gets you part of the way towards a possible solution. The Conference Board does not offer a solution except to suggest that HR has to become evidence-based. What it should have said is that the HR profession has finally reached its Rubicon; the same one that medicine had to cross in the mid-nineteenth century. Maybe the HR Profession needs its own Julius Caesar?

'We're alright as long as we're all wrong'

So who will make the HR profession change its ways? Whoever comes forward will have to be prepared to say out loud just how naked HR is without proper measurement. If it is going to come from an existing HR director they will be putting their career on the line. HR is now a classic case of the 'Emperor's new clothes'. The mindset in HR has become one where everyone feels alright as long as they are *all* doing it wrong and no one is stepping out of line. HR people are particularly prone to this syndrome because there is something in their collective character that makes them not want to rock the boat. CEOs do not usually hire boat-rocking HR directors. This explains why none of the CIPD's 140,000 members rose up against their Board and CEO for buying a consultancy in clear conflict with their own interests. It also explains why SHRM's 250,000 members did not 'storm the palace' in Virginia after The Conference Board had exposed HR measurement for what it is. If HR people allow themselves to be trampled over by their own professional bodies what chance do we have of them standing up to hard-nosed executives and political masters?

Even if there were a 'Julius Caesar' among them, and probability theory tells us there must be, he would find his troops to be anaemic after being fed a relentless diet of HR products with little evidence of nutritional value. They are demoralized and have stopped caring about what they came into HR to do. Turning an entire profession around is going to require a Herculean effort as part of a very well-conceived, multi-pronged strategy. This was neatly summed up by an Australian HR consultant and auditor, Richard Boddington[8] when he posted a comment in response to a blog posting about the CPH standard entitled 'American "HR metric mania" is a concrete lifejacket':[9]

> HR often becomes engrossed in tactical activity and processes, rather than clearly linking to the organization's strategic objectives. HR can provide a valuable service but may not be providing an effective service (to achieve 'value-for money', an activity should be effective, efficient and economic), as HR often directs its efforts and resources to the 'here and now', current needs, and transactional rather than strategic effectiveness. One recent interviewee described this mode of operating as 'the cycle of fury'; another as 'being caught in the activity trap'.

> Over recent years, outcome based management (OBM) and reporting have been promoted in the Australian public sector, in particular. What is OBM? It focuses on why things are done not just what is done, and facilitates managing for results, and provides outcomes and Key Performance Indicators (KPIs) against which performance can be measured. Australian audits, however, have found deviance from best-practice OBM. For example, the Victorian Auditor-General's report of June 2008 examined performance reporting by councils. 'It concludes that much of the performance data reported is not useful ... and that important data on the cost-efficiency and quality of council services, and on the achievement of outcomes is not being reported'.

> This was followed by a 2010 report which concluded that 'the focus of performance reporting in Victoria has largely remained on output performance measures' so that only a few departments were able to demonstrate the extent to which objectives had been met. In these circumstances, departments were not able to demonstrate effective use of allocated funds to Parliament and the community.

> So, if the focus on HR and/or public sector KPIs is on 'what is done' rather than 'did we achieve our objectives', stakeholders are less likely to see demonstrated value-for-money effectiveness. **The draft CPH Standard appears to suffer this syndrome**. The Australian National Audit Office (2004) proposes that a good performance reporting framework should include specified desired outcomes and measurable performance indicators

for those outcomes. This proposition could equally apply to HR departments.

The audit department might not be everyone's first choice for convivial company but they do have an acute eye for the detail in systems thinking. This auditing ability could be put to much greater use in teaching organizations how to manage human capital.

Auditing learning

The consequences of failing to understand value measurement are particularly important in learning and development. L&D departments are wasting astronomical amounts of valuable time and money in their own cycle of fury by measuring training days, happy sheets and the average cost of training; meanwhile the organization is not learning the most valuable lessons it can. Auditors need to know how to audit an organization's ability to learn because learning is one of the prime sources of value creation. So we asked auditors how they presently audit training, to see what education they might need to raise their own professional standards. A letter was sent to several auditing journals in 2010 with the question 'how do you audit the training budget and how would you know whether it offers best value?' The letter was really designed as a more general enquiry about auditing methods for the less tangible aspects of organizational management. Several replies were received, which were almost uniform in taking the question very seriously and offering a well-considered, highly intelligent, response. Here is one representative sample, from an FCA, a Fellow of the Canadian Institute of Chartered Accountants:

> The audit of the 'training budget'
>
> The audit of training activities is no different to any other audit activity, i.e. it is a process built around the theory of auditing, including the audit objectives, knowledge of the client's business, the client's business objectives, suitable measurement and reporting criteria, and risk analysis.
>
> Auditing is generally concerned with either historic events or systems (the link to the future.) I do not have a definition of 'best value'. It sounds to me like a phrase that incorporates Frederick Winslow Taylor's concepts of economy, efficiency and effectiveness.
>
> Objectives should include:
>
> - a precise statement of the objective;
> - the units of measure of the objective;
> - who is responsible for attaining the objective; and,
> - the timeframe for achieving the objective.

> Objectives provide the units of output from any process, including training. All objectives must be stated in measurable terms, preferably in the same units of measure as overall business objectives. This last requirement facilitates the calculation of the contribution of training activities to the overall business objectives. If objectives are not expressed in measurable terms it can never be proven that they have been attained. The fact that non-financial objectives are not expressed in measurable terms is itself an important audit finding.

> The financial reporting paradigm is so powerful it has been extended to not-for-profits, who really should have their own accounting paradigm, though this should be based on the same conceptual framework as financial reporting.[10]

These are the words of someone who really knows their job and is totally confident working within a well ordered, theoretical and practical construct. He is a true Professional, offering his advice free of charge, to a fellow Professional seeking guidance. This is not a typical auditor's report though, is it? It is thoughtful and he does his best to adapt his framework to deal with the specific issues behind a particularly problematic question. He does not pretend that he has all the answers either. In doing so his Professionalism is not diminished in any way, if anything it is enhanced. His answer is also eloquent but its application, to an HR context, is nevertheless constrained by the conventional, accounting paradigm.

There is no reason why the L&D department should be excluded or excused from the Professional auditor's expertise and oversight. If this were to be the global standard for all learning and development expenditure the world would be a much better place. It is doubtful whether many trainers or L&D professionals would see it that way because their conventional wisdom, albeit non-evidence-based and unprofessional, is that learning is a special case. It isn't. The biggest hurdle to overcome, if the auditing and L&D Professionals are ever to be able to see eye-to-eye, is this issue raised by the FCA 'The fact that non-financial objectives are not expressed in measurable terms is itself an important audit finding.'

He is telling L&D professionals they have to accept *the principle of measurement*, even if they do not know how to apply it. This is now an extremely simple test to distinguish between Professional and non-professional L&D practitioners. Do you accept the principle of measurement or not? Once the principle is accepted the L&D Professional will need help in answering the next question: so how do I measure what I do? Accountants are not well equipped enough to deal with this. When there is not an obvious monetary sign in sight they tend to resort to vague, imprecise and unprofessional language. One other respondent to the auditing journal letter remarked that:

> The setting of non-financial objectives can, despite the best of intentions, soon become a game in which the participants revert to the old practices at the first opportunity. It can take several cycles of the planning process before

the setting of quantitative objectives becomes the accepted norm … recommendations may have to be repeated over 3–5 years before they are fully implemented.

It appears we are witnessing an evolutionary shift in the conventional management paradigm here. Intelligent auditors have already woken up to this: it might take another three to five years before HR will. Unthinking line managers would probably still love to be able to just get on with their job and not have to worry too much about HR complexities. It's about time they woke up as well. Everyone is going to have to get used to a much more searching audit of their people management practices. Even auditors themselves are going to have to finally acknowledge that human capital management requires a fresh perspective in auditing methodology.

An idiot's guide to auditing

The UK's National Audit Office (NAO), which exists to ensure that the nation's finances are spent wisely, is still trying to shoehorn 'HR auditing' into its own rigid and outmoded methods, the only ones it knows, by measuring what it can, activity and inputs, rather than what it should; value added.[11] One of the most commonly cited HR 'metrics' is the number of HR people per 100 employees (or FTE's, full time equivalents) and this has now been adopted by the NAO as one of its 'Primary indicators' of 'value for money' when in fact it does precisely the opposite. It indicates a waste of money measuring things that do not matter. The HR Professional would be able to tell them that such meaningless metrics are indicators of just how badly HR is doing focusing on inputs, not outputs. Pfeffer and Sutton would probably call it total nonsense.

This meaningless metric 'school of thought' can be traced directly to back Fitz-Enz, whose methods are actively promoted and sold by PwC.[12] Both PwC and the NAO are reinforcing some very odd concepts in the minds of HR departments, and their masters, in the fallacious belief that there is an 'ideal' or 'best practice' ratio to aim for. They also seem to regard HR as a necessary evil that should always aim to reduce its costs. You might be asking yourself how they manage to sell these ideas and their products to HR departments? Is it not like asking turkeys to vote for Christmas? Our guess is that HR is so inept and innumerate that it has managed to get itself into a double-bind: it is placing its head in a noose whichever way it turns. Option A is to zero-ize its own costs until it no longer exists. Option B, doing nothing, means being made to look bad against its own, spurious benchmarks. You cannot win with nonsensical HR metrics.

The NAO might try to pretend they view these as indicators of 'the organization's commitment to enhancing its capacity to deliver and improve' but they should already know, as do the auditing Professionals cited above, that such thinking produces illogical and absurd conclusions. Would it be better for total 'commitment' if 100 per cent of employee time was spent on training? Of course not. A judgement always has to be made about where 'best' lies on a scale from 0 per cent to 100 per cent.

Every profession will have its professionals and its Professionals. The least professional are those willing to put personal ambition, survival and pleasing their political masters ahead of any other consideration or intelligent response. When their tools are just not sophisticated enough for the job required perhaps we should not be surprised if they continue to hit everything they see with the same blunt instrument. In so doing, their cost-cutting logic becomes twisted and distorted. Sentient human beings will decide for themselves how much commitment they are prepared to give and they are likely to give less if they regard the auditors as idiots. The NAO has managed to create its own, two-headed monster, portraying HR as both a necessary evil and a positive sign of commitment at one and the same time. What a strange beast indeed?

Of course, one way to expose the fallacies perpetrated by unintelligent and unprofessional auditors is to turn their own spotlight back on them. Do auditing departments, like the NAO, have an equally fixed idea of the perfect ratio of auditors that should be employed by FTSE100 companies or government departments? Do they automatically assume that a lower ratio of auditors is good news or can they, for once, allow their intelligence some room for manoeuvre and admit it really depends on how much value their auditing ability adds? Perhaps the UK government should outsource its NAO to Canada, where common sense seems to prevail alongside very high, Professional standards?

If Arthur Andersen auditors had spent more time using their brains and doing their job properly, instead of shredding evidence, maybe Enron would still be around today, and possibly Arthur Andersen as well? How soon will it be before the UK government realizes it has an NAO that is not fit-for-purpose? The NAO needs an HR Professional to recruit new auditors who will start using their brains. The same HR Professional would also teach them some new tricks about how to audit human capital.

All HR activity divides easily into three simple categories

Anyone who has to facilitate meetings with groups of HR and L&D people will tell you it is like herding cats, although we offer our apologies to any cats who might regard this as a slight. HR people do not generally like being pinned down, which is at the root of their poor and non-existent standards. The attraction of joining the HR profession, for some new graduates, is probably that it is not at the sharp end: or that might have been their perception. We now know the world has changed and organizations cannot afford to have HR that is not in the front line, helping it to win some tough battles. Existing HR departments do not want to hear this bad news so it has to be broken to them gently. The 3 Box System shown in Figure 7.1 is one technique that was designed to do just that. It is comprised of three boxes, or categories, that cover every possible HR activity.

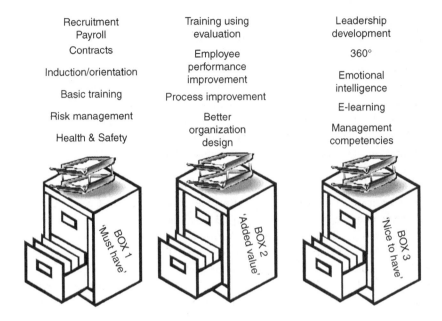

FIGURE 7.1 The 3 Box Management System

The Boxes are almost self-explanatory:

- Box 1. Must have: Standards dictated by statute, mandate, regulation or just minimum operating procedures.
- Box 2. Added value: Work designed to add value; with a clear line of sight to $'s (OCRQ).
- Box 3. Nice to have: You don't have to do it and no one knows what value it might add but you do it anyway.

For a much fuller description of the 3 Box System applied to HR see *HR Strategy* (Kearns, 2010, pp. 94–95) and for applications in L&D see *Evaluating the ROI from Learning* (Kearns, 2005, pp. 79–84).

Do not be fooled for one moment by the simplicity of the 3 Boxes. This is not an icebreaker or a game, it is a deadly serious, standard setting system with strict rules. Box 1 covers minimum standards; usually self-imposed or mandated by an external authority (e.g. you must have a financial adviser's qualification). Box 2 requires a well thought out, logical hypothesis that links these activities to dollar value. Box 3 should always be empty, if possible. You will notice that 'management competencies' have been put into Box 3 in Figure 7.1; even though competence should always be a minimum standard. The reason for this is simply that organizations rarely take the competence of their management as seriously as Box 1 demands. How many senior executives do you know that have a senior executive competence certificate?

This is not just an HR system it is a general management, standard-setting system. The 3 Boxes are also designed to be part of an integrated auditing system.

The Professional auditor's view on measurement is very simple: tell me how you want to be measured and I will measure you against that standard. They must have an audit trail, though. If every new employee has to receive induction the auditor will want to see a list of all new employees who have been inducted. If the HR director is working on organization design (shown here in Box 2) the auditor will want to know how they plan to measure an improvement in the newly-designed organization and what audit trail they could track? Organization design is obviously a more problematic area to measure than induction but the system demands that the HR director answers both questions seriously. The more exact they are, and the better the measures they use, the more Professional the HR director.

The other main purpose of the 3 Box System is prioritization: where does the organization spend most of its time, effort and money and has it got its priorities right? Any effort or money expended on Box 3 is likely to be wasted, or at least not as worthwhile as Box 1 and Box 2. Pet projects sponsored by senior executives should always start from Box 3; if they start at all. Efforts should then be made to shift their thinking so that the project can be safely put into Box 2 or Box 1. We will use this simple categorization from here on to distinguish between different priorities and levels of Professionalism. Box 3 pet projects are always unprofessional.

What will an evidence-based HR Professional look like?

The non-evidence-based, copycat mentality of HR usually encourages practitioners to follow what other high profile organizations are doing, like Google or Pepsico. When Pepsico declares that it wants to attract the best HR people, there is an assumption that it has managed to do so. Take leadership programmes for example: we have put these into Box 3. So if any leadership development people from Pepsico are reading this they might now be wondering which Box to put their own leadership programme in: they are bound to have one because everyone else does. If that is how they think then they have already missed the whole point of the system.

This system could be described as clinical and is looking to produce clinical outcomes. The HR Professional, as clinician, uses very precise, technical language. They will more accurately describe the 3 Box System as an *ex ante* analytical system (as opposed to an *ex post* process). An *ex ante* system *designs-in* success, right from the earliest beginnings, based on evidence gathered before policy implementation. An *ex post* process is not a system at all; it just tries to analyse what happened, much later, and after the event. In less professional language it is usually called hindsight.

'The failure of the Royal Bank of Scotland: Financial Services Authority Board Report' was an *ex post* analysis written after the executive horses had already bolted. Real Professionals would have started from an *ex ante* analysis, based on the best evidence they could get their hands on, and then reviewed the results from an *ex post* perspective against that original evidence base. Auditors would celebrate this approach. If you are now wondering why the organization that exists to guarantee the security of the UK financial system had no such *ex ante* system in place please join the back of the queue. Actually, that is slightly unfair. The FSA does employ *ex ante* analysis and had already spotted Fred Goodwin's failings as a leader, long before the bank ever failed. What they did not have, self-evidently, was an FSA leader or effective management system to prevent that failure.

Now, stop for a moment and consider the far-reaching and frightening implications of what we are saying here about this principle of *ex ante* management. Every off-the-shelf initiative, or product, ever used by HR and L&D is obsolete if it is just an *ex post* process. The HR Professional's method will always be an *ex ante* analysis, as standard.

Turning HR and L&D practitioners into *ex ante* Professionals will be a huge challenge because there is a fundamental Catch-22 in play. Traditionally, no one in HR wants to do anything that has not already been done by someone else; it is called 'catch up'. By the time they have caught up the one who got there first will already have moved on. Copying HR practice is also a bad idea if what you copy is not evidence-based. This is why management competence theory and practice has proved to be such an enormous disaster. The theory is shaky. There is no logical hypothesis that says you can develop managers according to a pre-prepared list of competencies. There is also no evidence that competence frameworks add any value (Box 2) or are treated seriously enough to become the mandatory requirements to do the job (Box 1). This means that management competence has always slipped into the nice-to-have Box. Thank god medicine is no longer run on this basis.

The most immediate, most obvious, difference between a conventional HR manager and an evidence-based, Professional HR manager is that the latter will eschew all HR convention and adopt instead a critical, *ex ante* mindset. Anyone wanting to be an HR Professional has to declare that as their intent. Professor Denise Rousseau, one of the leaders of the EBM movement, neatly sums up the gulf that currently exists between conventional HR and evidence-based HR in an article entitled 'Becoming an evidence-based HR practitioner'[13] stating that:

> Blind faith has no place in professional practice. The fundamental problem is not so much that a practitioner lacks scientific knowledge (though that is an issue). Rather, the key problem is the absence of a questioning mindset. Thinking critically is what good professionals do. Wondering what works, what does not and why is the first step towards improving practice. Critical thinking means actively exploring alternatives, seeking understanding and testing assumptions about the effectiveness of one's own professional decisions and activities ... The opposite of critical thinking is imitation, reliance on copycat practices from other companies, while ignoring widely available scientific findings regarding what works and what does not. Most insights from HR research do not reach the practitioner – despite the existence of evidence-based guides written with practice in mind.

After reviewing HR research literature the HR Professional may well end up using some practices that do not look dissimilar to conventional HR (as we saw with Google). For example, some form of employee review will still need to happen, but there is a world of difference between evidence-based and non-evidence-based reviews. The first will be a very focused, personal discussion while the latter will be blind adherence to a mechanistic process. The former will not be trying to achieve a spurious correlation with company performance because it will already be creating causal links. Similarly, if HR Professionals choose to use employee surveys at all (certainly not a foregone conclusion) they will not be purchasing Gallup's Q12 or any other, off-the-shelf product that makes claims of proof that cannot be substantiated. Their survey will be bespoke in every sense, not off-the-shelf. HR Professionals are not that puerile and so will never make themselves look stupid. Professional HR managers are the most mature managers you will ever find.

Evidence-based HR managers are the most mature of all

In *HR Strategy: Creating Business Strategy with Human Capital* (Kearns, 2010) the extent to which organizations understand the relationship between human capital management and business strategy is expressed as a scale of organizational maturity, a continuum along which the various roles expected of an HR function are explained through six evolutionary stages of development. We have included a version of that same continuum here in Figure 7.2 to illustrate how the move towards better evidence is a journey not just for the HR function but for the organization as a whole (see also the Institute of HR Maturity at www.hrmaturity.com).

On this occasion we will take a quick look at each aspect of this Maturity Scale from a Professional's perspective but we should not lose sight of the fact that this builds to a complete, holistic picture where the brushstrokes blend; it is not a

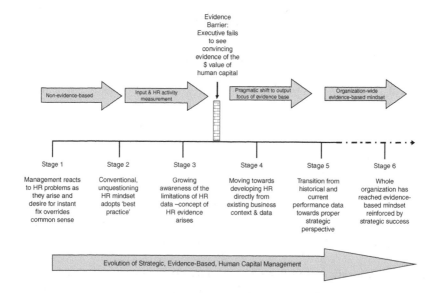

FIGURE 7.2 The HR Maturity Scale and the evolution of evidence-based HR

painting-by-numbers set. The general impression should be a historical shift from left to right. It starts from a non-evidence-based position (Stage 1), requiring no measurement, through a phase of measuring inputs and activities (Stage 2). After the Stage 3 realisation that simplistic measures are not asking the right questions ('Does this add value?') the organization starts to focus more on OCRQ. This gradually moves it towards Stage 4 where HR expertise works with the business to measurably improve, say, sales. It then passes through a transitional, experiential learning phase (Stage 5) towards the eventual realization that being evidence-based has to be a whole system, organization-wide philosophy. The whole evolution takes a lot less time if the CEO understands Stage 6 from the get-go.

There is a major barrier to progress though in the form of a conceptual 'wall' of Executive ignorance; one where no one has been able to articulate just how much potential value could be created by managing human capital more effectively. This could also be described as the 'human capital reporting barrier', which could have been resolved if SHRM/ANSI's 'Investor Metrics' standard had been better conceived. This is actually a dual barrier though. In Figure 7.2 it describes this barrier as the 'Executive fails to see convincing evidence of the dollar value of human capital' and this can be read as shareholder value in a very conventional, capitalistic, profit-driven enterprise. However, it should really be viewed in much broader terms as the executive not understanding their role in societal value; not squaring the people-profit circle in their own minds.

If the Executive team have short term objectives and want to maximize their own bonuses, or achieve their own objectives at the expense of society's best interests (e.g. oil companies polluting the environment or over-paying striking tanker drivers), how can they possibly expect their human capital to perform to their full potential? This barrier applies equally to not-for-profits as well because there can be no automatic assumption that a charity is valuable. Its Executives must also articulate exactly what value they are bringing to society in the absence of profit. For example, a charity housing homeless people has to decide how many homeless people they can house per dollar of funding raised. As this debate is much more fully explored in *The Value Motive* (Kearns, 2007) we will leave it there. Let us concentrate here on applying the Scale to reputable companies, governed by fully accountable executives, who take all their responsibilities very seriously; both the financial and the societal. Even in such organizations judged 'great' by the standards of today there is enormous potential for more societal value from human capital.

The 2012 share launch at Facebook, an IPO partially managed by the investment bank Morgan Stanley, was mired in controversy after it was alleged[14] that Morgan Stanley analysts, just before the launch, had held a more pessimistic view of Facebook's prospects than they had admitted in public. When the share price subsequently tumbled by 10 per cent, within the first few days of trading, other investors were understandably upset. Morgan Stanley analysts may feel they had a duty to look after Morgan Stanley's interests but society might argue otherwise. From a pure, dollar value perspective many more investors have since lost out as the Facebook share price continued to tank; suffering nearly a 50 per cent fall from its launch price by August 2012. Another value consideration is the litigation costs that Morgan Stanley itself now faces. We could also, of course, have a debate here about business ethics, and the impact on Morgan Stanley's reputation, but the HR Professional would maintain their sharp focus on both the Box 1 (legal and regulatory) impact and the Box 2 $ value; before jumping to any ethical conclusions. They will harbour the same innate belief as any other human being that Morgan Stanley's practice seems unethical; in the same way that a doctor might believe an unnecessary abortion is unethical. Nevertheless, they will remain pragmatic in dealing with the situation that faces them directly whilst hoping for a more ethical future.

Returning to the Maturity Scale, underneath each of the Stages in Figure 7.2 is a short, representative description of what they mean from a data and evidence perspective. It is very important to recognize the insidious ways in which a lack of evidence can influence the way people are managed:

- Stage 1. There is no philosophy at play here. Managers react to problems, as with oil companies and the tanker drivers' unions.
- Stage 2. HR professionals are taught that there is such a thing as 'best practice', which they tend to regard as absolving them from any accountability or responsibility for subsequent policy failings.
- Stage 3. Eventually the failings of HR 'best practice' are noticed, if not entirely understood, and HR departments react by measuring their activities, as with the CPH metric. HR then gets stuck at Stage 3 unless and until someone convinces the Executive that what they really need is not single metrics, such as CPH, but the complete version of value (OCRQ) that comes from hiring the right candidates who perform well.
- Stage 4. The more Mature HR Professionals, working towards a higher purpose than HR activity, do realize that evidence can only be defined in terms of dollar value. They manage to convince the Executive of this fact and this revelation brings a much greater level of certainty regarding human capital management. If the Executive does not deploy a better human capital strategy the whole organization will be stuck behind the barrier at Stage 3.
- Stage 5. The Executive barrier can only be removed through education which means that business schools need to offer a much better EBM curriculum than they currently do. This transitional phase is going to take some time. New methods for collecting and disseminating human capital management evidence have yet to be devised. Even the most enlightened executives will take some time to really tap into the full potential of their human capital.
- Stage 6. Toyota arrived at Stage 6 some years ago as they built the best example so far of the complete and holistic organization. This was constructed from the best materials of a philosophy of continuous improvement; a learning system; the principle of measurement and a closed-loop, quality system called Plan, Do, Check, Act. Even at Stage 6 standards can easily slip and this will translate into inferior performance and a loss of reputation: as with Toyota's significant vehicles recalls in 2009/10. This is why the Maturity Scale has no end point.

Even the best, or should we say only the best, will ever know what it is like to be out at the leading edge and the new problems this can create.

The Maturity Scale was never intended to be an invention; it is a reflection of reality. All executives, and all of their HR people, have always been in relative states of maturity. The Scale just offers a way of plotting their current position, their Baseline, with some hints as to how they might progress. Executives who know nothing about HR strategy, do not want to know or have been misinformed, will all be at a relatively immature stage in thinking and managerial decision-making. Some of those decisions, like attending non-evidence-based leadership development programmes, will be seen as just plain stupid once they mature. Sending executives on leadership courses when they are immature makes them worse because they reinforce the infantile notion that leadership is a 'course' to be attended.

The best leaders become the best by always wanting to be better. This is what underpins the Maturity Scale but 'best' has to mean best societal value. When it comes to getting the best returns on human capital, boards of directors have had a very easy ride so far because there has been no one reporting on their human capital management record. Even investment analysts, who are paid to spot unrealized potential, have failed to develop the methods for identifying where organizations have latent human potential that is not being realized. This has huge implications for whole economies.

Our recent, shared, history of poor leadership in the financial crisis of 2008 (and ongoing), the Eurozone crisis (ongoing), the viability of the whole EU project (ongoing) and increasing challenges to the legitimacy of the capitalist model (ongoing) reveals just how far we have to go in making our economic and social models work better. One of the goals of leadership is to have as many willing citizens as possible behind a model that works. This is the simple notion behind the grand vision and we can start to take some tentative steps in that direction through better management education.

Developing the new, Professional management curriculum

As we saw in Chapter 3, the academic community is still struggling with EBM as a concept, a scientific methodology and a practical management methodology. So we cannot look to existing business school teachers yet to produce the finished article in evidence-based, human capital management. However, if you were forced into choosing a management programme tomorrow would you go for a non-evidence-based programme or one where they were at least asking intelligent, evidence-based questions? The latter might not be perfect but it should be the better option. It would then be in your interest, as a paying customer, to help your chosen business school develop the programme further by asking them your own, evidence-based questions:

- Does your business school believe there is such a thing as EBM?
- Is it a strong advocate of EBM methods and if so how long has that been true?

- Could you please define what you mean by EBM and give me at least two simple examples of how it might immediately influence my management practice?
- Is your teaching faculty's research based on case studies of conventional management or EBM?
- Would they be able to distinguish clearly between the two and if so what would be the defining characteristics of each?
- Is EBM in any way inferior to conventional management and could it actually harm my organization?
- If management has not been evidence-based in the past then on what basis were management decisions made?
- Is EBM particularly relevant to people management and, if so, why and how?

Another indicator of the better EBM programmes will be a much more precise use of language around people management. HR taxonomies already exist at professional Level 1, with job classifications and categorizations of conventional HR activities, but the terminology for Levels 2 to 4 needs much more clarity. The recent drive towards ISO HR standards recognizes this; the days of HR being 'pink and fluffy' are over. Terms such as 'soft skills' and 'hard results' have been bandied about, without adequate definition, for far too long. There is still no single, universally agreed definition of 'coaching' and there are as many different methods of coaching as there are coaches. Some even use the words 'counselling' and 'coaching' interchangeably without any difference in outcomes expected.

There has to be a universal lexicon of key HR terms and we are not going to provide one here but we can start the ball rolling. SHRM's attempt at 'Investor metrics' already includes 'human capital', a term which has slipped into HR parlance without having had to pass any systematic test of precise meaning. This is slapdash and highly unprofessional. The UK Mirror Committee for ISO Technical Committee TC260 on HR standards therefore proposed a working group be established to address the whole issue of HR terminology as a best practice, first step in quality management systems. In Table 7.1 we have offered a few working definitions of common words. Common understanding is much more important than abstract definition. If we cannot achieve a common understanding then we should take these words out of circulation.

This short list has been specifically chosen to highlight the problems of using imprecise and sloppy language when it is part of a serious, HR management discussion. Here are some examples of problems that are likely to arise:

- How often is the term 'value' used without specifying which of these alternatives you mean – money or personal principles? Can we achieve the highest monetary value without matching it with our personal values?
- 'Training days' is an input, as are the costs of training and the training department itself. Measuring inputs reveals nothing about the value of training, except as a contraindicator.

TABLE 7.1 A sample taxonomy of important, everyday HR terms

Term	Dictionary definition	HR context definition
Value (money)	What something is worth compared to the price paid	A monetary assessment of an HR activity in whole value terms of OCRQ
Value (personal view)	Personal judgement of what is important	Personal beliefs that underpin principles and behaviour
Input	Time, cost, energy expended	Time, cost, energy expended
Output	What does the organization produce from the inputs?	What does the organization produce from the inputs?
Outcome	Ultimate consequence of a series of actions	Ultimate consequence of a series of actions
Investment	The action of investing money for a profit or return: not to be confused with cost	The action of investing money for a profit or return NB.
Cost	Money expended	Money expended
ROI	Rate of return on an investment	Hypothetical or estimated rate of return on an investment in people
Talent	Natural aptitude or skill	A specific aptitude or skill possessed by specific employees (e.g. he is a talented negotiator)
Leadership	The actions of a person who leads or commands a group	The ability of a person to provide direction and purpose that encourages others to follow (Not to be used interchangeably with 'management' – especially as in 'leadership team')
Engagement	A formal agreement to get married	A strong psychological bond between an employee and the purpose of the organization

- The only output from training that is worth anything is a physical output: did the customer receive a better service; did efficiency improve on the production line?
- Is training expenditure a cost or an investment? Do accounts treat it as an investment or as a cost? If they measure it as a cost is that simply because they don't know how to calculate the return on this investment? Is it acceptable to base decisions on ROI estimates and hypotheses?
- Do all employees have talents? Have they been identified? Why do some talent managers refer to the whole workforce, generically, as 'talent'? Should an organization only develop the talents of part of the workforce?
- Is your senior management team now called the 'leadership team'? Not all senior managers are leaders. If you want to call it a leadership team have you tested its leadership capability?

- Is there a happy marriage between employer and employee or is it just an engagement? At what point does engagement turn to commitment? How important is that bond in value terms and what are the likely costs of divorce?

Imprecise language not only creates confusion it is likely to be ridiculed. No sane employee would believe that re-naming the executive team the 'leadership team' suddenly transforms ordinary managers into leaders. This sort of linguistic distinction does not make the HR Professional a pedant; it enables them to influence and persuade. Calling a manager who exhibits no leadership capability a 'leader' devalues the term and makes it meaningless. Equally, the head of a company, government department or political party should not automatically be called its leader. Only followers can decide who their leaders are. If 'leader' becomes a meaningless term what chance do we have of defining or developing better leadership in the future?

The other, perhaps more obvious, abuse of language is jargon. Every profession has its own unusual, and sometimes peculiar, language to differentiate parts or specify technical details. Most ordinary UK householders will know what a window sill is but perhaps only a professional builder knows the difference between a sill and an architrave. Doctors have a vast array of medical terms that an ordinary patient could never be expected to learn. So should they translate or spell everything out? What does HR need to spell out? What is the best way, for example, to describe the process of assimilating a new employee? Should it be induction, orientation or onboarding? How is that perceived by the new hire and would a different word be required in different languages or cultures?

One of the founding family members of Toyota, Eiji Toyoda, in his book on the company's history (Toyoda, 1987), literally used the word 'brainwashing' to describe the process of inducting employees into the Toyota Way. We can all create different perceptions, and send mixed signals, through our careful or careless choice of words. Toyoda admitted that he hesitated to use this term in his book and would probably not have dreamed of telling an employee this to their face. However, he would have no hesitation in telling them that they have to fully understand, and commit to, Toyota's total philosophy.

Precise, Professional language is the most honest form of communication. So why, when the time comes for someone to leave a company, do we use so many euphemisms for 'sacked' or 'redundant'? IBM referred to one of its many large scale redundancies, in the early 1990s, as 'career transitioning' and came up with different titles for each of several, subsequent rounds of further job losses. What impression do such words create? Does being 'outplaced' make the leaver feel any better or more human? Doctors are trained that when they have to give bad news they do it in a way that minimizes patient distress but, if the patient wants to know the truth, they have to give them the unvarnished truth.

What about remuneration? It is a difficult enough word to say never mind understand so why not use pay and benefits instead? What signal does the term 'compensation' convey? That someone has to be compensated for working for the company because there is no other reason to work there? More recently we have been introduced to the terms 'metrics' and 'analytics' being used in HR when all they mean are measures and data that can be used for analysis. The OED just defines 'analytic' as 'another term for analytical'. Yet again HR is inventing unnecessary words and more jargon. The Professional always chooses the simplest, plainest language they can think of and frequently checks understanding and interpretation.

Of course the term 'HR' itself is still regarded as jargon by many ordinary human beings. Some make fun of HR by referring to it as the 'human remains' department or some other derogatory play on words. The advent of 'human capital' management is probably not helping matters and yet it is probably the most complimentary way to view people in an organizational context: they are valuable and valued. So what's in a name? If HR wants to be taken seriously and seen as a force for good, rather than as a necessary evil or a cumbersome and costly bureaucracy, then probably the least an HR Professional should aim to do is start by using language that everyone understands. Then they can move on to the really important steps.

8

TEN STEPS TO BECOMING AN HR PROFESSIONAL

Step 1. Taking the HR Professional's Oath

Hopefully the earlier chapters will have prepared you for what you need to do to call yourself a Professional manager and developer of people. If you are not quite there yet let us just reiterate that the sort of Professional we have described here is only a very distant relative to what most organizations would regard as HR. It would be more accurate to describe most HR and L&D practitioners today as nothing more than personnel and training administrators who support basic, operational needs. The larger the organization the bigger and more complex this administrative task becomes but it never becomes anything more than just administration. Whereas, to refer to Professional HR as a 'support' role would be an oxymoron because it is essentially strategic. What we are proposing is also a much more wide-ranging role with a purpose that is higher than any immediate or short-term goals of the organization. So the first step towards this higher level of Professionalism, Level 4, is to openly acknowledge the sheer scale, nature and onerous responsibilities such a role entails. What better way to do this than to swear an HR version of the doctor's Hippocratic Oath?

The Professional HR Oath

> I swear to help organizations and those whom they employ to the best of my ability and judgement; to create as much value as humanly possible through the application of the best principles of evidence-based management to the management and development of people. This value will include profit, where appropriate, but ultimately value has to be societal value – the greatest satisfaction of the greatest number – and this applies to all organizations whether they be governed by profit or not.
>
> I will not offer any prescriptions for managing or developing people without a proper diagnosis and I will always search for evidence that my methods have had the desired effect and impact.

I will respect any hard won lessons of those HR Professionals in whose steps I walk and gladly share such knowledge as is mine with those who are to follow.

I will remember that there is art to Professional HR as well as science, and that warmth, sympathy, and understanding may outweigh any cold-hearted logic or impersonal, scientific analysis.

I will also remember that I can only influence individual human beings, whose ability or inability to learn, develop, perform and improve may have an effect on their family and economic stability. My responsibility includes these related problems, if I am to care adequately for all of those who come within my Professional practice.

I will always remember that I remain a member of society, with special obligations to all my fellow human beings.

I will not be ashamed to say 'I know not', nor will I fail to call in my colleagues when the skills of another are needed for an organizational or employee benefit.

Prevention is always preferable to cure so I will always help employees to learn and plan today to avoid the problems of tomorrow.

If I do not violate this oath, may I long enjoy life and art, and be respected while I live and remembered with affection thereafter. May I always act so as to preserve the finest traditions of my calling and may I long experience the joy of seeing people develop and improve, especially those who have sought my help.

This is a serious suggestion. Hopefully Hippocrates would forgive us for borrowing his medical oath and would welcome our attempt to apply his highest ideals and principles to the purpose of societal value creation through people. Our oath is adapted from a modern version written in 1964 by Louis Lasagna, academic dean of the School of Medicine at Tufts University, and apparently still in use in many medical schools today. It is entirely in keeping with SHRM's ethical code and marks Professional HR out as a true vocation.

That is only the second time we have used that word – vocation. It is a word that seems to have fallen out of common parlance; more is the pity. Professional HR is a genuine calling and so an oath is appropriate. When personal or commercial gain squeezes out the values of a vocation it is a sad day for humanity. When those forces start to influence a field such as medicine, or any other Profession, something very important is lost. Maybe now, when healthcare is under the joint pressures of escalating demand and cost, it is a good time to try and rebalance the human equation. Perhaps re-injecting a heightened sense of vocation will help to improve both care and its finance?

When medicine was still regarded as a vocation and a doctor climbed out of bed at 3.00 am to visit a poorly patient it brought with it admiration and respect. The patient not only appreciated the effort and dedication but knew the doctor had their best interests at heart and was not doing it just for the money; or the threat of litigation. A return to those values might reduce the high cost of the American healthcare industry, where malpractice alone costs \$55.6 billion[1] (2.4 per cent of total healthcare costs) and also ensure that the UK's NHS will survive long into the future? Maybe banking could also, once more, have values that we respect? Professionalism does not discriminate between profit and not-for-profit and should be respected by both.

Any manager of people can take a similar oath as testament to their Professionalism but only if they have the interests of wider society uppermost in their mind. There is no reason, for example, why private equity partners should not take this oath. It would reveal who was in it purely for personal gain and who saw private equity as a more positive and natural part of the normal cycle of capitalism renewing itself. It could become mandatory for CEOs to take the oath before they dream up any mission statement about double digit growth or market dominance. A very public display of taking the oath would send some very strong signals to the market and the workforce. If a CEO cannot reconcile their day job with such a higher vocation we should wonder why we have allowed them so much power over resources and people in the past. If that is too much to expect then we must hope that we can find many more HR Professionals who are willing to accept that responsibility on their behalf.

Try saying the oath now, out loud, to see if it makes you feel more passionate and determined or just ridiculous. Look at yourself in the mirror and try not to blush. If that is too much of a challenge you can put it to one side until a later date. Whether you take the oath or not, the next test is to do almost the exact opposite of committing yourself to doing good works; you are going to try and get yourself struck off.

Step 2. Help to create a Professional register that can strike you off

This might sound like an odd step to take but of all the possible indicators of true Professionalism the ultimate indicator is the existence of a body that monitors and controls Professional standards. A General Council that controls entry to the profession and has the power to strike off those who fail to meet its tough standards. Professional HR will only be taken seriously when it is controlled by a GHRC. A code of conduct is not a strong enough sanction.

The CIPD recently published a revised 'Code of professional conduct',[2] which came into force for all its members on 1 July 2012 and covers four key areas:

- Professional competence and behaviour.
- Ethical standards and integrity.
- Representative of the profession.
- Stewardship.

Announcing the changes, the ex-President of the CIPD and chair of its professional conduct committee, said:

> The CIPD promotes high standards of behaviour and practice in the HR profession. This is critical given the powerful role of HR in ensuring organizations have the trust, integrity and capability to deliver not just success today, but sustainable performance for the future.

She has spent much of her long career in HR working for large HR consultancy firms and only retired from Towers Watson in 2012; the same company that we saw passing off correlations as causation. This illustrates how questionable practices and products can undermine the professional integrity and probity at the very highest levels of the HR profession. She also remarked that the new code:

> marks a raising of the bar in terms of the maintenance and enforcement of clear, simple, rigorous standards in HR professional practice.

How easy would it be to enforce such standards when the professional credentials of the guardians themselves are open to question? Non-existent and low standards in HR have created a management crisis of epic proportions: the governors no longer have the requisite credibility for governing. Any CIPD President that wants their words to be taken seriously has to be beyond reproach and Towers Watson have some questions of their own that need to be answered publicly. Those upholding a proper, Professional register would have to set an example by taking the oath. This is such an obvious point that has yet to be acknowledged by the professional body.

Do we need to keep reminding ourselves what has happened in the banking industry? Banking is essential to modern society and it should be obvious that we cannot afford to let our standards drop. Yet even as late as July 2012 Barclays bank was fined £290 million because its traders had manipulated LIBOR – the London Interbank Offered Rate – one of the most important interest rates that affects literally trillions of dollars in inter-bank lending. Even if these traders have not committed any crime it reveals something of the mentality and culture that still exists in the banking system as a whole, not just at Barclays. Aside from the legalities, did the Banking Code of Practice not result in any of them being struck off? The issue of professional registers with the power to strike members off goes much wider than HR. To call these people professional with a small p, never mind a capital P, would be a travesty. The fact that the Chairman and CEO of Barclays both had to resign over the matter is not just an indicator of public outrage but also the outrage of other, more respected, City figures that still possess some vestige of integrity. They do not work in banking just for the money but because they know a successful society demands a successful banking system and rightly deem this to be beyond the pale.[3]

Several General Councils are obviously called for. It is a big step but anyone brave enough to adopt our standards will only want to associate with those who work to the same, highest standards. It will also be in their own, long term, personal interests to set standards that only the best will be able to meet and there is nothing wrong with that. True Professionalism, the type that creates great value, should be well recognized and well rewarded. It would not take many dedicated souls to form the first GHRC and item one on their agenda would be establishing objective criteria that HR Professionals have to meet. The over-arching principle governing all practitioners would be to demonstrate that they are evidence-based.

Step 3. Pass the test of an avowed, evidence-based Professional

We have already covered developments in EBM at some length, even though there is still no universal consensus as to what constitutes the 'official' version. So we are going to set our own standard here for evidence-based Professionalism; knowing that some will take issue with us. Our primary criterion for the evidence-based HR Professional is to offer a practical solution to a client's problem. So what does this mean? Well, for a start, it means that every organizational context is unique and requires a bespoke prescription that cannot be bought over the counter. It also requires specific evidence being used as a basis for any prescription. Only after the Professional has carried out a thorough examination, analysis and diagnosis will they decide what tools might be required. More often than not they will design their own solutions; in the same way that leading surgeons have had to design their own tools for very specific, surgical procedures.

HR managers who continue to re-heat pre-cooked products without questioning their relevance or validity will have to understand that a GHRC would regard this as malpractice. HR practice that is not constantly refreshed and reinvigorated can produce a rigid bureaucracy (as with job evaluation and grading schemes) and with that comes stasis, not the renewal that capitalism is supposed to create. Moreover, once a Professional CEO sees what an evidence-based HR Professional has to offer they will want nothing less. They will be reassured by the HR Professional's solid discipline of always creating a Baseline that has been subjected to the most rigorous test possible – a generic set of seven Baseline Questions.

The seven Baseline Questions

Examining value

- Question 1. Will this add value?
- Question 2. How will it add value: what is the initial hypothesis?

To answer Test Question 1 the only 'evidence' that will qualify is evidence of value (OCRQ); or at least a clear line-of-sight towards a goal of value. The HR Professional frames everything they do in terms of its potential value but they also have to produce a sound, causal hypothesis for that line-of-sight. If the culture of the organization is an issue, for example, then it first has to be articulated as a value question. In the case of Barclays bank this might be 'how do we avoid another £290 million fine for fraudulent behaviour?' The HR Professional does not accept the concept of intangibility though and culture is certainly not an intangible phenomenon, far from it. Culture is the lifeblood of an organization and its flow, pressure and temperature need to be regularly checked and monitored. If pressure is building up in one area (LIBOR) the system will burst unless something is done to reduce that pressure and avert any misbehaviour that might follow.

Test Question 2 establishes hypothetical causality. It forces the HR Professional to posit a rough, working hypothesis of what the problem is. This will establish the effect that needs to be alleviated and what the causes of that effect might be. It is a standard question that can be applied to any HR or L&D intervention – 'If this works, how will it actually add value?' It is a much more focused and appropriate question than just asking 'Why are we doing this?' Asking 'why' too often can irritate those in the executive suite and is in danger of appearing patronising: 'where is the value' is a much more acceptable and legitimate question. If the C-suite does not want to answer this pin-sharp question that, in itself, is evidence of a dysfunctional organization working below par. Once the hypothetical causality is made plain you can move onto the diagnosis.

Diagnosis and hypothesis

- Question 3. Have you fully diagnosed the problem?
- Question 4. What is your initial hypothesis?

The rough hypothesis needs some more work before it is refined enough to act as a basis for action. The mindset of the HR Professional is the same as that espoused by Pfeffer and Sutton (2006); always regard the organization as a prototype that requires further experimentation and refinement. The hypothesis is there to be tested, iteratively if necessary, to get it closer and closer to the truth of the situation. It might even take the organization somewhere it has never been before or imagined possible.

Hopefully the hypothesis will prove to be sound but equally, if the hypothesis fails, then the organization has to learn from this experience: that requires a learning system. You might ask do 'we need a system to learn?' and, strictly speaking, the answer is no, at least not at an individual level. However, Professional HR imposes a much tougher standard; everyone who needs to learn has to have access to learning and only a complete system will allow that to happen. The learning system depends on accurate diagnosis though and so the HR Professional uses their diagnostic tools assiduously before attempting to implement anything. This usually involves a chicken-and-egg situation: what comes first, the hypothesis or the diagnosis? The reality is a mix of the two.

The City of London is already saying that 'the UK banking culture must change'.[4] But how can they know that the problem is one of 'culture' when the whole system is comprised of so many disparate yet connected elements? Also, why is this just a 'UK' culture problem when banking is supposed to be a global system?

Headlines might get the diagnosis completely wrong but headlines can influence readers who do not know any better. Even if one of the root causes is a cultural issue, how might it be resolved and how long will it take? The HR Professional will slice through such inexact terminology and hasty diagnosis as easily as a potter's wire cuts through wet clay. A professional potter will also ensure their clay is centred on the wheel before they can mould it to their own design. So it is with the HR Professional: people management problems are malleable lumps of indistinct shape that can be fashioned into a thing of beauty. They realize that beauty is always in the eye of the beholder though so first have to establish what shape will please everybody. This is where the evidence comes in.

Establish the evidence-base

- Question 5. What question are we asking and what evidence will answer it?
- Question 6. Where are we starting from? (point A)
- Question 7. Where are we hoping to arrive? (point B)

If we stick with the real-life Barclays example, for now, we find the authorities were already setting up an inquiry. The HR Professional would immediately want to write down the questions this enquiry is designed to answer. That could be a very broad-ranging set of questions about fraudulent behaviour, the governance of Barclays Bank or even a more serious question about the whole banking system and its regulation. Some still regard Barclays' ex-CEO, Bob Diamond, as a very talented investment banker and that may well be true but the role of a CEO is not just to make money. His replacement, Antony Jenkins, admitted just after he was appointed in August 2012 that 'We have made serious mistakes in recent years and clearly failed to keep pace with our stakeholders' expectations.'[5]

The CEO has to create the right culture, or find someone competent enough to mould it into a shape of their choosing. In this sense Barclays and RBS were exactly alike, a strong CEO who produced a damaging culture. Maybe we need even more banking failures before we finally realize that this is a generic, organizational problem? One view already expressed by the Governor of the Bank of England, Mervyn King, is that no more regulation is required. Perhaps, as a former academic, King had never been taught about evidence-based solutions to systemic problems that are caused by culture and its consequent effects on peoples' behaviour? Yet it is now clear that a central bank governor has to understand these elements in economic, banking and financial stability systems if they are to be deemed competent enough to do their job.

The HR Professional would start by framing the question in terms of what success looks like. This is not a new idea and the 'why' question will never be far away either. Why do we have LIBOR anyway; what is its purpose? Is 'success' the smooth and flawless operation of LIBOR or is it the fate of the trillions of dollars in trading that depend on it? How will we know when success has been achieved?

How could it be measured and what other indicators might be acceptable evidence? Are there already any minimum standards being set for the operation of LIBOR? If so, why have they been by-passed or otherwise unenforced in the past? These relentless questions have to continue until the evidence-base is established. Everyone needs to agree what 'point A' is and what we hope 'point B' will look like. Only then can a Professional plan be hatched to move us from A to B.

It is worth mentioning here that the level of Professionalism required directly corresponds to the level of complexity and scale of the issues at stake. Strategic organizational issues, such as culture, are wicked problems. Professional OD specialists will tell you that 'culture kills system', which is precisely what has been happening within the banking sector. If those same OD specialists had enough credibility and status to have advised Mervyn King then maybe this fiasco would never have happened? Doing nothing about the LIBOR problem allowed it to fester and it eventually caused so much damage that it erupted into a very public scandal. When bad behaviour continues unchecked for so long it is extremely difficult to eradicate and often requires radical surgery, including amputation, which is why there is now a call to sever the investment banking limbs from retail banks. If ever there was an argument for a proper HR Professional, now is the time. When they are called to the scene of the accident they will have their trusty toolkit – their 'doctor's bag' – with them.

Step 4. Become a consummate master of the evidence-based Professional's forensic toolkit

This step requires mastery of a complete set of analytical and diagnostic tools. Some are very old, while others have been specifically developed for the new role of the evidence-based HR Professional. Knowing how to combine these tools into a total management methodology is as much art as science. So what tools are we talking about?

- A very clear strategic framework (see Figure 8.1) that provides the HR Professional with a map and a checklist, all in one. It is their anatomy chart for the organization. The map identifies all the components needed for strategy and the sequence of analysis. Each component has to be mentally ticked after checking that it is in good, working order. The real art of the HR Professional is in helping the organization to articulate, in very simple language, all of the important connections between vision, values, principles, dollar value and what all this means for every single, individual's role
- HR strategy techniques to articulate to the C-suite how a competitive advantage can be gained from Professional human capital management (see Kearns, 2010, pp. 11–13).
- Learning strategy techniques to help the organization reach a maturity level where it can learn from its failings and mistakes, as well as any successes. The key tools here include an evaluation model that starts from a clear Baseline and

the intelligent use of ROI formulae to run 'what if', cost-benefit analysis, scenarios to educate and convince executives and line managers about the value of learning (see Kearns, 2005).

- Structural analysis. The organization has to be designed to offer the best structure possible and that includes ensuring that accountabilities and responsibilities are placed with the most appropriate people, in the most appropriate roles, with clear reporting lines.
- Systems analysis. This is analysis of both the whole system and all of the sub-systems. Being able to describe and influence the whole system is probably a skill and art of the very highest order that any Professional can ever achieve: it equates to organizational neurosurgery. This has particular relevance to the HR Professional because they have to deal with the most complex of all organizational systems, the human system: how people behave, how they are prepared to perform and what rewards they expect. This all has to come together in complete harmony.
- Cultural analysis. The skill here is in articulating the apparently intangible in very clear, tangible terms. One technique is to offer many varieties of organizational model. Does the organization want to be like an army, an orchestra, a family, a bureaucracy, a jungle or what? Whichever model is chosen has to be the most appropriate for achieving the organization's goals. The culture 'circle' shown in Figure 8.1 includes the organization's leadership behaviour, its values and principles, its ethos, the level of trust and cooperation, the willingness of its people to share knowledge and their eagerness to learn. All of these are separate items on the checklist but the HR Professional never forgets they are really inseparable elements in a blended, cultural cocktail.
- People measurement and human capital management indicators have to be much more advanced than the simplistic type of CPH metrics beloved of old-fashioned, HR bureaucrats. This is a developing field but one template suggestion is to be found in 'HR Strategy. Creating business strategy with human capital' (Kearns, 2010, Chapter 9).
- Process analysis is already a well-known technique that has been used to great benefit to reduce costs and strip out wasted activity. Here it is allied much more closely with the structure and system analyses. Looking at individual steps in a process and asking 'who does this step?', 'where do they sit in the structure' and 'which bit of the system are they protecting or enabling' is one way to crystallize many connections and interdependencies. Of course, once these questions have been answered the capabilities of a particular person for a particular role can be assessed, right up to the highest levels such as central bank governors and government ministers.
- Maintaining a value focus at all times is essential. This can be done remarkably easily by only using the four value variables of OCRQ combined with a 'line of sight' version of critical path analysis. What is the critical path to enable us to move from A to B? How do we get to value creation as soon as possible; what is going to get in the way or slow that process up?

- Pareto analysis. This is the 80:20 rule for prioritising actions in conjunction with the 3 Box System. Pareto analysis is just a technique for prioritizing and targeting the added value and risk management opportunities in order of size. This has a specific application at a strategic level in HR because organizations are very poor at identifying human opportunities and risks. For example, how much extra value could a supermarket create by training its checkout operators to gain $1 more from each customer on every shopping trip? How much, in dollar's, would Barings, Societe Generale and UBS have saved by spotting their rogue traders sooner?

- Cause and effect analysis, or root cause analysis, is a very simple fishbone diagram at Level 1 on the professional scale. It takes on a whole new meaning when it is applied to wicked problems at Level 4 where you cannot deal with a specific, measured effect in isolation from all of the other causes. Some of the causes of the LIBOR scandal are the numerous, systemic weaknesses running throughout the global financial and banking systems. If UK banking culture is the *effect* produced by some of those weaknesses why is it being treated as a *cause* of the problem by the Governor of the Bank of England? If it is a cause of other effects (bank share prices) then it is only one cause amongst many. The HR Professional will not confuse causes and effects; especially where people are involved. Moreover, when it comes to solving these problems they will never get the arrow of causation the wrong way round. They will never pretend that a correlation (e.g. the way banks report) can be used to solve a problem (systemic weakness).

- The most powerful weapon in the HR Professionals armoury will always be their unshakeable belief in probability theory and the normal distribution, bell curve, of human behaviour. This predicts that for every great executive or board member who gets between 8 and 10 there are equal numbers getting 1 to 3. They will be looking for the potential 10's and trying to root out the 1's; doing everything they can to mobilize the 6's and 7's by getting them out of their comfort zone and giving advance notice to the 4's and 5's that the curve keeps shifting inexorably to the right. Complacency is not allowed.

- All of the above tools can only be deployed in an organization that is dedicated to creating value. Once that philosophy is adopted the simplest, yet most profound tool of all, PDCA (Plan, Do, Check, Act) can come into play to ensure all actions start with a measure and feedback success or failure for learning purposes. This is an iterative cycle that only works to full effect in organizations with a philosophy of never-ending, continuous improvement. Declaring as much is a good indicator of a nascent learning organization.

- At the more sophisticated end of complex learning (Stages 4 to 6 in HR Maturity – see Chapter 7, Figure 7.2) the HR Professional educates the executive, and eventually everyone else, about the crucial differences between single and double loop learning.[6]

This revelation will fundamentally change the management style of the organization into one where silos disappear and trust begins to blossom. No one jumps to conclusions in a learning organization because, at this level of complexity, they know that wicked, systemic, organizational problems are immune to simplistic solutions. At this level of sophistication blame cultures become redundant; simply because everyone acknowledges they are all part, collectively, of one system.

This is an extremely demanding syllabus and only HR Professionals with the right blend of intellect and pragmatism will be able to cope. There is an online, introductory, personal development programme - 'The Consummate Professional Series'[7] designed for this role but do not expect to find a ready-made 'product' or 'magic pill'. All it will do is to make you think more clearly, more effectively. Once you have thought everything through you can then use whatever tools you find useful but you might find you do not need any other tools. A conventional HR director might also conclude that they do not need many of their existing policies or practices either. If you are wondering why the series is not called the Consummate 'HR' Professional that is because it is not an HR programme at all; it is a Professional leadership and general management development programme. HR Professionals must demonstrate strategic leadership as much, if not more, than their CEO.

Step 5. Lead on strategy – don't follow

We have accused HR and L&D of committing many sins but the most mortal of these is their failure to link what they do to strategic priorities. This is a well-recognized problem within HR circles. SHRM's choice of cost-per-hire (CPH) for its first international standard is ample proof of this point. Whether intentional or not, it has sent a clear signal that HR is primarily concerned with administrative detail and bureaucracy. HR seems more bothered about cost than value. If CPH was meant to herald a new dawn for HR standards then SHRM has set its own horizons very low. Their first HR standard should have been a standard for gauging the quality of HR strategy: the only logical place to start in standards is from the highest point.

So why did SHRM not start with HR strategy? Simply because it does not understand HR strategy. Their CPH 'standard' is a symptom, an underlying indicator, of the illogicality of poor organizational measurement and when a strategist spots such symptoms they search for other manifestations of the same disease. These can be found all over HR and L&D. L&D Professionals will stamp out meaningless measures such as training days per employee. 'Training days' is neither a measure of the cost of training nor the value of learning. If the American Society for Training and Development (ASTD) understood this it would have changed its name to the 'American Society for Learning' and already be teaching its professional members accordingly.

This is why the complete strategic framework in Figure 8.1 is incomplete without Professional HR. No one can pretend to be running an organization to

FIGURE 8.1 The total, holistic, strategic framework

maximize value, of the shareholder or societal variety, unless the totality of the people aspects of the framework are being Professionally managed.

There is absolutely nothing new in this framework, it is the standard, generic version and can be used as a gauge for assessing how well any organization is designed. One important modification though is the reference to a value statement instead of a typical mission statement. Mission statements and value statements already exist but the latter tend only to refer to values as beliefs. The clear purpose of the value statement in Figure 8.1 is to make beliefs and dollar value synonymous.

The value statement of a bank should be clear. Its profits should only be maximized by being based on a clear set of societal (ethical) values. In the case of Barclays bank there has been a serious mismatch between traders, who think a global bank can get away with manipulating LIBOR, and the need to maintain the bank's integrity. Values should be clear and the behaviour of the senior team should reflect those values. That is why the Chairman and CEO of Barclays had to resign, irrespective of profit performance and whether they had sanctioned illegality. When poor organizational values at the top stink everyone starts to give off a bad smell. Conversely, where a CEO's behaviour represents the very best of mankind the workforce is more likely to follow in the same spirit. This is not new either. The intention here is not further insight or being more 'savvy' but the practicalities of solving a very old and common problem. The HR Professional will always encourage 'honest dealing' and do everything within their power to design the organization accordingly, not because it is a nice idea but because there is growing evidence that dishonest dealing is not going to be the best value option in the future. We just need to make that the normal, working hypothesis.

Step 6. Always start with a causal hypothesis

We have already covered much of the debate around correlation and causation but the academic discipline of statistical significance is still valued by the HR Professional who will happily borrow whatever devices they believe to be valuable. One such device is called Null Hypothesis Significance Testing (NHST), which requires the construction of both positive and null (zero), alternative hypotheses. This is primarily an academic concept and is still hotly debated in academic circles but that does not mean the tasty kernel of the idea cannot be adapted to help resolve a particularly tricky, practical problem. It offers a good opportunity for the academic and practitioner to join forces in the cause of evidence-based practice.

The practical 'problem' is trying to 'prove' a negative. Proving that something does not exist, or does not work, is almost impossible. If you believe in a god that is your faith (assuming you cannot prove your god exists) and no one is ever likely to be able to prove that your god does not exist. Hence we often agree to differ on such matters when it only affects our personal lives. We do not have that luxury when we work in an organization: alternatives have to be considered and choices made. The new HR Professional knows they have to chip away, tirelessly, at the resistance of those who have faith in false gods. How do you prove to someone that attendance on a 'leadership' programme is a waste of time and money when they have just told you how much they *enjoyed* it? Pointing out to them that they were not there to *enjoy* themselves is not going to win them over and telling them they are being unprofessional will not help either. NHST has an elegant answer to this conundrum and it has the added bonus of being academically blessed. So how does it work?

If academic researchers want to determine whether 'leadership development' has any impact on performance they first have to construct two hypotheses:

- Hypothesis 1 – Null – 'There is no relationship between leadership development and performance'.
- Hypothesis 2 – Alternative – 'There is a positive (or negative) relationship between leadership development and performance'.

Let us now assume that many different researchers have started researching many different leadership programmes to test these two hypotheses. Let us further assume that there is pleasing evidence to support the alternative hypothesis (2) with a positive correlation. Meanwhile, however, other studies support the null hypothesis (1) with no statistically significant relationship being found between leadership programmes and business performance; essentially showing zero impact. Now let us consider how a non-evidence-based, head of L&D would approach this situation compared to a new, evidence-based, Professional head of L&D.

The non-evidence-based head, by definition, does not care about evidence. If they use any 'evidence' at all it will only be the variety that supports their own practice: they will gather happy sheets from happy executives. They will also be 'savvy' enough to know that 'null' hypothesis research might put them out of a job. Whereas the new, evidence-based, Professional, head of L&D will visit the university library to read this research and try to make sense of the apparent contradictions. They will not arrive with any preconceived ideas, other than those based on their own experience, and will be willing to entertain the possibility of forming an entirely new hypothesis that fits their own context and avoids a 'null' result. They take greater care in developing leadership and will certainly not just be sending any more senior managers on leadership courses offered by non-evidence-based providers.

If they wanted to convince a non-evidence-based colleague to change their own thinking (following Step 2 above) they might ask them 'So which hypothesis are you following?' This seemingly innocuous question forces the non-evidence-based L&D practitioner to countenance the possibility that their practice will have zero impact. So they have to reply in the positive, 'Hypothesis 2', at which point the L&D Professional comes back with a supplementary question: 'So how do you tell the difference between Hypothesis 1 and Hypothesis 2 leadership programmes?' In doing so the apparent obstacle of having to 'prove a negative' is immediately avoided by automatically shifting the focus to the evidence that might support their Hypothesis 2. Happy sheets do not count.

This simple device, without any detailed academic research being required, should help us to predict, with some confidence, that non-evidence-based, unprofessional, leadership 'experts' are probably going to be much rarer in the future. By lowering the probability of ineffective practice we raise the probability of developing better leadership as a direct result of evidence-based thinking. The evidence-based, academic theorists and evidence-based practitioners are at last working in harmony to real practical effect. The HR Professional will then go even further in asking the non-evidence-based to spell out their causal hypothesis (see Step 4). You can practice this yourself by asking what is the causative hypothesis that lies behind any popular HR practice. Instead of leadership why not 360 degree feedback and while you are pondering that one you might want to consider whether the 180 degree or 540 degree varieties of the same concept have to subscribe to the same or different hypotheses? As you start to formulate a hypothesis you realize that it has to be based on theory as much as evidence. If something does not work in theory it cannot work in practice. So what is the theory of human-to-human feedback? For example, is honesty an essential ingredient of the theory of human communication and feedback?

On 4 July 2012, CERN scientists finally announced that they had found the elusive Higgs Boson particle. The original theory that eventually led to this discovery goes back to the beginnings of particle physics but it was Peter Higgs, in 1964, who postulated the theory that his eponymous particle existed. This theory encouraged CERN physicists to build the LHC (Large Hadron Collider) at a cost of about \$10 billion.[8] At this stage, we still do not know with absolute certainty that the Higgs Boson really does exist. So theories and hypotheses can easily run ahead of themselves, incurring huge costs in the process, without any immediate payback.

Nevertheless, CERN scientists now at least have some evidence pointing in the same direction as Higgs theory and that offers a much higher degree of confidence that quantum theory is still on the right track.

HR Professionals are in exactly the same position. They definitely want a sound theory to work to but they also want to predict, with a very high degree of probability, sound practice. So they want to know if there is a theory that says receiving feedback from everyone is good for you and the business. If they are being pressurized to copy what every other HR department is doing (see the SHRM member's own evidence in Chapter 3) then they will ask whoever is putting them under duress to explain their own hypothesis on 360 degree feedback. To help test any hypothesis they will apply it to an imaginary manager, somewhere, whose results come at a cost. This cost could either be the toll it takes on their team or a negative impact on other departments in the organization. For example, a high pressure sales manager leaves other problems in their wake, in terms of extra delivery costs, after sales service arrangements, unsupportable customer expectations and contractual disputes. This sounds like a perfect candidate for 360 degree feedback from everyone concerned.

At this level the hypothesis sounds valid and will particularly appeal to anyone in the sales team who wants to exact revenge on their domineering boss; especially if they know that their part of the 360 degree feedback process will be anonymous. It would have to be pointed out to them, of course, that revenge is not really the purpose of the exercise, even if it is the most cathartic, therapeutic and enjoyable aspect of it. So, having thus described the 360 degree process, are we now more tempted, or less likely, to give it a try? This might still not deter the most ardent, copycat HR director so a few other ground rules need to be established. Number one on that list is a definition of the problem that 360 degree feedback is supposedly designed to solve?

If we look at the entire sales process, from end to end, from the original sale to a satisfied customer who has paid the bill, what value does feedback add? Where, specifically, will 360 degree feedback add any value, how much value will it add and who is going to have to add that value? If you ever receive sensible answers to all of these questions you might at least try 360 degree feedback, confident that everyone's focus will be on value and not vengeance. Without this value discipline it could be a waste of time and only end in acrimony, especially if the sales manager improves his behaviour but achieves lower sales. This same discipline, of thinking through how an intervention applies to one individual, will provide the basis for every causal hypothesis the HR Professional is ever likely to need. However, now we are going to broaden out our concept of value to work for the whole system.

Step 7. Produce a whole system, value hypothesis

To do that we need to formulate a whole system hypothesis. Whole system hypotheses look at all of the underlying, systemic causes. In the scenario outlined above there are already many additional facets that should have been considered:

- Are senior management setting strategic objectives that turn ordinary sales managers into domineering managers?
- Is senior management tacitly approving such 'bad' behaviour?
- What culture already exists? If you do not like how your colleagues are working, can you legitimately raise the issue in a forum designed for that purpose? Or do you need to find a different employer, with a different culture?
- To what extent are people encouraged to voice their views without fear of reprisal or retribution?
- Is there a culture of genuine cooperation here or is it every man for himself (or indeed every woman)?
- To what extent does the system reward and encourage selfish or narrow interests?
- How mature is the organization in developing the best processes (the complete end-to-end process) and does the organization's structure facilitate or hinder cross-functional collaboration?
- To what extent can the organization admit to itself that it has a fundamental problem with honest feedback?

Against the weight of these valid questions any decision to use the 'treatment' we call 360 degree feedback is likely to have as much impact as inoculating a very large elephant with a tiny syringe. Matters are made even worse by not knowing exactly where to stick the needle. Exactly the same challenging thought process can be applied to a whole list of conventional HR activities that are almost regarded as 'givens' without any clear Hypothesis 2 or any supporting evidence. They include policies on:

- Ageism.
- Competence frameworks.
- Diversity.
- Engagement.
- Leadership development.
- Performance management.
- Succession planning.
- Talent management.

All of these topics should be relevant, and probably had some theoretical justification originally, but if you try to trace a reliable source you might find that correlative research has undermined any validity they might once have had.

Take succession planning as another example; do we need a theory to plan succession? Well, you could have no theory, and no planning, and instead just appoint or recruit people as and when vacancies arise. The theory the HR Professional is seeking is not one about filling vacancies, per se, but one that predicts a higher probability of filling the right vacancies with the right people who then go on to create as much value as possible. Filling vacancies is an administrative matter; strategic succession planning is another action entirely. That sounds like a no-brainer, doesn't it? Who would question that? Well maybe the senior executive who has just moved abroad, as part of a planned career transfer, only to find that a much better job has just arisen back at his old office after somebody else left unexpectedly. We should never assume that a policy is good; we should always check its progress against its original hypothesis. That means we have to measure 'successful career transfers' and that necessitates a theory on how to measure them.

The other consideration of the HR Professional is the principle that all human beings are unique; so one-size-fits-all policies are not likely to be the most effective. They would go further in doing everything they can to ensure that every individual is respected for their individuality and managed accordingly. If the practice of 360° feedback is to have any validity it not only has to work for the individual receiving the feedback but those giving it as well. You might remember from Chapter 1 that we used the engineering profession as our comparator for developing technical specialists into professional managers. In keeping with that choice it is interesting to see that 360 degree feedback has been introduced into the education of engineering students[9] in a paper entitled 'Implementation of a 360 degree feedback assessment process for the development of the leadership competence of senior engineering students.' The abstract for this academic paper remarks that:

> Over the last decade, 360 degree feedback has been widely used in leadership development practices. This paper describes the implementation of the 360 degree feedback process into the Project Management in Practice course. Within the scope of this implementation, a 'Leadership Competency Questionnaire' was designed and applied as an online tool. The effectiveness of the 360 degree process was evaluated in terms of obtaining students' reactions and perspectives about its implementation.

Note the use of the term 'leadership competence', which required the creation of a 'Leadership Competency Dictionary' and also note that 'evaluated' does not refer to any value, only 'students' reactions'. The HR Professional has a right to ask whether any of these engineering students will make better managers in the future? One feature of the competency model used in the article is 'Integrity' and the paper raises the issue of 'compassionate confrontation' to challenge those who do not have integrity. Good luck to them. We all want to see integrity in our managers and leaders but organizational life has a habit of squeezing the life out of those with integrity; unless there is a conscious and concerted effort made to design in, and reinforce, integrity at every juncture. 'Outright confrontation' might not sound as nice as 'compassionate confrontation' but it might be a more appropriate and effective competency in dealing with the world's current crisis of integrity. An HR Professional would certainly not beat about the bush in trying to root out those engineers without integrity.

Step 8. Start to offer a higher degree of management certainty

In principle, HR Professionals would want to construct hypotheses for every single HR policy and practice but, as with all principles, it is unrealistic to stick to them 100 per cent. They will probably have to introduce this discipline of hypothesis formulation into an organization that still has a perception of HR as 'pink and fluffy', intangible and unmeasurable. So the HR Professional will not be spending all their time formulating hypotheses; they will install a simple system that demands a working hypothesis from each manager to support their own decision-making. This system is easy to audit by walking up to a manager and asking them what hypothesis they are working to at any particular time. How about the manager who has just taken their team on an 'awayday'? What hypothesis lay behind that activity? Any blank looks should be taken as failing this simple test. Clear-headed answers pass with flying colours.

We are finally entering the realm of management certainty based on observable management standards. This is not proof of anything, and we are not seeking absolute proof, but managers who have actually thought through what they are doing, in terms of a value hypothesis, are more likely to be creating value. The alternative, null, hypothesis is the 'hammer hypothesis'; just keep striking everything with the same hammer until you hit the right spot. Keep going on team-building courses and awaydays and hope that something rubs off on the team. Of course, hitting people with the same blunt instrument is bound to cause head trauma eventually.

The 'hammer hypothesis' produces unnatural management methods that deprive us of our need for clarity and certainty. CEOs love certainty and cannot get enough of it, yet they will also sanction activities with uncertain outcomes. We might all enjoy an awayday but if we have genuine and deep-seated concerns about the way the team is working, and they are not resolved at the end of the day, we will be anxious about our own future. Certainty is one of the greatest human motivators; we like the feeling of having achieved something at the end of a hard day's work. Management uncertainty is just bad management. The professional healthcare worker works in healthcare because they care; so they want to know if the patient is doing well. That is as much in their own interest as it is in the patient's. They realize they can only play a part in the end-to-end treatment process but are dedicated to accomplishing what they can. If managers suggest any activity that does not contribute to that process they have every right to regard it as poor management practice.

Professional HR is about disavowing senior managers of the notion that managing people is in some way different to managing any other resource. Paradoxically, regarding people as a resource, as human capital, should make management more human, not less. People management is never going to be as predictable or as certain as building a brick wall but it should be just as solid. Human capital management is not more jargon, it is moving people management up the agenda and further away from being a hit-or-miss affair. It can be managed much more strategically and humanely, with a greater degree of predictability and certainty. This does require a much greater degree of measurement though because you cannot manage anything that you do not measure. This is why the HR Professional will only install a measurement system to measure those things that are clearly valuable.

As long as an organization's board of directors is confident that it has a consummate HR Professional running the HR show it will have less need to be constantly checking, questioning or micro-managing HR policies. This does not mean it will resort to rubber stamping HR policies though. The most mature, Professional board members are evidence-based and will be critical of anything that does not appear to have been tested against evidence-based criteria. 'Diversity' is a meaningless concept when used in a non-evidence based context. Whatever the organization's head of diversity is doing they have to reassure the board that its legal obligations (Box 1), shareholder needs (Box 2), and societal responsibilities (Boxes 1 and 2) are being effectively met. Professional board members will not sanction Box 3, diversity activity that serves only the purpose of public relations.

This level of Professional certainty and confidence should filter down throughout the entire organization. If the overall system is designed according to the principles of closed loop feedback systems individual employees only need to know:

- what the desired outcomes of their own actions and behaviour are (e.g. patient satisfaction at the lowest cost, treating all colleagues and patients with respect); and
- the crucial importance of honest feedback to the organization if they cannot achieve those outcomes (e.g. cost saving opportunities are not being realized, some colleagues are treating patients badly).

Honest feedback is not just a process it is the bedrock of a culture that encourages all feedback; both the positive and the negative. Above everything else, the consummate HR Professional knows that following these two simple rules, every day, will help to build a very solid and sustainable learning organization that is more valuable and, from a risk management perspective, less likely to experience the sort of shocks currently jolting many banks and other large organizations.

As an aside, have you noticed how difficult it is to explain all of this in simple enough language for anyone to see the sense in it? Anyone outside of HR and L&D hearing such terms as the 'learning organization', 'whole system thinking' and 'psychological contracts' is likely to regard it as jargon. Organizational neurosurgery on this grand scale needs neuro-HR Professionals of the highest calibre who can explain themselves in simple language. Level 4 neurosurgeons are the ones that not only perform fantastic surgery but can put their patient's mind at ease at the same time.

Step 9. Develop human value systems

The concepts of 'certainty' and 'systems thinking' cannot be separated; effective management systems are designed to bolster management certainty. The most effective management systems are those designed to cope with whatever feckless and fallible human beings can throw at them because all system failure can potentially be brought back to a human cause. It is the human system that ultimately dictates how effective mechanical or accounting systems can be. If a human being wants to ignore the traffic lights, or the auditors report, they will do so. When the human element fails the whole system fails. If only the banks and regulatory authorities had made sure they had human systems in place. If only they had employed proper HR Professionals at the highest levels.

Conventional HR has always fallen badly at the system hurdle by focusing only on the process; being concerned with activity, not outcome. The majority of conventional HR practices have no clear connection with value at all. Job evaluation is usually very costly to the salary bill so why is it so ubiquitous? Because it enables the administration of pay and grading, not because it is the best way to manage people. The need for bureaucracy has trumped the need for performance from every single individual. Similarly, why do organizations try to measure training days or numbers attending courses? Because it gives an impression that someone is managing the training budget, not because it will reveal anything about the value of learning. Measuring the number of performance reviews each year is measuring the process of review not the performance outcome.

The real problem with focusing on the process, rather than the system and the outcome, is that it encourages process-only behaviour. Another, more common, expression to describe this tendency is 'playing the system'. Job evaluation becomes a game where managers try to work the system to get more for their people, not because they are better but because it makes the manager's life easier. Or they offer staff more training days as a pat on the back, not because they need it to perform better. The HR Professional does not become too judgemental about these natural, human, personal survival strategies from intelligent people, they expect it to happen in poorly designed human systems and know the only answer is not admonishment – 'the culture needs to change!' – but more meaningful measurement to encourage more meaningful and mutually beneficial behaviour.

Apparently Einstein was supposed to have said 'Not everything that counts can be measured and not everything that can be measured counts'. Who would be prepared to say that a genius like Einstein might have got it wrong? The HR Professional would. Everything in management can be measured and, what is more, it already is. Take the most 'immeasurable' thing you can think of. How about your relationship with one of your colleagues or someone outside your department? Or how much care you think one of your colleagues has for customers or patients? Or maybe even something as obscure as how well your boss listens or what their mood is on a particular day? How would you measure all of these? Admittedly, none of this shows up as specific measures in the company accounts, yet, but the whole system thinker would point out that their effects are nonetheless being felt in a very tangible way, somewhere in the system.

Consider your last week at work and try measuring how many days were 'good', 'bad' or just 'OK'? Don't spend too long thinking about this because you have already done your calculation. You have already told your spouse/partner/colleagues that you had a good or bad day. But then they already knew what day you had, before you told them, because they know you so well and had already read the signs and the body language. Either Einstein got this one badly wrong, which is highly unlikely, or his wicked sense of humour knew that many would misread what he was saying. There is not another species on the Earth whose innate capabilities come anywhere close to the sophistication of human beings in terms of measurement. We measure absolutely everything we do, and everyone we meet, and often those measurements are instantaneous; they have to be. We only survived as a species by developing this sixth sense, a combination of all our other senses, to enable us to instantaneously gauge what is in front of us. If our ancestors' ability to measure risk had been slower than any of our predators' ability to strike we would not be here; we would have been easy meat.

So you have already made a mental note of which days last week were good or bad but you have not recorded your assessment anywhere or been asked, by an external observer, to make your thoughts and judgements more explicit or systematically put them into any order. If you want to have some fun by annoying whoever runs your annual engagement survey then suggest to them that they should incorporate this next year. Everyone should be asked to give each day at work a score from 1 to 10 (being the best day) and then tell them to collect and collate that data for everyone to produce a bell curve – see Chapter 1, Figure 1.2. It might be an interesting exercise but we already know what the outcome will be because probability has already predicted it for us. Over a year of, say, 250 working days, most of your days will fall into the 4 to 7 range and a few will be particularly bad (3 or less) and a few particularly good (8 or above). This just makes the common, subjective view of work, 'oh, I have good days and bad days', a bit more scientific.

Einstein was right, of course, in suggesting that some things count for more than others and we can easily interpret that as some things have a higher value than others. So did your own scores for each working day relate at all to how efficient or productive you were? Did you achieve greater sales figures on the days that were great? Or was it the other way around? Did the great sales figures make those particular days feel much better? If you look back in more detail, were the best days a mix of just more footfall in the store, the fact that the sun came out or the beer you had with a colleague after work? That causation thing keeps popping up all the time doesn't it, yet there is an extremely serious and practical point here. It is even more than that; this is a fundamental question of management philosophy. Should companies be interested in how employees feel on any particular day or should they only be concerned with what they produce?

The philosophy that has been espoused throughout this book, from the very outset, is that the best value strategy is likely to be one where how we feel about work matches how we perform at work. If we think smoking is a nasty, horrible habit (and are afraid our kids might smoke) would we give our all if the only job we could find was in a tobacco company? Maybe keen smokers and irresponsible parents would be the most appropriate selection pool for a tobacco company? Or possibly those who just feel very strongly about an individual's right to choose? If we get this philosophy wrong, if the logic becomes twisted then we are all in trouble. Imagine if the people who work in healthcare or drugs companies are primarily motivated by money and not by patient care, should we be at all surprised if they try and sell us drugs that we don't need?

The Economist ran a 2012 story under the heading 'Mis-selling drugs. The Settlers'[10] and reported that GlaxoSmithKline had just agreed a $3 billion payment to settle 'a pile of criminal and civil charges … (in the) largest health-fraud settlement in American history' for 'promoting drugs as treatments for conditions for which they were not approved'. An HR Professional would immediately read this as GSK having managed to create for itself a perverse, *health-fraud value system*. Law abiding citizens do not generally break the law unless they are coerced or believe their behaviour is being sanctioned by their employer. So this GSK system must have been built in a way that encouraged its employees to behave in this way. It may even have factored in a nominal ROI calculation, a cost benefit analysis that showed a net return in profit after the cost of the fine had been accounted for. Otherwise why would GSK have sanctioned such behaviour? So here is evidence of an ethical drugs company that has managed to transform itself into an unethical drugs company. This is quite a feat of human engineering when one considers how many of their researchers probably gave their all to GSK because they thought it was supposed to be relieving pain and saving lives. Presumably some of them even believed GSK's 2012 Responsibility Report[11] when it declared its 'behaviour' as 'open and honest in everything we do'. Some might even have thanked the Queen of England for knighting CEO, now Sir, Andrew Witty, and still believe him when he says on the same page:

> At GSK, we firmly believe that operating in a responsible and ethical way is essential for the success of our business. We have come a long way but recognise that there is much more we can do and we will continue to challenge ourselves.

We should all be very afraid when an industry that should be a beacon of integrity has a human system in place that contains no integrity. Once an evil human system is in place it is the worst type of cancer. This fraud was not down to a single rogue executive; if it were then the guilty executive should be punished, rather than the whole organization and its shareholders. Maybe the shareholders should lobby to appoint an HR Professional to the board of GSK and get them to replace the entire HR department who must have been as much a part of the whole health-fraud system as anyone else? They might even have helped to design and administer the reward system, installed the performance management system that encouraged this bad behaviour and even trained the perpetrators how to perpetrate the fraud.

The Economist helpfully includes a chart in the same article showing other drug companies that have also been fined for 'promoting drugs as treatments for conditions for which they were not approved'. The list includes Abbott Laboratories, Merck, AstraZeneca, Pfizer and Eli Lilley. It looks like this management cancer is spreading; it is not just banking that needs better governance. We do not need to dream up measures for GSK's own intangibles of 'openness', 'honesty', 'trust' or 'governance'; we have all the evidence we need in the form of a cost to the business of at least $3 billion, a similar cost to the health service and the cost of any subsequent litigation from patients, assuming they are still with us. It is a pity that the only part of this whole sorry affair that will show up on GSK's conventional profit and loss account is the net profit. The real value, or should we say negative societal value, will not appear.

The HR Professional is not dissuaded from measurement by Einstein's genius. Anyone who understands the sophistication of the innate human measurement system, but puts it to good use, has to be one of the best measurement experts you will ever find. They do not get sidetracked, make false distinctions between hard and soft measures or subscribe to the notion of intangibles. Dishonesty and a lack of integrity can always be measured in very tangible terms. There are employees at GSK, as we speak, who did not benefit directly from GSK's mis-selling but either chose to say nothing or were too afraid to do anything to stop it. If GSK had encouraged its employees, in its annual engagement survey, to measure the integrity of their bosses on a 1 to 10 scale, and protected them from any reprisals, maybe this shocking incident would never have happened?

Is it too idealistic to hope that one day a normal board of directors, and their Executive committee, will be populated by Professional leaders and mangers who subscribe to a total value philosophy that requires the installation of a total measurement system that is also a total performance system and a total learning system? All of these can be physically observed, checked and audited: there is nothing intangible about any of them once simple measures are introduced. Shareholders, even those with purely selfish interests, should be sending in HR Professionals to install such systems. If necessary, this should be over the heads of the executive committee, because they are obviously either unwilling or unable to do it themselves. That is why Step 10 is required to close the loop on the whole human capital management system.

Step 10. Close the loop with a detailed report on human capital management

If all of this is new to you it should not be. It has been going on since the pyramids were built and probably before. All of the organizational issues outlined above have been well recognized for many years; long before the problems of 2008. For evidence just look at the laws and regulations put in place to mitigate the worst effects of human behaviour. Yet the bad behaviour continues in spite of the legal restraints, so a more recent suggestion was to ask companies to report on how well they are doing in terms of their corporate social responsibilities. As with many CSR reports, GSK's seems to bear no relation to the reality on the ground. What executives say and what they do are obviously two very different things. In GSK's case they have already dropped the 'corporate' and the 'social' and the mis-selling fine shows they finally got around to dropping the 'responsibility' as well. What they cannot drop is accountability. Every one of the pharmaceutical companies on *The Economist's* list seems to be saying – 'we cannot perform well enough within the rules so we have to break them'. This is a complete and utter abdication of board accountability and the signal it sends to the executive committee is that they do not have to be responsible for what their people are doing in their name.

What has been absent so far is any universal framework for dealing with this universal problem. If you just leave companies to manage people unProfessionally they will behave badly. It is crying out for Professional people management of the highest order, not because that is idealistic but because it is imperative. This is why human capital reporting is back on the agenda after a few false starts. Human capital is not just another word for 'employees', as SHRM's Investor metrics standard would have us believe. HCM is a different management philosophy, and very different reporting paradigm, that places human value and risk at the very heart of corporate governance. Such a report is of great interest to all citizens as taxpayers and as employees, to governments, to shareholders and investment analysts. In fact the only people who do not have a vested interest in producing an HCM report are precisely those executives who we do not want running our companies.

The need for a human capital report is not just about risk management though; it should have a much more positive outlook and this was addressed in HR Strategy along with a sample of what such a report might look like (Kearns, 2010, pp. 189–199). This report was predicated not only on the CEO embracing the concept and practice of human capital management but actually staying in the driving seat for all people management matters: that recommendation is echoed here. So if the first version was a very basic sample of a human capital management report what other indicators might now need to be added?

- A specific individual tasked with the role of Professional HR.
- A wide ranging education and development programme for all board directors, executives and managers to become fully conversant with the requirements imposed by higher, Professional HR standards.
- Active support for the development of better, international, Professional HR standards and moves towards a GHRC.
- A complete re-statement of the organization's value statement in terms of how it reconciles its obligations to shareholders with its obligations to societal value.
- Re-thinking and re-framing its corporate social responsibility strategy to be entirely consistent with its value statement.
- A strategic plan that includes many more people related measures and indicators.

- Clear accountabilities and responsibilities assigned to named board directors and executives to cover every aspect of corporate governance, including human governance.
- Those measures and indicators to be included in monthly management reporting procedures so that any transgression can be picked up very early.
- A conscious move to EBM, with a particular emphasis on evidence-based people management. This would have to be auditable with clear evidence of progress on the ground.

Surely this is where any civilized version of capitalism should be heading anyway?

9

WE NEED MORE PROFESSIONAL MANAGEMENT FOR A MORE CIVILIZED WORLD

Clearing out the HR stables

We have presented plenty of evidence of corporate greed and poor governance and those of us who work in HR should be asking ourselves what have we been doing about this? The answer appears to be nothing but then HR was never designed for that purpose. So HR now has a decision to make; does it want to rise to these challenges or not? The most important role required from HR today is human governance and if it does not want to become involved then it needs to get out of the way. A significant proportion of HR's day-to-day, personnel administration will disappear and the configuration of HR, and the emphasis in its workload, will naturally shift. As HR's professionalism moves onto a higher plane, the capabilities of the vast majority of existing HR and L&D people will slip backwards in relative terms, when judged against evidence-based standards, as shown in Figure 9.1 below. The professionalism of the present HR and L&D population is shown as the dotted line on the right. When

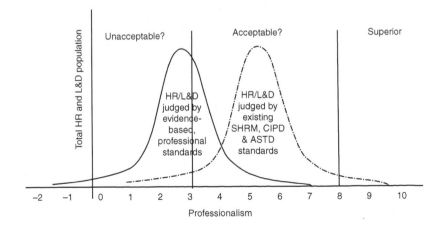

FIGURE 9.1 The backward shift in HR's performance curve

tougher criteria are introduced this whole curve shifts to the new curve on the left: what was acceptable yesterday will no longer be acceptable today. Spending money without any corresponding evidence of benefits will rightly be seen as a waste of resources.

This is what must have happened to the world of medicine in the mid-nineteenth century: it was probably a difficult and painful transition with plenty of practitioners in denial. Even the best practitioners of today, those who naturally collect some evidence of what they do, will only reach a score of maybe 6 or 7 because evidence-based HR is not an occasional reference to evidence, it is a conscious decision to move up several gears to a different mindset.

This shift can only lead us to two conclusions:

- The worst of the existing population (-2 and -1) have to be removed from the field because, by the higher standards demanded of evidence-based Professionalism, they will have slipped into negative territory; actually doing harm.
- To replace the old bell curve it will be necessary to repopulate the profession with many new, evidence-based Professionals. It is unlikely that many of these will come from within the present ranks.

This might sound rather drastic and there may be an assumption that it is HR administrators who will bear the brunt of any job losses, but that is not the case. The real crisis in HR is not at an administrative level, it is within the ranks of the most senior postholders. They are in a position to make a significant difference and are the ones who have the most resources at their disposal. If they are not producing evidence of their value and demonstrating they can use resources wisely then this will be the area for the greatest fallout. Here are just a few of the most public examples to illustrate what we mean.

In October 2008 London Mayor Boris Johnson launched an enquiry into racism in the London Metropolitan police force (the 'Met'). *Personnel Today*[1] reported the Black Police Association as saying that the Met had:

> made the working environment for its existing black staff a hostile atmosphere where racism is allowed to spread and those who challenge it are either suspended, told to shut up or subtly held back in relation to career development.

Six months later, in April 2009, *HR Magazine*[2] interviewed the then HR Director at the Met, Martin Tiplady, and opened its piece with the words:

> HRD Martin Tiplady rebuffs accusations that the Met has failed to tackle deep-rooted racism. Great strides have already been made, he says, and workforce diversity is his priority.

Two years later, in April 2011, *HR Magazine* reported[3] that Tiplady, 'currently number four on *HR magazine's* ranking of Most Influential HR practitioners', had decided he was retiring from the Met.

The following year, in May 2012, a new headline read[4] 'Boris Johnson launches Met anti-racism drive. Racism within the Metropolitan police force will not be tolerated, says London mayor.'

Is this what the terms 'vicious circle' and 'cycle of fury' really mean? The Met's HR director might not have made any difference but what about his boss, the Commissioner of the Met? Is he also accountable for failing to deal with racism? Racism is a really nasty and difficult issue to deal with and if conventional HR is not working then what would the Met have to lose by appointing a Level 4, evidence-based HR Professional? If nothing else, they would help by simply defining and measuring the problem. Racism is committed by racist individuals and the problem can only be resolved by re-educating or removing that racist element: there should be no ambiguity on this.

Sometimes HR's ambiguity will perpetuate, rather than resolve, such problems but on occasions HR just completely contradicts itself. Consider these comments from the ex-HR Director of Royal Bank of Scotland, Neil Roden. Just after he left RBS in January 2011 Roden was interviewed by *HR Magazine*[5] and said of his time there:

> There's a debate here about what HR can reasonably be held accountable for. People think HR runs companies. I say, stop getting carried away; HR is a support function, no more or less important than sales or IT. HR critics are way ahead of themselves; they need to get back inside their box.

Compare that comment to what he told PwC's *Hourglass* magazine (Issue 9, 2008) after RBS's disastrous takeover of ABN AMRO and just before RBS collapsed into UK taxpayers' hands:

> I was personally involved in the group executive committee on whether or not we should proceed with ABN Amro.[6]

So was HR at RBS administrative or strategic? Roden subsequently joined PwC to take on, according to the PwC spokesman, ' ... a wide ranging role advising clients on all aspects of HR ... focusing on the role of the HR function, how to optimize its activity and the critical impact of people on business performance.' So how good will the quality of Roden's advice be for PwC clients? The evidence of RBS's fate does not augur well.

Our third example comes from the world of learning and the failed BBC leadership programme. The architect of that programme, the BBC's head of learning, Nigel Paine, was advertised as a speaker at a 'Learning Live'[7] conference in 2012, where his personal biography included the following:

> Appointed in April 2002 to head up the BBC's Learning & Development operation where he built one of the most successful learning and development operations in the UK. This included an award winning leadership programme ...

Because there are no universally accredited standards in L&D it is quite possible that a leadership programme that was condemned by one independent body can be given an award by another. There will always be differences of professional opinion, even in the medical profession, but who is collating all of these conflicting and contradictory opinions and synthesising lessons learned into common standards? We all need a clear answer to a simple but challenging question – are these very senior practitioners doing a professional job or not? If they are, let us see the evidence. If they are not, is their behaviour serious enough to warrant being disbarred from practising? The medical profession has to make the same tough choices and we should all be very thankful that they have a strong, ultimate authority in their General Council.

Anyone seriously interested in raising professional standards will not see this naming of names as invidious and a GHRC could not work on a basis of anonymity. These individuals are not harmless, academics tucked away between dusty university shelves but practitioners supposedly at the top of their game. They are in the news because they choose to be in the news. All three stories only surfaced because of the protagonists' willingness to offer personal testimony to the media. So what impression does this leave in the minds of all of their fellow professionals who might have read these articles? Where is the professional institute's considered view of the evidence and what would their analysis conclude? We need a clear and objective answer.

HR can no longer be viewed as just an indifferent presence, beavering away in the administrative background. Racism affects the policing of London on a daily basis. RBS has gone bust. The BBC still needs better leadership. There is a real need for unquestionable, Professional standards in HR. A Profession cannot be a mix of good practice and bad practice, or effective and ineffective HR directors; it can only consist of properly accredited, evidence-based Professionals. If not, then PWC's clients, along with everyone else, will just have to keep their fingers crossed and hope for the best.

Everyone thinks they are a people expert

Any experienced HR professional will testify to the fact that one of the most annoying and frustrating aspects of their job is that many managers already think they are people experts: even the ones who have just called in HR to help them sort out their people problems. Self-irony is not usually evident in these 'experts'. Of course, some managers are naturally more perceptive, and can read people well, but that has absolutely nothing to do with Professional people management practised by proper Professionals. Even the most experienced and effective line managers will have a great deal to learn from a real Pro. Whether they are prepared to see it that way is just another hurdle for the HR Pro to overcome.

One really serious consequence of this assumed expertise is that it leads CEOs, who might not have much respect for HR people, to believe they can appoint anybody to do the top HR job. There are still numerous examples of senior operational, financial and legal executives being given responsibility for HR with literally no human resource management expertise or experience, whatsoever. In 2005 Siemens promoted a 62-year-old engineer to the top HR job; presumably because they thought he could do a better job than HR? For all we know he could prove to be the most effective HR director ever but what does his appointment say about the Siemens view of those who have spent their entire careers working in HR? In what other 'profession' would so little heed be paid to professionalism? Who would allow someone to act as a top lawyer, doctor or finance director without many years of relevant training and experience and the necessary qualifications? In fact, how many top lawyers, doctors or accountants can practise without the relevant documentation? At this point in our exposition of HR it is easy to see why it only has itself to blame. If HR were a true Profession, based on mandatory qualifications valued by the business community, it would never have been usurped in this way. This might be a tragedy for some dedicated HR people but it is more of a tragedy for the organizations that really need good HR, like the London Met, and the police officers and citizens on the rough end of its racism.

There is a much deeper, underlying issue at play here. Surely Siemens could not have expected its 'new' 62-year-old HR director to bring anything really valuable to the role? If he had always wanted to work in HR why had he left it so late? Had he always been a keen reader of HR books? If not, what was the thinking behind Siemens' decision? Let us consider two possible hypotheses:

- They were just putting this ageing engineer out to grass and they felt HR was the safest place for him. This is quite possible based on many similar instances.
- They perceive HR to be a purely administrative, support function and do not trust their HR department to deliver an efficient, operational service.

There are other, even less kind, interpretations that we could put on this decision but it is very difficult to think of a positive reason. Yet any true HR Professional, who has followed the history of Siemens over recent years, could easily argue that the one role they needed to fill with a proper Professional is this one. In December 2011 eight former executives from Siemens were charged by US authorities in connection with a $100 m (£64 m) foreign bribery scheme. It does not matter whether they are eventually found guilty or not, these executives should be beyond reproach and further reputational damage was being added to the previous damage done back in 2008 when 'Siemens agreed to pay $1.6bn to the US and German authorities to resolve charges of corrupt practices in connection with the case, and helped in the investigation of those charged.'[8] This is not just about eight executives; it is about the entire culture and system at Siemens.

Credit rating agencies and investment analysts have every right to downgrade their future forecasts for Siemens based on these allegations and fines. What is not so clear, in the absence of a really intelligent HR strategy at Siemens, is what they can do about the management cancer that has taken hold. How can Siemens convince the markets, and authorities, that it is in remission? Trust and reputations take years to build and only seconds to destroy. Can any organization perform the necessarily radical, self-surgery without bringing in someone from outside who is untainted and has no loyalty to colleagues who may have been led astray?

This is not an indictment of Siemens, per se; although they were chosen for having a particularly unenlightened view of HR. It is an indictment of general management around the world that probably thinks the odd bit of corruption in business is the norm and to be expected. That is probably the reality of having to deal with some countries that have the lowest standards of probity: even if your company is not corrupt someone else's will be and they will take the business off you. It is naïve to think otherwise but there is a world of difference, in governance and culture terms, in accepting corruption as a fact of life rather than formulating a longer term strategy of building a corruption-free reputation. Such a strategy would essentially have to be a corruption-free-people strategy.

None of this would surprise students of Machiavelli's *The Prince*. They would expect executives to behave badly at every turn unless there is proper governance in place. Machiavelli was a sixteenth-century genius who only had personal observation and the history books of the time to formulate his thesis. Yet his understanding of the essential nature of the way humanity works is as relevant today as it was then. If he were to write a belated second edition of *The Prince* he would not have to change any of the content or the advice, it can all be adapted to a modern context: better governance cannot happen without better governance of human capital. The only difference today is that history is written instantaneously on the web and many more of the dots of corruption and malpractice become joined up, much more quickly, in the minds of ordinary citizens and shareholders. These same citizens can also use the web to vent their anger and dissatisfaction and force politicians to listen and react more quickly. Let us not confuse 'reacting' with responding though.

The crash of 2008 and the many scandals in the business world, and the public sector, have given us all a sharp reminder that the standards of the 'old norm' were set far too low. When times were good no one bothered to check whether the underlying framework was solid and robust. When it eventually collapsed, new designers should have been appointed right away to build a better model but as there is no accredited, evidence-based, 'School of Professional Organization Design' there are no new designers ready to start work on this. In the short term the best we can hope for is that government ministers and CEOs care enough to renew any interest they might have in professional management.

The advent of the caring, sharing CEO

Have you ever laboured under the misapprehension that to 'get to the top' one has to accept a significant increase in one's personal level of responsibility? If so, in the light of unfolding events since 2008, has anything changed your view? It appears that we have many CEOs at the top of banking and pharmaceutical companies, among others, who might have big responsibilities but who do not seem to care at all about the consequences of their actions. On paper, the CEO has to accept full responsibility for the running of the organization but, in reality, they don't. Ex-RBS CEO Fred Goodwin still seems to believe he was not responsible for the collapse of the bank and Angelo Mozilo of Countrywide successfully defended his own actions in court. We often confuse responsibility with accountability. Fred Goodwin was held accountable but had to be forced to resign; he was not fired. So it is his mindset, and the collective mindset of the RBS board (chaired by the ex-CEO of AstraZeneca), that is of most interest to an HR Professional. A CEO who has no sense of personal responsibility for their decisions is unlikely to take any responsibility for the people in the organization.

Conversely, we might hypothesize that nice people, who really do care about other people, are afraid to take on the greater responsibility that comes with more senior roles precisely for that very reason, because they care too much. Their mindset is one where they take their responsibilities so seriously they really cannot countenance failing; they would find it difficult to live with themselves if there were any adverse consequences from their actions. If these two, apparently opposing views of the world contain any element of universal truth then it might be the basis for an interesting management theory. Appointing senior executives is a classic Catch-22, where the uncaring and irresponsible get to the top by dint of the fact that they do not care. Meanwhile, those who care so much for their fellow man rule themselves out because of the insufferable burden that would place on them. If this holds any water at all then it is time to ensure that an HR Professional, who fully accepts their responsibility to care for people, sits alongside the CEO to ensure that all decisions take this into account. This has nothing to do with nice people becoming HR Professionals; they will be as eagle-eyed as any other executive when it comes to profit and long term value. The only difference is that the HR Professional is ahead of the CEO in seeing how to reconcile profit and value with employee values. Fred Goodwin might still be at the helm of RBS today, and making the most of his own particular talents, if he had been counter-balanced by a Professional HR director with a particular talent for people management.

It is inconceivable that a modern day CEO should be allowed to run a large corporation without such expertise, advice and guidance when they are responsible for the livelihoods of thousands. This is especially true in businesses that have to play the long game. Take the airline manufacturing industry as a case in point. The two biggest manufacturers, Boeing and Airbus, are likely to face much greater competition from both China and India in the future so are these companies geared up to compete? We should also ask, as consumers of air travel, whether we want China and India to compete with them on Professional people management practices. Of course we do. We will all be better off if standards across global industries start to rise. They should all be putting in place open cultures, learning systems and flexible organization structures so that they will be providing us all with the best value possible. If they all remain at a lower Stage of HR Maturity; if their management is relatively amateurish; if they promote 62-year-old aircraft engineers to the top job in HR; that is not in anyone's interest. Perhaps we need to help CEOs understand what it will feel like to move from a state of 'amateurish' management to Professional management? A sporting analogy might help.

Rugby union used to be an amateur sport up until as recently as 1995, when it turned professional. Rugby players always had a very strong ethos of playing hard but fair; of knocking hell out of their opponents on the pitch but having a beer in the bar afterwards. Any keen rugby fan, who has followed the development of the game since the dawn of professionalism, will have noticed several significant differences between the amateur game and the professional era in terms of its character and culture. That list includes:

- the higher intensity of the game;
- the sheer pace of play;
- the greater levels of player fitness required;
- referees having to match the increasing professionalism of the players;
- the complete business model for rugby had to change, as did its governance and infrastructure;
- the traditional values of the game have been under constant pressure, especially the culture of sportsmanship, with greater temptation to cheat;
- in the UK, a salary cap was placed on clubs to prevent a few rich clubs dominating the league, while in France no cap was imposed, which means many players have been lured by French clubs.

The world of rugby is not totally analogous to organizational management but at least it highlights the dynamics of a changing market, changing values and the people dimension. These are all lessons for the CEO who wants to move away from the amateur game. Ever-increasing commercial pressures are usually transmitted down through every level of the organization. One tempting strategy is to tell the players 'do whatever it takes to win and we will reward you accordingly'. That usually leads to bad behaviour and militates against teamwork. An alternative strategy, the more mature version, aims to involve and empower; to harness the latent talent in every single person in the team, not just to tighten the pressure valve. Greater competition does not have to mean greater stress if it can be converted into a creative force for channelling everyone's best behaviour.

The more Boeing and Airbus put pressure on their people, to cope with more global competition, the more they will have to be sensitive to the people issues. Their fundamental business model is definitely going to have to change but so will the pace, intensity and fitness required to work in that environment. Their values will be sorely tested and there will be many temptations to cheat the system with bribery and corruption. Under such pressure CEOs can be tempted to reach for the instant release valve of executive 'compensation'. This is the one area that we have not looked at in any depth, so far.

In Pfeffer's *Harvard Business Review* column ('Management a Profession? Where's the Proof?', September 2011) he tells the tale of the remuneration consultant he met at a company where he is a non-executive director. He asked the consultant, whom one might have expected to be a professional expert in such matters, whether he was aware of research showing a poor relationship between executive reward and performance. The consultant, not to put too fine a point on it, paid little heed to Pfeffer's advice, thereby failing even the most basic, entry level test of professional respect and courtesy. However, the research evidence will not influence compensation practice unless we can influence, or control, the influencers. So what expectation will future Boeing and Airbus executives have regarding their performance and rewards? Will research evidence come into play from a proper, Professional, reward consultant? Will that consultant take into account that the world has shifted, that we live in a new paradigm? Executives should only be allowed to take on a contract, and the corresponding rewards, with their eyes wide open. They are likely to face challenges unknown to their predecessors and will have to accept much greater accountability and responsibility; lip service will not be acceptable. Their new world will be one in which the 'norm' has changed. So what is this 'New Norm' and how will it feel?

The New Norm

It might help you to get the picture if you consider how you would feel if your internet provider's system went down for more than a few hours. Years ago, when the internet was in its infancy, you would probably have been quite philosophical about it and put it down to the inevitable teething problems of new technology. Since then, not only have you come to expect a much smoother and undisrupted service but you have also become used to higher connection speeds and are much more dependent on the internet and email than you ever were before. You cannot imagine going back to a time before the internet; your expectations have already been transformed; there is just no going back. Start thinking of your old style of organization in the same way as the old postal service, with its 'snail mail', and you might get a sense of what this new super highway of Professionalism might have to offer.

The real beauty of Professional HR is the huge advantage that comes from managing people effectively. Once you turn them fully on they become self-propelling, like a jet engine, but with infinitely more applications. All it takes is a simple but radical shift in thinking in government policy, boardrooms and executive suites. Most CEOs will not understand this yet because they allowed themselves, for reasons known only to them, to be led by their present VP-HR without evidence of value. The few CEOs that might have some insight into the New Norm will probably have learned it from the few, exceptional organizations that really do try and get the best value from their people. If they cannot copy the best, maybe they can at least ensure that they do not make the same mistakes as the worst. There are plenty of examples in that category.

In July 2010, Aviva's group HR director wrote in *Personnel Today*[9] about the insurance giant's strategic move to a single, global brand and how 'employees were engaged in the changes'. Just over a year later, in November 2011, he was admitting to *Personnel Today*[10] that 'getting the HR teams in different locations to act as one "global HR function" has not been an easy task.' Only six months later again, in May 2012, the architect of Aviva's re-branding, CEO of five years Andrew Moss,[11] was ousted in the face of shareholder anger at the company's poor performance under his tenure. The shareholders did not immediately ask for the Group HR director's head despite the fact that nowhere in these two articles were the words 'shares' or 'shareholders' ever mentioned (although the Group HR director was concerned about 'shared HR processes'). He eventually stood down in a management shake up in July 2012.[12] Meanwhile, 'old norm' investment analysts are probably not reading *Personnel Today*; nor any other HR journal for that matter. Even if they were, they would not be able to join the dots up adequately without the help of a forensic HR Professional.

Aviva, and all of its competitors, have been adversely affected by the global downturn and if they are all still seeking a competitive advantage surely the only option left open to them, other than more mergers and acquisitions (M&A), is the way they manage their people. If Aviva had been able to manage its human capital to its own advantage there are no indications or evidence of that here. Certainly none that would convince any investment analysts including, ironically, Aviva's own investment team. The Group HR director originally concluded his 2010 article with the line 'It's early days and there is some way to go but our strategy is starting to pay dividends' – not according to his shareholders it isn't.

If Group HR Directors and investment analysts are so clueless where can they get a decent education? What is being taught on the subject of human capital strategy on all of those MBA programmes? The reality appears much more prosaic than the textbooks, the post-hoc case studies of success and HR's own hype would have us believe. Old norm, conventional, management practice is not holistic, it is piecemeal. It was designed that way because the paradigm has always been a simplistic one that you can maximize profits by deconstructing every management problem. This is why, as a management philosophy, it has lost coherence recently. The simplistic correlations made between management practice and profit have fallen apart. The investment analysts of the world already know this because they see the evidence in the figures every day. The only conclusion they can possibly reach from the evidence is that profit is no longer an adequate indicator of success. The conventional paradigm is too narrow to incorporate the complete, societal perspective on which economic theory and sustainable capitalism are predicated. The New Norm that is emerging places people right at the heart of the equation as producers, customers and taxpayers; all at once. This requires a much more holistic management strategy, of which an essential ingredient has to be human capital strategy, and that requires a much more sophisticated level of Professionalism. The intrinsic logic is actually quite simple and elegant.

This does not remove the harsh realities of human existence for one moment. Human beings know that redundancies are bound to happen and they might just be in the wrong place at the wrong time. Life can be very cruel but most of us still lean towards a sense of fairness, even if we cannot agree how to define it, and know that cheating is wrong. We judge fairness by our own standard. This tells us that s★★★ happens but, when it does, it should have been anticipated, planned for and handled as Professionally and as humanly as possible. If we believe that to be the case we come to accept our misfortune much more readily, if not less painfully. On the other hand, if we deem the organization to be acting unfairly then all bets on our commitment to the paradigm are off.

The question of whether employees are entirely engaged in what their organization is trying to achieve is not as straightforward as HR's laborious engagement surveys would suggest. Some employees, possibly many, are still disengaged from the main tenets of capitalism and the profit motive. They certainly do not leap out of bed every morning determined to do their best for shareholders; who they are unlikely ever to meet. It therefore behoves management to square the people-profit circle effectively enough in their own minds before trying to help their people to feel the same way. David Erdal in his excellent book *Beyond the Corporation: Humanity Working* takes this argument to its logical conclusion in suggesting that the most engaged and motivated workforces are likely to be those that own their organization. This may well be the endgame for capitalism one day.

In the present norm, HR people recognize some of these issues but their policies are often nothing more than a band-aid, a finger in the dyke, and they find themselves adhering to the principle of the lowest common denominator. When a very loyal, hardworking individual asks for a concession, say a bit of leeway when their child is ill, the risk-averse HR adviser immediately thinks of the contractual and legal implications rather than the particular plight of the individual. They are afraid to sanction a concession that others might abuse. In doing so, a small, kindly gesture can so easily be blown into something bigger; with all sorts of policy implications.

A true HR Professional, still with warm blood flowing through their veins, empathizes with this genuine, hard-working employee and wants to help them resolve an apparently helpless situation. The HR Professional is equally aware of the knock-on, policy implications but reconciles these apparently conflicting pressures in their own mind before trying to reconcile them in the minds of everyone else. They know that consistency in decision-making is a sound management principle but they also know, as Ralph Waldo Emerson told us, that 'a foolish consistency is the hobgoblin of small minds'. Fortunately HR Professionals are not small-minded or mean-spirited and adopt the principle that everyone should be treated equally: knowing that does not necessarily mean they should all be treated the same. Their precise use of language and terminology makes a crucial distinction. People who deserve time off, from an employer that deserves their time, will get equal treatment and be allowed time off. People who do not deserve time off will no longer be employed by the company. This is a totally rational and coherent solution that forms a very strong psychological bond. In practice, the people who have time off for questionable reasons will be questioned systematically and their absence closely monitored. As a policy, it works with the full reality of the bell curve of human behaviour and is ready to deal with each employee as a unique individual. It also deals with those who are just trying it on.

Very minor incidents such as this, that will cost the corporation virtually nothing, can become the defining moments in the psychological contract; especially where a well-worked policy does not already exist. The best in human nature should be encouraged to naturally rise to the surface and then it will not degenerate into a drama of several acts involving HR jobsworths. When employees are not sure how the organization is going to react to the unexpected it is incredibly reassuring for them to learn that the corporate beast manages to react in a very human way. It further reassures all of their colleagues, and everyone else they speak to outside the organization, who might want to join them one day. Instead, many organizations have taken conventional HR management advice that produces rigid policies stating exactly when, and in what circumstances, an employee can have time off. As we saw earlier, with the principle of 'women and children first' and the policy that kept the brave police officer from entering the water, what makes sense to most of humanity can so quickly be replaced with inhuman nonsense. When this happens the loyal employee's perception becomes that of the victim of an untrusting and unsympathetic, organizational bureaucracy: one that does not value their previously unblemished record nor the value of their future commitment.

The HR manager's policy document, possibly even written by the legal department these days, sends more and more signals of mistrust. It is designed to avoid similar concessions being granted to those who are less-than-committed, the ones the organization does not trust and can do without, but it is bound to tar everyone with the same brush. Unprofessional union representatives tend to reinforce this principle of policy rigidity by being prepared to support any paying union member, regardless of the merits of their case. Even the more professional union representatives, who are mature in their own thinking and can see the sense in flexible policies, will know that for every unscrupulous employee there is probably an equally unscrupulous manager whom they cannot trust. And so the downward spiral of mistrust revolves once more.

Normal, 'professional' HR practice has become a breeding ground for very insidious organizational diseases with ineffective policies and activities that have no impact. Such diseases would be completely and utterly eradicated in the New Norm, where the peer pressure of dedicated employees is likely to be even more effective than any HR policy document. As with all diseases though, the whole system has to be disease-free if we are to prevent a recurrence.

Professional politicians need national, human capital strategies

The Prime Minister of the UK and the President of the USA, or the nominal leader of any other nation for that matter, might not immediately see a connection between a nation's grand economic and social strategy and a father or mother needing a couple of days off work to tend to a sick child. What can we expect our national leaders to do about such an apparently minor detail when they are preoccupied with much more important matters of state? Well, first they need to know that everything that happens within an organization, within a nation and across the whole globalized world is part of one system. It might not look like one system but the peasant still toiling in the fields of China and the limo driver in the US are both part of the same system. This should not be news to intelligent world leaders.

It would not be news either to point out to these leaders that the system is in need of repair and improvement. They are only too aware of that as well. Where they might take a renewed interest is in the notion that there are already some well-tried-and-tested design modifications that could be quickly introduced to make the whole system start working better. These modifications would not change everything overnight but they would certainly offer a better prognosis. However, none of this will ever happen unless there is a well conceived strategy to make it happen. Some of the component parts of that strategy have already been identified and are very obvious but, as of today, they are still just separate elements that have not been joined together as a coherent whole. They include a need for:

- A better form of capitalism focused on value.
- Better corporate governance allied to better human governance and greater accountability.
- Better management of meritocracy, responsibility and reward.
- Better evidence-based policy making and management.
- Better auditing and reporting mechanisms.

There have been many attempts to come up with better human capital reporting mechanisms in the past. The UK had its own 'Accounting for People Taskforce' in 2003 but its aims were unclear and its case studies of 'best' HR practice from conventional, non-evidence based HR departments, just produced long lists of meaningless activity data and false correlations. This threat of greater bureaucracy frightened off the business community and led to the government withdrawing their plans to revise company law. This has not deterred investment analysts though. They still want indicators that connect intangibles such as culture, human systems and an organization's ability to continuously learn to tangible, dollar figures. We are also now witnessing much stronger shareholder reactions to executive packages that appear to reward failure. More and more of the dots of systemic failure are being joined up.

The Professional HR advice to our political leaders is to stop producing non-evidence based policies, like throwing money at education and training, and hand it over to the HR Professionals who will know how to spend it wisely. Stop producing ridiculous political slogans about what you can do for the country unless you have a clear strategy to make the most of the valuable human capital you already have at your disposal. This is just a taste of the New Norm and it will taste bitter to senior management teams unless they can taste the sweetness of the value it will bring. It is time to resurrect human capital reporting but this time we have the right, evidence-based technology.

Political leadership has to be translated into organizational leadership but this will not involve sending anyone on the type of 'leadership' programmes run by the BBC. If the truth be known, most senior teams are actually afraid of HR strategy and do not know how to get their heads around the concept of people as capital because they fear it undermines their own value. It actually suits them to pass this problem over to an ineffective HR Director. In the worst cases, as we saw with diversity and racism at the Met, the chief officers have an easier life if there is an ineffective policy in place. Writing in *The Times* about 'recruiting more women at all levels' the Global Head of Diversity at Vodafone,[13] stated that they 'genuinely believe that the company will be higher performing if it has a range of different perspectives at the top'. She did not offer a single statistic to support this contention. If the board of Vodafone genuinely want to introduce some valuable, 'different perspectives' they should first recruit an HR director who adopts an evidence-based perspective, irrespective of gender.

Very little progress will be made without the necessary reinforcing mechanisms in place. In the future, CEOs who declare they will achieve 'double digit growth', or some similarly headline-catching utterance, will have to back it up with 'and this is the part that our people will have to play.' During M&A the team for due diligence and investment appraisal will have to include an HR Professional alongside the Chair, CEO, CFO and head of investor relations. CEOs like Andrew Moss at Aviva should have been asked, from the start, how human capital strategy had been integrated into his business strategy and how it was likely to produce a competitive edge that other insurance companies could not easily match. Any hint that Aviva had exactly the same HR policies as all other insurance companies would then be seen, in the eyes of the investment analysts and shareholders, as a contraindicator of future performance. Any of Aviva's 'HR' activities that were neither mandatory (Box 1) nor showed any evidence of value (Box 2) would have to be aborted immediately. Now do you see all the connections?

Politicians who want votes are missing a trick here. Any politician who can convince citizens that they can help them to maximize the value of their own human capital potential are more likely to be re-elected. This takes real political leadership though and broad-brush policies such as 'new deals', job creation schemes and subsidized training places will be a thing of the past. Any Government initiative would be evidence-based and publicly tracked in the full glare of the media to show what was and was not working. Scarce resources would be targeted at the schemes where the evidence was convincing. Meanwhile, political parties would have to devise and promote their National Human Capital Strategies, not just fine words and PR spin.

The New Norm is a new form of capitalism because we already know what can happen in the old version. The opposite of a National Human Capital Strategy has been perfectly illustrated for us by Greece's present predicament. For many months in 2012 the whole of the Eurozone crisis hinged around Greece's national performance. It has a bloated and inefficient public sector that produces little value and yet there is tax avoidance on an epic scale. Greece also has a long history of belligerent unionism and an economy too dependent on tourism (18.2 per cent of GDP in 2008[14]). There was also an expectation among the public that someone, somewhere, would bail them out even if they did not accept the terms of that bailout. The same public voted to stay in the Euro even though this was dependent on accepting those terms of austerity. In short, Greece is a perfect example of a totally incoherent, political, economic and social mess. Other Western countries may not be dissimilar.

It is already recognized that social democracy can produce a culture of high expectations, in terms of state welfare standards, without each and every one of us having to earn them. National culture and organizational culture cannot be separated. Indeed, employees of commercial companies are reminded every day that the way we work dictates the benefits we can accrue. Therefore, none of us can afford to tolerate under-performance within our ranks and we will only be fully signed-up participants to that social contract if all the other pieces of the jigsaw are in place. A few more of the bigger dots need joining up. A National Human Capital Strategy requires re-visiting the social contract. For the ordinary citizen, who makes their living as an ordinary employee in a profit-driven organization, what is the deal? They should already be paying their taxes but if they want to take part in the nation's wealth and wellbeing they have to sign up to creating as much value and wealth as possible. Otherwise, earning a salary from a poor performing organization means they have to be subsidized by someone else. Asking ordinary citizens to put in even more effort to create even more wealth is likely to be a non-starter though if their failed, ex-CEO has just resigned and walked away with a multi-million dollar severance package. In the same vein, public sector employees, who might genuinely believe in a public sector ethos, will have to start demonstrating that their ethos provides the best value to their fellow citizens. On that score, there is enormous room for improvement in the UK public sector and probably everywhere else as well.

The necessary reform required in the UK civil service will have to be quite brutal. There is no way around this; the present civil service paradigm has to change. The evidence of failure in every civil service department is regularly seen from Ministry of Defence procurement waste, on a huge scale, to daily horror stories about the management of the NHS and wasted education spending. A new civil service for the New Norm requires a completely different intake. The civil service's present 'fast track' recruitment policy has turned very bright graduates into the very worst type of jobsworth. The sort who draws up a manual to stop brave and intelligent police officers from jumping into a three-foot lake to save somebody's life.

This is why the current president of the CIPD, Gill Rider, was drafted into the Cabinet Office (which oversees senior civil service development) after a long HR career with Accenture. Presumably someone believed she would bring some much-needed HR expertise with her? She retired after five years in the post, in 2011, and reported[15] on the results she had achieved. She had been following the CIPD's 'Next generation HR' rulebook, which apparently:

> ... transforms the existing (civil service) departmental model of HR delivery. Instead of each department having its own full HR function there will be shared centres of expertise that will lead on HR for the whole civil service. We are on track to introduce the programme in April (2011) and ultimately it will deliver anticipated savings of £300 million and a best in class [sic] staffing ratio of 1:100.

So after five years it was still a case of jam tomorrow and pursuing meaningless 'best in class ratios'. This did not seem to worry her boss, the Permanent Secretary, Gus O'Donnell (whose initials earned him the nickname 'GOD') when he said:

> Not only has Gill led some amazing work to transform the HR profession, she has seen through a transformation of the senior leadership of the civil service. The development of the Top 200, capability reviews and talent management programmes, such as SCS (senior civil service) Basecamp, are just three examples of the impact (sic) she has made on the Civil Service.

When the highest ranking civil servant in the UK, GOD (now Lord GOD), can refer to such inputs as 'impact' and think he can get away with patronising any serious, intelligent, Professional readers we are truly witnessing the death of an institution. What signal does this send out to future generations of fast-track, bright young things? Is this an organization with a higher purpose? Does it have a cause to which you would want to dedicate the rest of your life?

The lesson that the cynical reader will take from this is that to get to the top of the UK civil service you only have to say the right thing, not do the right thing. You can pretend that activity, or even failure, is success. This is the very opposite of meritocracy and you can get promoted for all the wrong reasons. You can avoid accountability and take no responsibility for your own actions or those of your own recruits. If these are the values of the Permanent Secretary of the UK, who acts as the 'CEO' of the entire civil service and is meant to be the very embodiment of its ethos, what sort of people will the future civil service continue to attract? The most virulent form of management cancer is to be found in the most politicized environments. This brings us round, yet again, to the question of how we educate our leaders.

A National Strategy has to address the whole of the education system. This means making teachers and university academics much more accountable for what they teach. We need clear evidence that students are not only learning something useful but applying it as well. This would require a complete overhaul of most education systems and, if the general belief that 'education is good' is to survive, then it will have to survive by evidence. Our present, blind adherence to the 'education is good' mantra is crumbling in the face of hundreds of thousands of unemployed graduates and the illiteracy and innumeracy of thousands of others who have come out of the education system. Shaking up education will also have an immediate effect on research. Only the clearest line of sight to value should be supported from public funds and researchers should be required to demonstrate progress and success; or at least a high probability that their research that might see the light of day and result in a real application in the real world. This is a huge challenge for academia.

UK research councils[16] spend about £3 billion a year on research, the majority of it on science, medical and engineering research. In 2002 the Roberts Report[17] encouraged the UK government to provide £150,000,000 extra funding to increase 'stipends, length of doctoral programmes and provide training for their funded researchers.' It also demanded that any training for researchers had to be evaluated. Ten years later, in 2012, a report entitled 'Evaluating and exploring the evidence of the impact of training and development activities for researchers'[18] revealed what progress had been made. In Appendix 4D it compares 'outcomes' that were expected in 2008 with actual outcomes reported in 2010, see Table 9.1.

This reveals that ten years after the Roberts report came out we are still no wiser as to the value of researcher training. Does this help to justify continued 'government investment in research training and skills development'? Are academic professors taking the training of researchers seriously? Would you put those that evaluate properly at the top of your list for the next round of research funding?

HR Professionals do not subscribe to the academic philosophy of 'learning for learning's sake', especially when the demands for scarce funding are so great and potentially so valuable. Their Professional calling means they can only support a policy where the focus is on applied learning, just as medicine has to always focus on health improvement, eradicating disease or alleviating illness. By following a Baseline approach to evaluation they will significantly raise the probability of 'potential outcomes' becoming actual impacts with tangible benefits. Based on this report alone it appears that scientists are not applying any of their own scientific methods to the development of their researchers.

Is there a connection here between attitudes to training in academia and the fact that there are thousands of unemployed graduates in the UK?[19] If so, the HR Professional will see this as a multi-layered problem. Academics, who are supposed to value education so highly, do not take the evaluation of their education seriously

TABLE 9.1 Evaluating researcher training and development

	Appendix 4D – Higher complexity/longer time-span	
	Suggested potential outcomes (2008)	Actual examples of impact (2010)
Funding bodies	Better equipped and more highly skilled academic and research workforce	Evidence was not reported in this area in the report 'The impact of researcher training and development: two years on'
	Ability to demonstrate value for money and justify government investment in research training and skills development	

enough. This results in costly and unfocused education, with no obvious return. The Government does not want to be seen as not supporting education though because voters still believe that education is 'good for you'. So the Government continue to pour money into education knowing that it is being wasted. This is evidence of the mismanagement of a nation's human capital on a truly epic scale. Any nation that stays locked into this vicious cycle will not have much of a future if other nations manage to get themselves into a virtuous cycle.

What is actually happening in higher education is a move towards a more capitalistic, market-driven model where students are 'customers' who pay their own way. As customers they can take their business elsewhere and it can be very painful, financially, for a university to lose this source of income. Economics professors will tell you that competition is a good thing for society but does the same theory apply to their own market? When we purchase a can of beans we can be very confident it will contain what it says on the label. The same confidence cannot be gained from reading a university course syllabus. In tough economic conditions there is always a temptation to reduce costs by reducing quality and hoping the customers will not notice. This tendency applies as much to universities under pressure as it does to producers of beans. The big difference is that it is more difficult to assure the quality of education and so less reputable universities will be sorely tempted to pass sub-standard students to keep them paying their course fees: reputable academics will be replaced by quackademics who are only too willing to oblige. Thus begins the first cycle of the principle of the lowest common denominator. Other universities, despite having a reputation, might have to follow suit in order to survive, especially if educational choices are based on price, rather than some indistinct and indeterminate, educational outcome. These are scary questions, even for the HR Professional, but they have to be asked because we need to seek the truth of the matter. If education is as important as we all say it is then dropping standards must come at a cost. If education is not as important as that then why are we spending so much resources on it? The only reason we trust our doctors is they started seeking the truth in medicine over 150 years ago. We had better start seeking the truth in human capital management as soon as we can if we want to catch up. The only way we will all have a sustainable future on this planet is by constantly seeking the truth and managing ourselves accordingly.

A physicist might never find out *why* we are here but they are certainly doing their best to discover *how* we came to be here. These will remain legitimate questions for scientific discovery until a satisfactory answer has been found. Sometimes such questions have to be asked for many years before we get even close to an answer, as with CERN's search for the Higgs boson. It might be a cliché to say that such endeavours require visionary leadership but it might also be an over-statement. Evidence-based management is nothing new in the sense that it keeps asking questions until it finds the truth. Once this premise is accepted everything else should start to fall into place. Highly intelligent permanent secretaries and presidents of professional bodies that do not set out to seek the truth are making themselves look stupid by perpetuating an HR system based on nonsense rather than common sense. The ordinary man or woman in the street, with common sense, can usually spot falsehood and dishonesty when they see or hear it and are less likely to tolerate it today.

If you were completely free and unconstrained in choosing where to work would you choose the UK civil service, a large bank or pharmaceutical company, Microsoft, Google, Facebook, a workers cooperative, a trust, a social enterprise, a not-for-profit education or healthcare organization, a charity, an employee owned enterprise, an ethical consultancy or a group of like-minded freelancers? Would that choice be determined by your values more than any other consideration? If you chose banking would you choose the bank that paid the most or the one that clearly wanted to serve society? When you know that your best human values are perfectly matched by your employer's then you are experiencing what the New Norm really has to offer.

We started out by saying that HR's obvious failings have huge implications for society and have presented evidence in support of that highly provocative contention. Maybe the evidence is mounting so quickly now that it no longer appears contentious? There is a plentiful supply of equally damning evidence and the internet makes it very easy to find and disseminate. Management ignorance about the best way to manage people used to be easy to hide; that is no longer the case. When the vast majority of citizens, as employees, come to the same conclusions, there will be nowhere for leaders and managers to hide their obvious failings. They will have no other option than to join the inevitable march towards a much more Professional, more civilized future.

NOTES

1 Introduction

1 www.boston.com/business/articles/2009/03/03/hsbc_ends_us_subprime_lending/
2 www.livemint.com/2012/07/24233038/Green-has-8216regrets8217.html?h=B
3 Definition of 'fit-for-purpose' from /www.askartsolutions.com/iso-9000-lead-auditor-training/Quality-Definition.html
4 Global Polio Eradication Initiative: www.polioeradication.org/
5 'The failure of the Royal Bank of Scotland: Financial Services Authority Board Report' www.fsa.gov.uk/library/other_publications/miscellaneous/2011/rbs.shtml
6 http://blogs.wsj.com/deals/2011/09/15/why-your-ceo-could-be-in-trouble/
7 Assessing the professional performance of UK doctors: an evaluation of the utility of the General Medical Council patient and colleague questionnaires http://qualitysafety.bmj.com/content/17/3/187.abstract
8 'Just 17 teachers are struck off for incompetence in 10 years.' http://www.dailymail.co.uk/news/article-2080087/Just-17-teachers-struck-incompetence-10-years.html#ixzz1n1H5NJvO
9 www.thetimes.co.uk/tto/news/uk/crime/article3299317.ece

2 Professionalizing the management of people

1 http://en.wikipedia.org/wiki/Evidence-based_management
2 http://news.bbc.co.uk/democracylive/hi/europe/newsid_9159000/9159048.stm
3 UK Privy Council has the authority to grant chartered status http://privycouncil.independent.gov.uk/royal-charters/chartered-bodies/
4 UK Engineering Council www.engc.org.uk/
5 The Chartered Engineer Standard www.engc.org.uk/ecukdocuments/internet/document%20library/UK-SPEC.pdf
6 Retail Distribution Review www.fsa.gov.uk/about/what/rdr/professionalism
7 'Goodwin in FSA pact' www.thesundaytimes.co.uk/sto/business/Finance/article1021896.ece
8 www.30percentclub.org.uk/how-to-balance-your-board/executive-search-firms/
9 Michael Woodford settles Olympus claim www.bbc.co.uk/news/business-18258542
10 www.thetimes.co.uk/tto/business/industries/banking/article2159024.ece
11 *Economist* – 'Field of dreams' www.economist.com/node/21541045
12 Denise Rousseau, 'Designing a better business school' http://onlinelibrary.wiley.com/doi/10.1111/j.1467-6486.2011.01041.x/abstract

13 Milton Friedman www.youtube.com/watch?v=MBB7l-SfoK4
14 Francesco Guerrera of the *Financial Times*, www.ft.com/cms/s/0/294ff1f2-0f27-11de-ba10-0000779fd2ac.html#axzz1lhh2IFg1
15 Jeff Immelt on You Tube www.youtube.com/watch?v=CCVy7OxThGo&feature=related
16 Mo Ibrahim African Leadership Index www.moibrahimfoundation.org/en/pressrelease/media-centre/press-releases/news-release-ibrahim-prize-announcement-2010.html
17 www.economist.com/node/21547815

3 The definitive, Professional manager

1 www.infosysblogs.com/leadership/2012/05/inspiration_innovation_influen.html?goback=.gde_936527_member_118102426
2 https://wpweb2.tepper.cmu.edu/evite/ebm_conf/conference%20bd%20HR%20paper.pdf
3 www.scotsman.com/news/rbs-losses-mis-selling-scandal-pay-outs-mean-bank-losses-hit-15-billion-barrier-1-2448260
4 www.peoplemanagement.co.uk/pm/articles/2009/04/performance-management-at-rbs-looks-beyond-financial-results.htm
5 www.evidencebasedhr.com/evidence-statistics-and-damn-lies/a-travesty-of-eb-hr-principles-a-book-review-of-transformative-hr-by-john-boudreau-and-ravin-jesuthasan/
6 www.actuaries.org.uk/regulation/pages/regulation
7 www.aomonline.org/
8 AIM UK www.aimresearch.org/
9 www.microsoft.com/education/en-us/Training/Competencies/Pages/dealing_with_ambiguity.aspx/
10 www.dailymail.co.uk/news/article-2104358/Simon-Burgess-drowned-firemen-refused-wade-3ft-deep-lake-health-safety-rules.html#ixzz1xf1iwYOZ
11 http://en.wikipedia.org/wiki/September_11_attacks
12 www.serco.com/instituteresource/subjects/contractman/publicservice/index.asp

4 Educating the Professional, evidence-based manager

1 www.belbin.com/rte.asp?id=3
2 www.cipd.co.uk/blogs/cipdbloggers/b/angela_baron/archive/2011/04/13/is-engagement-always-good.aspx
3 www.trainingjournal.com/news/articles-news-high-engagement-scores-can-spell-trouble-for-companies-cipd-say/
4 http://hbr.org/1998/01/the-employee-customer-profit-chain-at-sears/ar/1
5 www.personneltoday.com/articles/2012/02/15/58347/employee-engagement-at-tesco-optimising-two-way-communication.html
6 www.thesundaytimes.co.uk/sto/business/marketscrisis/article1042237.ece
7 www.cochrane.org/about-us/history/archie-cochrane
8 http://news.bbc.co.uk/1/hi/4304290.stm
9 www.aimresearch.org/
10 www.aimpractice.com/our-products/toolkit?id=14
11 www.roiinstitute.net/
12 www.managers.org.uk/
13 www.management-standards.org/standards/standards/

5 Human capital management recognizes the new order

1 www.sciencecouncil.org/content/what-science
2 SHRM have since dropped their proposals in the face of industry opposition

6 What should we do with HR and L&D?

1 www.histansoc.org.uk/timeline.html
2 www.chstm.manchester.ac.uk/research/areas/medicalprofession/
3 www.cipd.co.uk/hr-resources/factsheets/history-hr-cipd.aspx#link_2
4 www.thetimes.co.uk/tto/news/politics/article3388438.ece
5 www.payscale.com/research/UK/Job=Registered_Nurse_%28RN%29/Salary
6 www.tes.co.uk/article.aspx?storycode=6000186
7 www.mirror.co.uk/money/city-news/at-last-fuel-strike-averted-as-tanker-829365
8 www.ncsl.org/issues-research/labor/at-will-employment-overview.aspx
9 www.standard.co.uk/news/politics/beecroft-report-letting-us-sack-staff-we-dont-like-will-be-good-for-the-economy-bosses-tell-downing-street-7770808.html
10 www.fastcompany.com/53319/why-we-hate-hr
11 www.personneltoday.com/Articles/09/04/2008/45340/dave-ulrichs-model-defence.htm
12 www.cipd.co.uk/cipd-hr-profession/hr-profession-map/
13 www.bridge-partnership.com/

7 Establishing a universal, evidence-based standard for HR

1 www.shrm.org/about/news/Pages/StandardsEffortRatified.aspx
2 www.shrm.org/about/pages/code-of-ethics.aspx
3 www.shrm.org/hrstandards/publishedstandards/documents/cost-per-hire%20american%20national%20standard.pdf
4 www.tc176.org/about176.asp
5 www.guardian.co.uk/media/2003/may/16/bbc.broadcasting
6 www.cfo.com/article.cfm/14577155?f=singlepage
7 www.hreonline.com/HRE/story.jsp?storyId=461233863
8 www.talent2.com/our-people/meet-our-team/richard-boddington
9 www.evidencebasedhr.com/?p=473
10 This quote is in response to a letter sent by the author to the Canadian Institute of Chartered Accountants. The name of the fellow is unknown
11 www.nao.org.uk/publications/0607/vfm_in_public_sector_corporate.aspx
12 www.saratogapwc.co.uk/index.html
13 http://onlinelibrary.wiley.com/doi/10.1111/j.1748-8583.2011.00173.x/full
14 www.telegraph.co.uk/technology/Facebook/9290132/Morgan-Stanley-may-offer-refund-to-Facebook-investors.html

8 Ten steps to becoming an HR Professional

1 www.reuters.com/article/2010/09/07/us-malpractice-usa-idUSTRE6860KN20100907
2 www.cipd.co.uk/pressoffice/press-releases/cipd-unveils-new-code.aspx
3 www.bbc.co.uk/news/business-18685040
4 http://news.sky.com/story/954031/uk-banking-culture-must-change
5 www.bbc.co.uk/news/business-19420310
6 www.instructionaldesign.org/theories/double-loop.html
7 www.paulkearnshr.co.uk
8 www.economist.com/node/21558254
9 www.sefi.be/wp-content/abstracts/1134.pdf
10 www.economist.com/node/21558313
11 www.gsk.com/responsibility/

9 We need more Professional management for a more civilized world

1 www.personneltoday.com/Articles/06/10/2008/47766/London-Mayor-sets-up-racism-inquiry-at-Met-Police.htm#.UA9-h6OQN-U
2 www.hrmagazine.co.uk/hr/interviews/1014895/interview-martin-tiplady-human-resources-director-metropolitan-police-service
3 www.hrmagazine.co.uk/hro/news/1019390/breaking-news-martin-tiplady-leave-role-met-police-hr-director
4 www.guardian.co.uk/uk/2012/may/31/met-police-anti-racism-drive
5 www.hrmagazine.co.uk/news/1048531/Former-RBS-HR-director-Neil-Roden-joins-PwC/
6 www.evidencebasedhr.com/wp-content/uploads/2011/12/RBS-Neil-Roden-PwC-Hourglass9-Feb2008.pdf
7 http://conference.screencastacademy.com/conference/speakers/
8 www.bbc.co.uk/news/business-16166354
9 www.personneltoday.com/articles/2010/07/30/56345/how-hr-at-aviva-boosted-employee-engagement-during-its.html
10 www.personneltoday.com/articles/2011/11/07/58132/personnel-today-interview-embedding-recognition-at-aviva.html
11 http://uk.reuters.com/article/2012/05/08/uk-aviva-idUKBRE84707X20120508
12 www.insuranceage.co.uk/insurance-age/news/2189438/aviva-shakes-senior-management
13 www.thetimes.co.uk/tto/career/article3520153.ece
14 www.oecd.org/cfe/tourism/tourisminoecdcountries2008trendsandpolicies.htm
15 http://network.civilservicelive.com/pg/pages/view/533417/
16 www.rcuk.ac.uk/Pages/Home.aspx
17 www.vitae.ac.uk/policy-practice/1685/Roberts-recommendations.html#invest
18 www.vitae.ac.uk/policy-practice/375-555681/New-from-the-Impact-and-Evaluation-Group.html
19 www.guardian.co.uk/commentisfree/datablog/2012/jul/02/graduates-future-prospects-debt-unemployment

BIBLIOGRAPHY

Boudreau, J. and Jesuthasan, R.(2011) *Transformative HR: How Great Companies Use Evidence-Based Change for Sustainable Advantage*, Jossey-Bass.

Daniels, A. (2000) *Bringing out the Best in People*, McGraw-Hill.

Drucker, E. (1998) *On the Profession of Management*, Harvard Business School Press.

Erdal, E. (2011) *Beyond the Corporation: Humanity Working*, Bodley Head.

Friedman, M. (1962) *Capitalism and Freedom*, University of Chicago Press.

Green, S. (2009) *Good Value: Reflections on Money, Morality and an Uncertain World*, Allen Lane.

Hubbard, D.W. (2010) *How to Measure Anything: Finding the Value of 'Intangibles' in Business*, 2nd edition, Wiley.

Kahneman, D. (2011) *Thinking, Fast and Slow*, Daniel Kahneman, Penguin.

Kearns, P. (2005) *Evaluating the ROI from Learning*, CIPD.

Kearns, P. (2007) *The Value Motive: The ONLY Alternative to the Profit Motive*, Wiley.

Kearns, P. (2010) *HR Strategy: Creating Business Strategy with Human Capital*, 2nd edition, Routledge.

Khurana, R. (2007) *From Higher Aims to Hired Hands: The Social Transformation of American Business Schools and the Unfulfilled Promise of Management as a Profession*, Princeton University Press.

Machiavelli, N. (ca 1532) *The Prince*.

Pfeffer, J. and Sutton, R.I. (1999) *The Knowing-Doing Gap: How Smart Companies Turn Knowledge into Action*, Harvard Business School Press.

Pfeffer, J. and Sutton, R.I. (2006) *Hard Facts, Dangerous Half-truths and Total Nonsense*, Harvard Business School Press.

Senge, P. (2006) *The Fifth Discipline: The Art and Practice of the Learning Organization*, 2nd edition, Random House.

Slater, R. (2002) *29 Leadership Secrets from Jack Welch*, McGraw-Hill Professional.

Smith, A. (2007) *Theory of Moral Sentiments*, Filiquarian Publishing.

Thaler, R. and Sunstein, C. (2008) *Nudge: Improving Decisions about Health, Wealth and Happiness*, Yale University Press.

Toyoda, E. (1987) *Toyota: Fifty Years in Motion*, English translation, Kodansha Publishing.

REFERENCES

Baldwin, T., Pierce, J., Jones, R. and Farouk, S. (2011) 'The Elusiveness of Applied Management Knowledge: A Critical Challenge for Management Educators', *Academy of Management Journal*.

Careers Research and Advisory Centre (CRAC) Limited (2012) *The Impact Framework 2012: Revisiting the Rugby Team Impact Framework*.

Gibbons, J. and Woock, C. (2009) *Evidence-Based Human Resources' Conference Board Report Research Report* E-0015-07-RR.

Learmonth, M. (2006) 'Is There Such a Thing as EBM?', *Academy of Management Review* 31.

Learmonth, M. and Harding, N. (2006) 'Evidence-based Management: The Very Idea', *Public Administration* 84(2): 245–66.

NAO (2007) *Value For Money in Public Sector Corporate Services. A Joint Project by the UK Public Sector Audit Agencies*.

Pfeffer, J. (2011) 'Management a Profession? Where's the Proof?', *Harvard Business Review* column.

Rousseau, D. (2011) 'Becoming an Evidence-based HR Practitioner', *Human Resource Management Journal* 21(3): 221–35.

Rousseau, D. (2012) 'Designing a Better Business School', *Journal of Management Studies* 49(3): 600–18.

Rucci, A.J., Kirn, S.P. and Quinn, R.T. (1998) 'The Employee-Customer-Profit Chain at Sears', *Harvard Business Review* 76(1): 82–97.

INDEX